Social Movements in Advanced Capitalism

The Political Economy and Cultural Construction of Social Activism

Steven M. Buechler
Minnesota State University, Mankato

New York   Oxford
OXFORD UNIVERSITY PRESS
2000

Oxford University Press

Oxford New York
Athens Auckland Bangkok Bogotá Buenos Aires Calcutta
Cape Town Chennai Dar es Salaam Delhi Florence Hong Kong Istanbul
Karachi Kuala Lumpur Madrid Melbourne Mexico City Mumbai
Nairobi Paris São Paulo Singapore Taipei Tokyo Toronto Warsaw

and associated companies in
Berlin Ibadan

Published by Oxford University Press, Inc.,
198 Madison Avenue, New York, New York, 10016
http://www.oup-usa.org
1-800-334-4249

Library of Congress Cataloging-in-Publication Data
Buechler, Steven M., 1951–
    Social movements in advanced capitalism : the political economy
and cultural construction of social activism / Steven M. Buechler.
        p.   cm.
    Includes bibliographical references and index.
    ISBN 0-19-512603-3 (cloth: alk. paper).—ISBN 0-19-512604-1
(paper: alk. paper)
    1. Social movements.   2. Collective behavior.   I. Title.
HN13.B84   1999
303.48′4—dc21   98-42230
                                                                      CIP

Printing (last digit): 9 8 7 6 5 4 3 2 1

Printed in the United States of America
on acid-free paper

Once again, to Sue

Contents

PART TWO

Sociohistorical Structures and Collective Action   59

Introduction

The contemporary social world is an historical product. Its contours are the result of past purposive action as well as unintended and unanticipated consequences whose complex effects are inscribed in the social world. Among the most intriguing purposive actions are social movements. Throughout the modern era, diverse groups have banded together in explicit efforts to transform the social order. Although such efforts rarely met with complete success, their cumulative impact has been substantial. Alongside other influences, the contemporary social world is the product of prior collective efforts to transform old social orders into new ones.

The historical nature of the social world is rarely recognized in everyday consciousness. Such consciousness is present oriented, with little sense of the linkages among past action, present realities, and future possibilities. It is natural to take the existing world for granted—as if it could not be and never has been other than it is. An ahistorical perspective has also been a dominant feature of much twentieth-century American positivist sociology as it followed a restricted notion of social science. In pursuit of this goal, positivist sociology has reified social reality and obscured its historical shaping by past collective action.

In the subfield of sociology devoted to the study of collective behavior and social movements, there are new opportunities for restoring a more profoundly historical understanding of collective action. Social movement theory and research have recently become some of the most active areas within the discipline, producing a tremendous volume of work on diverse aspects of collective action. As with other rapid advances in knowledge, the growth in this area has exceeded our ability to assess, judge, and critically reflect on how this specialized body of knowledge is related to the broader discipline of sociology and to our everyday understanding of the social world. This book provides one such assessment of these larger issues through six overlapping themes.

First, I argue for the centrality of social movements to the development of contemporary society and the shaping of modern sociology. This is an attempt to restore a more historical consciousness to our understanding of the modern world and to provide the foundation for a richer analysis of collective action.

Second, I provide a series of reflections and commentaries on the state of social movement theory. In these reflections, my goal is a balanced but critical evaluation of the strengths and weaknesses of various paradigms as well as the overall status of social movement theory.

Third, I identify a prevalent problem in much recent theory and research. Among other things, this problem is evidenced by a fragmented, ahistorical, decontextualized approach to collective action that has made it difficult to see the structural roots and historical consequences of collective action.

Fourth, I propose an alternative in the form of a structural approach to social movements. This approach is presented through a paradigm for social movement analysis organized around four levels of social reality that identify the multiple contexts in which collective action is inevitably embedded.

Fifth, I integrate the subfield of social movements with more general theoretical traditions within the discipline by analyzing how these traditions have informed social movement theories and by using these traditions to articulate the multilevel paradigm within which social movements can be located and analyzed.

Sixth, I draw on critical theory to restore a normative dimension to social movement analysis. For all its incisiveness, this tradition has been too hampered by cultural pessimism to offer much of interest on these topics. Alternatively, mainstream social movement analysis has been devoid of the critique that animates the social movements it studies. In the name of a critical social science, I seek a productive dialogue across these traditions.

These overlapping themes mean that the book is addressed to diverse audiences. My hopes are that specialists will be nudged toward a somewhat different approach to our common subject matter, that nonspecialists and generalists will find some bridges across subfields and theoretical traditions, that graduate students will find a serviceable guide to some leading issues in the field, that undergraduates will find a helpful introduction to the study of social movements, and that general readers will gain an appreciation of what the sociological imagination brings to understanding the dialectic between collective action and social change. Only these respective audiences can judge the extent to which these hopes have been realized. Regardless of the audience, a brief overview of what follows may be helpful.

Part I consists of two chapters that may be read almost as free-standing essays. The first chapter makes the case for the centrality of social movements to the modern world and the sociological enterprise. Social movements and sociology are twin siblings of the modern era, and a family reunion is long overdue. The second chapter presents a critical primer in collective behavior and social movement theory. I evaluate these approaches through a sociology of knowledge analysis that is attentive to both the scientific and extrascientific forces that have contributed to the rise and fall of various theoretical approaches.

This chapter also critiques the state of the art in social movement theory as a foundation for the remainder of the book.

Part II develops a structural approach for the analysis of social movements. The central premise is that social movements are best understood through an historical, dialectical, and "structurational" approach to collective action as it is embedded in four levels of social organization: global, national, "regional," and local. Each of the four chapters in Part II explores one of these levels through a parallel organization. In the first part, I draw on diverse theoretical traditions within sociology to characterize the distinguishing features of a given level of sociohistorical structure; in the second part, I explore the implications of these features for collective action as well as the impact of collective action on each respective level of sociohistorical structure. Within this framework, a number of current theoretical controversies are addressed.

Part III consists of two chapters that address some remaining substantive questions about contemporary social activism. The recent shift from political to cultural issues in social movement theory provides the framework for these chapters. The first addresses the political dimension of social movements and offers an heuristic distinction and discussion of the differences between "state politics" and "social politics." The second addresses the cultural dimension of social movements through extended discussions of collective identity, ideology, and organization in social movements.

In the course of writing this book, I have often felt as if I were swimming against the currents that dominate the study of social movements today. Such a position has its benefits. For instance, I have not had to worry about being scooped by someone else working on the same ideas. My hope is that there will also be collective benefits if this effort can refocus our attention on some vital questions that link social activism, the sociological enterprise, and the contemporary world.

My work on this project has benefited from a rich combination of institutional, collegial, and personal support. The Department of Sociology and Corrections and the College of Social and Behavioral Sciences at Minnesota State University, Mankato provided valuable release time on several occasions throughout the project. In my department, Mac McCormick, Tom Schmid, and Bill Wagner have not only sustained my respect for diverse theoretical traditions, but also cultivated an intellectual climate that has been vital in sustaining this effort. I would especially like to thank Tom Schmid for his collaboration on various projects and his friendship over the past 13 years since I arrived at Mankato.

Benigno Aguirre meticulously read and thoroughly critiqued an earlier draft of the manuscript. Although we see many issues very differently, his review prodded me to rethink some of my claims and to incorporate a broader range of work into the manuscript. At Oxford University Press, S. Layla Voll has been an enthusiastic supporter and insightful editor as we have brought this book to fruition.

Finally, I would like to thank Susan J. Scott for her unqualified support of my work. This project took longer than I expected (and she hoped), but her tolerance of my work habits, her encouragement of my efforts, and her emotional support throughout this process have been invaluable.

Social Movements in
Advanced Capitalism

Part I

The Sociology of
Social Movements

1

Social Movements and Sociology
Siblings of Modernity

Social movements have profoundly influenced the contours of modern society and the discipline of sociology. Despite this dual influence, the analysis of social movements within sociology has only begun to receive systematic attention in the past 20 years. Prior to this time, social movements were treated as a subcategory within an amorphous area called collective behavior that itself was tangential to the core of sociology. The historical marginality of social movements within sociology is ironic given the standard textbook definitions of the discipline as concerned with the study of "social statics" and "social dynamics." A survey of those textbooks, as well as the discipline, reveals that for myriad reasons sociology has focused on social statics and regarded social dynamics as a residual category. Perhaps it is an indicator of disciplinary maturation that the study of social change and social movements is now acquiring a new significance within sociology.

An historical consciousness suggests that this is not so much a new development as it is a return to the origins of sociology. The discipline emerged in a time of massive social change, and sociology sought to understand and explain those changes by placing them within the more comforting frames of "progress," "development," and "modernization." Additional comfort was offered through the promise that these changes had their own internal logic that could be understood through an application of the techniques of natural science to the social world. The emergent discipline of sociology thereby disciplined and normalized an unruly world of social turmoil by offering the first social–scientific accounts of the causes and consequences of that turmoil and its role in a process of social evolution.

Much of the turmoil that sociology sought to normalize was expressed in the collective action that emerged in response to state making, urbanization, proletarianization, and industrialization. As these massive social changes rippled across the European continent, large numbers of ordinary people became involved in initially defensive and subsequently offensive forms of popular mobilization to preserve old customs or establish new rights (Tilly, 1995). Although these repertoires of collective action have changed over several centuries, contemporary forms of social protest are still variations on themes established during the transition from feudalism to capitalism and the rise of modernity in Europe. As important as these actions were, the dominant sociological discourses have marginalized their role in social change. From the perspective of master categories such as rationalization and modernization, collective action appears as an unfortunate and excessive response to strains and dislocations rather than an integral part of the process of change itself (Eder, 1993). As a corrective to this marginalization of movements, we would be well advised to recognize that "struggle has its own partly autonomous history, a history that does not reduce simply to a reflection of the changing organization of production or of the changing structure of state power, a history that in itself influences the organization of production and the structure of state power" (Tilly, 1995:37). Such a recognition would also require us to "constitute our theoretical notion of modernity not as a master narrative but in a way that reflects both its heterogeneity and contestation and that takes full account of the central place of social movements within it" (Calhoun, 1993:418).

The histories of sociology and social movements thereby reveal strong family resemblances. Both emerged as part of a massive social transformation that we typically summarize as "modernization." Both contributed to and were shaped by that transformation. Both continue in the present day when the effects of the postmodern can be felt in each arena. But the family resemblance is most firmly rooted in a fundamental premise shared by each of these siblings. In contemporary language, this premise is that the world is a social construction. For sociology as an academic discipline, this means that the world stands in need of explanation via sociological concepts. For social movements as a form of collective action, this means that the world stands in need of transformation via popular mobilization. Despite these differing responses, the premise that underlies both sociology and social movements is a distinctively modern one that has structured a dialectical relationship between understanding and changing the world for the last two centuries. The renewed recognition of the importance of social movements within sociology is thus long overdue.

THE ORIGINS OF THE SOCIAL MOVEMENT

There are countless discussions of the origins of social movements that focus on a particular movement and analyze the factors that contributed to its emergence in a specific time and place. Less attention has been paid to a larger version of this question about the historical origins of the social movement itself as a form of mass mobilization and social transformation. Perhaps this question is posed less often because there have always been episodes of collective action in diverse societies throughout history. Nevertheless, collective action underwent a qualitative transformation at a particular moment in history that can be identified as the origins of the social movement.

This historical moment was part of European societal modernization. The term modernization obscures the depth and disruptiveness of the wide-reaching changes and dislocations associated with the transition from feudalism to capitalism, the consolidation of modern nation-states, and the transformation of masses of people from rural peasants to an urban proletariat. The extent and rapidity of these changes were blunt testimony to the fact that social order was not a given but rather a contested, historical creation subject to profound transformation. At this same historical moment, society was becoming an object of scientific scrutiny for the Enlightenment philosophers. In Durkheimian terms, their fundamental sociological insight was that social facts are best explained by other social facts. The linking of social facts to provide explanations was guided by the scientific method, including empirical investigation and theoretical speculation. This approach had yielded dazzling insights about the natural world, but the outer limit of natural science was the premise that nature was a "given" whose laws might be uncovered but could never be reconstituted. As this method was applied to the study of society, its implications became even more radical with the gradual awareness that the "laws" of society were malleable social creations that could be altered by the conscious intervention of social agents (though often in ways they neither intended nor anticipated).

It was the confluence of these intellectual currents with state building and the rise of capitalism that gave rise to the social movement as a distinctively modern form of collective action. Despite superficial similarities with earlier forms of such action, social movements brought a new dimension to collective action because their participants saw the social order as contested and malleable rather than as natural and given. In the words of two European scholars, "[t]he idea of conscious collective action having the capacity to change society as a whole came only with the era of enlightenment" (Neidhardt and Rucht, 1991:449). As a result, "[s]ocial movements are genuinely modern phenomena. Only in modern society have social movements played a constitutive role in social development" (Eder, 1993:108). Indirect evidence of this shift is provided by the fact that this period also became an age of ideology. As society came to be understood as a social creation, and as one possible social creation among alternatives, both the given society and its possible alternatives stood in need of ideological justification. Hence, there was a tremendous flowering of ideological debate and argumentation that was geared either to defending the existing social order or to legitimizing some alternative. Whereas traditional social orders had rested on some type of metaphysical doctrine (and prophets had periodically challenged them with a differing interpretation of that doctrine), the Enlightenment saw a qualitatively greater proliferation of possible social forms and conflicting social ideologies because the entire social order came to be seen as subject to challenge or in need of justification. Thus, although collective action has been a feature of all societies, "the social movement is a *historical* and not a universal way of mounting collective claims" (Meyer and Tarrow, 1998:4; italics in original).

The historically specific and modern nature of social movements is evidenced in several ways. One concerns the scope and the depth of the challenge they pose to social order. In the premodern era, collective action was limited by certain "metasocial guarantees of social order" that constrained the field of possible actions that movements might contemplate (Touraine, 1985). "Men thought they lived in a microcosm included in a macrocosm whose laws imposed a definition of human nature and legitimated social norms. All social movements . . . were referring to a metasocial principle which was called order of things, divine rule, natural law or historical evolution" (Touraine, 1985:778). Movements were thus limited to the relatively narrow range of their social fields that was not regarded as given and immutable in keeping with the dominant metasocial guarantee of social order. Modernity, however, ushered in a qualitatively new historical era. "In our times, we feel that our capacity of self-production, self-transformation and self-destruction is boundless. . . . The result is that the field of social movements extends itself to all aspects of social and cultural life" (Touraine, 1985:778). The domain of social movement activity has thus expanded qualitatively with the passing of metasocial guarantees in the modern era.

In Touraine's view, this change brought social movements to center stage in modern societies, and he argues that they should have a corresponding centrality in sociology as well. This belief is grounded in a complex theory of historicity, defined as the symbolic capacity of social actors to construct a system of knowledge and the technical tools that allow them to intervene in their own functioning, act upon themselves, and thereby produce society. It is the development of this capacity called historicity that makes possible the self-production of society (Touraine, 1977). This capacity has become more developed and refined with each succession of major societal types from agrarian to mercantile to industrial and finally to postindustrial or programmed society. The expansion of historicity corresponds to the shrinking of metaphysical guarantees for social order; both tendencies extend the capacity and the range of action which contributes to the self-production of society.

Historicity is also the object of ongoing conflict between classes in the form of social movements that struggle over the self-production of society and the direction of social change. Since contemporary society is more dominated than any other by its historicity, and since class relations are about control of historicity (expressed through social movements) it follows that such movements are becoming increasingly central in contemporary society. For industrial societies, Touraine largely follows the Marxist analysis of conflict over production between capital and labor as central to this social form and to struggles over historicity. With the coming of postindustrial society, however, Touraine argues that the popular class consists of consumers, the principal field of conflict is culture, and the central issue is self-management. The conflict over the control of historicity in postindustrial society thereby involves a battle over who will program the programmed society, with managers/technocrats and consumers/clients comprising the dominant social classes and social movements (Touraine, 1977). Although Touraine's approach is not without difficulties, his theory of the self-production of society provides one eloquent statement of the notion that social movements are a distinctively modern form of collective action that has become increasingly central in the social construction of contemporary society.

Another link between modernity and movements involves the sustained, systemic, and ideological nature of social movement challenges in response to modern relations of power. Thus, "it was not until sometime in the nineteenth century that continuing organized antisystemic political movements of the oppressed strata were first formed. In itself, this was a remarkable social *invention*, which has too long gone unheralded and unanalyzed" (Wallerstein, 1990:13, italics in original). This development may be traced to two effects of the French Revolution. First, it challenged the ideology of the old order so effectively that it became permanently on the defensive—an effect that rippled throughout the capitalist world system. And second, it established the main ideological motifs of modern social movements in the famous slogan calling for "liberty, equality, and fraternity." Although these ideals have a long history, the French Revolution amplified their power in three basic ways. It established a firmly secular basis for these social and political ideals for the first time. It made them socially legitimate to such an extent that self-consciously conservative thinkers began to appear to actively contest these newly legitimized challenges to the old order. And finally, the French Revolution contributed importantly to spreading these ideas throughout the European continent and subsequently throughout the world capitalist system where they continue to inform social movements and collective action to the present (Wallerstein, 1990). This specific analysis echoes Touraine's larger argument about the erosion of metasocial (or metapolitical) guarantees of social (or political) order and the expanding role of historicity and the self-production of society as defining features of the modern world.

Yet another connection between movements and modernity concerns reflexivity. It is a truism of sociology that heightened reflexivity is a hallmark of modernity, but it is rarely recognized that social movements are crucial sites of this reflexivity. This is most evident in the utopian element of movements that involves imagining an alternative to an existing social reality (Gusfield, 1994). Through their actions, however, movements also enhance reflexivity throughout the society. Movements "are something members of a society reflect on, think about, and are aware of. In attending to movements, members of a society recognize that social rules are at issue" (Gusfield, 1994:69). While promoting reflexivity throughout society, movement participants also exercise heightened reflexivity in conceptualizing their own action. If "social change theorizing and acting is the central and on-going process of every social movement," it logically follows that "[s]ocial movement practitioners are practical social change theorists who devise inter-related hypotheses and act on them, assess their actions, confirm or revise the theory, and act again" (Lofland et al.,

1989). As change agents, movements utilize a pragmatic version of the scientific method and instrumental action as they seek to transform modern social orders. Perhaps more than anyone, social movement activists merit the designation of "applied sociologist" to capture the dialectical relation between theorizing about change, testing those theories through strategic action, reformulating them based on outcomes, and proceeding to another round of social change experimentation. The reflexivity of social change agents also suggests the importance of collective learning processes that are most abstractly involved in modernization and development (Eder, 1993), but are more concretely embodied in social movement tactics and strategies as they evolve through successive rounds of collective action.

Movements and modernity are also linked through the social construction of identity and the central role of collective identity in movement challenges. "Collective actors of the past were more deeply rooted in a specific social condition in which they were embedded, so that the question of the collective was already answered from the beginning through that social condition that accounted as such for the existence of a collective actor" (Melucci, 1996a:84). In more recent social movement activism, collective identity is "becoming ever more conspicuously the product of conscious action and the outcome of self-reflection" (Melucci, 1996a:76). Melucci's argument thereby parallels Touraine's, but specifies it in terms of the collective identity that inevitably accompanies collective action. Earlier forms of collective action were rooted in a collective identity that rested on transcendent, metaphysical entities and metasocial foundations such as myths, gods, and ancestors. With the rise of modernity and the distinctively modern form of the social movement, the collective identities that undergird such action are contingent, historical, and reflexive creations of those involved in challenging social order. For modern social movements, both the social order they challenge and the collective identity from which they issue their challenge are ongoing cultural creations and social constructions (Melucci, 1996a:Chapter 4).

A final link between modernity and movements concerns how the defining characteristics of social movements emerged in interaction with the forces producing modernization. Rather than seeing movements as suprahistorical phenomena, they are better understood as specific historical inventions with distinct origins. A comprehensive analysis of contentious action in Great Britain from 1758 to 1834 thereby reveals that

> Britain's surges of collective activity represented the birth of what we now call the social movement—the sustained, organized challenge to existing authorities in the name of a deprived, excluded or wronged population . . . from the 1790s onward we can see a remarkable expansion and regularization of the national social movement not only in Great Britain but elsewhere in the West. (Tilly, 1995:144)

The emergence of this distinctive form of collective action was one response of ordinary people to the macrolevel changes associated with the concentration of capital, the augmentation of state power, and demographic pressures. These changes undermined the viability of older forms of collective action at the same time that they created new opportunities and promoted collective learning that led to the more modern form of collective action known as the social movement. Although movements were constrained by these macrolevel forces, they were not determined by them. They were rather woven into a complex process of social change that is best understood as contingent history, meaning that small differences in the sequences and combinations of events (including the impact of social movements) were capable of producing significantly different outcomes. On balance, however, social movements in Great Britain made a significant contribution to the broadening of citizenship, the nationalization of politics, and the expansion of democracy throughout the nineteenth century (Tilly, 1995).

This historically specific rise of the social movement involved a new way of claims making in which ordinary people intervened repeatedly in national affairs through large-scale coordinated action. The concept of repertoires of contention refers to learned cultural creations that predispose people at a given historical moment to use a relatively narrow range of all the possible forms of acting collectively. The emergence of the social movement signified a shift in the repertoire of contention from one that was parochial, bifurcated, and particular to one that was cosmopolitan, modular, and autonomous. In being cosmopolitan, the new repertoire was oriented to multiple localities and centers of power rather than being anchored in a single community. In being modular, the new repertoire was easily transferable across different settings rather than closely tied to particular uses. And in being autonomous, the new repertoire rested increasingly on the initiatives of claimants who established direct communication with national centers of power (Tilly, 1995:45–46). In organizational terms, these shifts signified new forms of social association, including special purpose organizations as political instruments to cultivate mass mobilization and articulate a national program that represented group interests and claims. The overall logic of collective action shifted from immediate forms of revenge or resistance directed at local targets to sustained, cumulative pressure campaigns on national centers of decision making. The new repertoire thus signified and promoted the increasing parliamentarization and nationalization of claims making (Tilly, 1995).

Whereas Tilly provided the most detailed research on this topic in a single country, Tarrow (1994) made similar arguments based on a synthesis of a broader range of empirical research by himself and others in a variety of national contexts. This research also locates the birth of the national social movement in the early nineteenth century as evidenced by a new repertoire of collective action that was national, modular, and autonomous. This repertoire, in turn, was made possible by the consolidation of nation-states, the expansion of roads and printed communication, and the growth of private associations. Tarrow places particular emphasis on commercial print media and new models of association that facilitated communication and the diffusion of movement strategies and tactics. These technological developments enhanced the modularity of new repertoires of collective action by allowing them to be transported and replicated in diverse places. The expansion of the state played a similar role, as its basic activities of making war, collecting taxes, and provisioning food became the target of sustained movement challenges. Anticipating Tilly's conclusion from Great Britain, this research also suggests that movements democratized states by broadening suffrage and winning acceptance for new forms of association, participation, and citizenship. An impressive accumulation of empirical research thereby supports a view of social movements as distinctively modern, historically specific forms of collective action that have been dialectically intertwined with the fundamental economic, political, demographic, technological, and cultural changes that define the modern age.

The most recent statement in this tradition explicitly conceptualizes social movements as an historically specific form of collective action, defined as "collective challenges to existing arrangements of power and distribution by people with common purposes and solidarity, in sustained interaction with elites, opponents, and authorities" (Meyer and Tarrow, 1998:4). Having offered this definition, the authors immediately clarify that the viability of movements as a way of making claims is inextricably tied to the rise of the nation-state, which "assured its citizens regular means of communication, created standard but fungible identities, and provided challengers with uniform targets and fulcra for acting collectively" (Meyer and Tarrow, 1998:4–5). They also clarify that movements are not the only vehicles for contention, but rather coexist alongside more sporadic outbreaks of collective action as well as more institutionalized forms of political struggle. For this research tradition, then, the historical emergence of the social movement is intertwined with the evolution of the nation-state as a political form; this linkage provides further evidence for the specifically modern character of social movements. Continuing this trajectory, the period of modernity has witnessed not just the emergence but the increasing centrality of social movements to the constitution of society. In late modernity, this centrality has assumed a quasi-institutional nature, as variously expressed in discussions of the social movement sector (McCarthy and Zald, 1977), of movements as a subsystem of the social (Melucci, 1996a) or of the emergence of a movement society of permanent, ongoing mobilization (Tarrow, 1994).

The works cited above represent profoundly different theoretical traditions in contemporary sociology. They nonetheless converge on a view of social movements as an historical by-product of the modern age. In this view, social movements evolved with the waning of metasocial guarantees of social order and the new understanding of society as contested terrain. As the sociopolitical world was increasingly understood as a social construction meriting either legitimation or critique, the development of ideology qualitatively expanded to rationalize each side in the battle over the new social order. As these battles unfolded, participants on both sides became increasingly reflexive social agents who acted purposively in the world, consciously cultivated collective identities, invented new repertoires of contention, and mounted increasingly sustained, organized, national campaigns on behalf of various social and political groups. Despite this convergence of views on the modernity of social movements, this formulation nonetheless recognizes that movements have assumed a variety of forms and levels of organization, ranging from formal social movement organizations (McCarthy and Zald, 1977) to informal social movement communities (Buechler, 1990) to loosely structured collective action (Oberschall, 1993). The crucial thread linking all these diverse forms is that they allow collective actors to achieve some degree of internal solidarity, to engage in conflict with an established adversary, and to challenge the limits of the system in which this action occurs (Melucci, 1996a:29–30). As a result of these dynamics, social movements have played an integral part in the making of the modern world.

THE RISE OF SOCIOLOGY

Just as there have always been forms of collective action throughout history, there have always been social thinkers and philosophers who pondered the world. Just as collective action took an historically new form with the origin of the modern social movement, so too did social thought take on a specifically sociological character at a particular historical moment. The origin of sociology as a modern social-scientific discipline is a story that runs on a path parallel to that of the emergence of the modern social movement. Unlike parallel lines, however, these paths have crossed in fateful ways. From its origins through its subsequent development to the present day, the central concepts, themes, and paradigms of sociology have been shaped by the challenges social movements have posed to social order and the responses of that order to those challenges. Far from being a detached observer, the discipline of sociology has been profoundly shaped by the dialectic of "order and progress" it has sought to discipline.

It was the Enlightenment that broke the intellectual ground in which modern sociology would ultimately take root. Among the dominant themes of this intellectual movement, the new emphasis on reason and rationality was perhaps most prominent. For the philosophers of this period, reason was the new alternative to unquestioning religious faith and it was to become the standard for judging truth. However, this was not a purely speculative endeavor. A second important theme concerned the role of observation and empiricism. Careful scrutiny and comparison within and between societies were essential to provide the raw material with which reason would investigate the foundations of social life. However, this was also not to be a purely scientific endeavor. A third theme involved the central role of negative-critical thought. For Enlightenment thinkers, the major function of reason was to criticize existing social institutions for the limitations they placed on human potentiality. The criticism of existing institutions presumed a fourth theme concerning the perfectibility of human beings. This perfectibility could be approximated only by eliminating social institutions that obstructed positive changes in the human condition. The theme of perfectibility, in turn, was buttressed by a final theme of progress envisioning a linear, developmental path of improvement in social life as the logical result of the application of Enlightenment thought to the organization of society (Zeitlin, 1987).

These intellectual developments did not occur in a vacuum. They were inspired by the growth of natural science and the development of the scientific method, which in turn were spurred by European trends of discovery, colonization, and conquest. And these ideas had a strong affinity with the class interests and ambitions of a rising bourgeoisie seeking to throw off the remnants of feudal society and to counter the power of a lingering aristocracy. Hence, the class struggle between the bourgeoisie and aristocracy over whether and how the world would change had its intellectual counterpart in the clash of Enlightenment ideas with religious faith and metaphysical speculation. Within a relatively brief time, the bourgeoisie appeared victorious over the aristocracy—a victory embodied in the French Revolution. Subsequent events, however, revealed that this would be a more protracted struggle that would unfold over decades before the bourgeoisie would establish firm control in France and the feudal heritage of social thought would definitively be transcended. It was precisely in this period of protracted struggle—both political and intellectual—that we may locate the origins of sociology as a discipline.

Just as the French Revolution provoked the Restoration, the Enlightenment provoked a fresh articulation of conservative social thought that sought a return to the *status quo ante*. This conservative reaction can be read as an attempted refutation of the basic premises of Enlightenment thought. More to the point, however, is the irony that these thinkers "unknowingly provided the major concepts that ultimately were to become the elements of secular social science" and that "philosophical conservatism is the source, historically, of major sociological concepts and ideas" (Zeitlin, 1987:38). The work of Louis de Bonald and Joseph de Maistre offers a convenient summary of ideas that were simultaneously an antidote to Enlightenment thought, a critique of postrevolutionary disorder, and a prelude to the founding of sociology as a discipline. These propositions were that (1) society is an organic unity with deep roots in the past; (2) society antedates the individual; (3) the individual is an abstraction; (4) the parts of society are interdependent and interrelated; (5) people have constant and unalterable needs met by societal institutions; (6) social customs and institutions are positively functional; (7) maintenance of small groups is essential to social order; (8) traditional forms of social organization are preferable to social change with its associated disorder and disintegration; (9) nonrational aspects of human existence have an essential importance and positive value; and (10) status and hierarchy are essential to society (Zeitlin, 1987:47–48). Only when the old order came under political attack and these ideas came under intellectual criticism did they receive such an explicit articulation. Once this was done, they stood ready for incorporation in the foundation of the sociological enterprise.

That task was accomplished by Auguste Comte. In contrast to the negative-critical thought of the Enlightenment, Comte characterized his system as a "positive philosophy." The term had several connotations. First, the label "positive" was intended as a direct rebuttal of the negative-critical orientation of

Enlightenment thought, which Comte saw as associated with social disorder and breakdown. Second, the term "positive" also meant affirmation, for Comte proceeded not only to describe the newly emerging social order but to underscore the positive contributions of each aspect of the new society to its overall existence and survival. Finally, the term also connoted "positivism": the belief that the natural sciences provide the best model for the newly emerging social sciences. It was this latter notion that allowed Comte to place all the sciences within a hierarchy in which sociology occupied the top position (by virtue of the complexity of its subject matter) as the "queen of the sciences." The science that Comte articulated was dedicated to the study of both social statics and social dynamics, and it represented a synthesis of several intellectual traditions including organicism, evolutionism, and determinism. The most important product of Comte's efforts was his theory of social evolution and the claim that the society of his day represented the establishment of the positive or scientific stage of social evolution that would leave behind the theological and metaphysical stages.

From its origins, sociology has thus attempted to discipline social change and disorder by framing them as part of a larger, evolutionary narrative. Comte's theory allowed him to acknowledge the passing of feudal order (unlike the reactionaries de Bonald and de Maistre) and even to acknowledge the legitimacy of Enlightenment thought as a necessary part of the process of historical change. But it also allowed him to assert the legitimacy of the new order against further challenge and to call for a healing, constructive, positive philosophy to replace the lingering vestiges of critical thought. The parallel paths of social movements and sociological science thereby intersected from the beginning; these intellectual developments did not occur in a vacuum but rather were an inseparable part of political and ideological struggles. As Comte himself wrote, "It is only by the positive polity that the revolutionary spirit can be restrained, because by it alone can the influence of the critical doctrine be justly estimated and circumscribed" (quoted in Zeitlin, 1987:65). From its origins, sociology was to be a discipline that not only studied but frequently supported the newly emerging social order.

Despite these tendencies, the new social order was not even consolidated before it too provoked resistance. These challenges had their roots in the emergence of capitalism, the proletarianization of labor, and the consolidation of states. With the establishment of industrial society and wage-labor as its characteristic form of domination, resistance increasingly took the form of socialist challenges to the new capitalist order. Struggles in the factories and the streets had their ideological counterparts elsewhere, as defenders of capitalism (including many early sociologists) provided justifications and rationales for this social order to counter the ideas of socialist thinkers. The central figure in this process was Karl Marx. More than any other socialist intellectual, Marx provided a coherent interpretation of history, a trenchant analysis of exploitation, and a compelling vision of a more humane society that could result from the transcendence of capitalism. In his critique of bourgeois society, Marx took up a position parallel to the Enlightenment thinkers who had offered a similarly sweeping appraisal of the old feudal order a century earlier. However, whereas the Enlightenment thinkers had targeted theologians and metaphysicians as their ideological opponents, capitalism had a new set of secular intellectuals who claimed this social order as their own. In challenging capitalism, Marx was also challenging the new social–scientific disciplines that had emerged with the new order.

The political legacy of socialist movements has shaped capitalist society in fundamental ways. Their challenges to capitalism and the responses of capitalism have become inscribed in the institutions and the contours of advanced capitalist societies. The intellectual challenge of socialist ideas has shaped the discourse of sociology in an equally fundamental way, and these debates are also inscribed in core sociological concepts and ideas. It is in this sense that a good deal of what we now consider the classical sociological tradition developed in a dialogue and a debate with the "ghost" of Karl Marx. In Zeitlin's interpretation of this process, the work of Weber, Durkheim, Pareto, Mosca, Michels, and Mannheim illustrates this influence, though it can be seen elsewhere as well (Zeitlin, 1987). This is not to say that the sociological tradition can be reduced to a debate with Marx, nor that there have been no other important influences on the development of this tradition. But it is to say that the classical sociological tradition is inseparable from an ongoing debate and dialogue with socialism; the latter has always been one of the central influences in shaping this tradition. If sociology has been significantly shaped by its debate with ideas challenging social order, and if these ideas derive from movements that contend for power, it follows that the origins and development of sociology have been inextricably interwoven with social movements that have challenged the existing order.

The European tradition of classical sociological theory was imported into U.S. sociology largely through Talcott Parsons. In his first major work, Parsons (1937) surveyed this tradition to develop a theory of the structure of social action. He also provided a widely used translation of portions of Max Weber's *Economy and Society* (1947) that introduced an entire generation of English-speaking sociologists to this major thinker. But in his own work and in his interpretation of others, there was a pronounced tendency to filter out elements of conflict, domination, struggle, and resistance that were central to the Marxist tradition and important in much of the rest of the European sociological legacy. The Parsonian import of classical European theory thereby offered a sanitized version that shaped its reception in the United States for many years. Parsons's theoretical inclinations fully emerged with the publication of *The Social System* (1951) and the establishment of structural-functionalism as the dominant sociological paradigm. With its concerns for integration, equilibrium, and the functional role of societal institutions, the sociological tradition in the United States remarginalized the conflict, struggle, and change that had prompted its development. The best testimony to the theoretical hegemony of the Parsonian framework is the fact that the alternatives of "conflict theory" offered by Coser (1956) and Dahrendorf (1959) did not really escape the functionalist paradigm as much as they offered one-sided and partial theories of what functionalism ignored. Even with a conflict focus, each of these works remained explicitly or implicitly tied to the central concepts of functionalist analysis (Ritzer, 1996).

There were lingering traces of other traditions that persisted alongside structural-functionalism in this period. The Chicago school and the symbolic interactionist tradition operated as a sociological subculture during this time. C. Wright Mills sustained a more historically oriented form of sociological inquiry rooted in both Marx and Weber. But these and other traditions were indisputably marginalized by the status achieved by structural-functionalism in this period. This theoretical predominance was due, in part, to the resonance between the prevailing themes of functionalist discourse and the philosophical conservatism that was central in the founding of sociology in Europe more than a century earlier. Zeitlin's (1987) characterization of this philosophical conservatism reveals how close a fit there was between the conservative reaction to Enlightenment thought and the core ideas of structural-functionalism. And the bridge connecting these two bodies of thought was Emile Durkheim. He developed his conception of sociology through an explicit reliance on Comte and St. Simon, he reiterated their underlying concerns with order, stability, and integration, and he provided the theoretical building blocks for contemporary functionalism as synthesized by Parsons. In this manner, a set of ideas initially articulated in response to massive social conflict and change in late eighteenth-century France came to define mainstream, mid-twentieth-century sociology in the United States.

Sociology, of course, was on the verge of changing again. As in the past, the changes were not primarily due to internal debates within the discipline. Sociology rather changed in response to the protest, conflict, and social movements that defined the 1960s as an era. Three forms of this change may be noted in passing. First, these events reestablished the legitimacy of the Marxist tradition, now in the form of critical theory and several varieties of neo-Marxism that went well beyond the "conflict theory" of the 1950s (Ritzer, 1996). Second, these events prompted a more reflexive turn within the discipline, evident in numerous attempts to develop a sociology of sociology that could understand the myriad connections between the prevailing social order and the place of sociology within that order (Friedrichs, 1970; Halmos, 1970; Reynolds and Reynolds, 1970). Third, and most specifically, these events prompted a rethinking of the nature of protest and the role of social movements, and led to new ways of theorizing such events. There was much work to do, because the sociology of the 1950s proved an abysmal basis for predicting subsequent decades. Parsons (1951) had portrayed a social order in general harmony and equilibrium, Daniel Bell (1960) had spoken of the "end of ideology," Smelser (1962) had characterized social movements as irrational and short-circuited, and even Mills's (1956) more critical theory of the power elite and mass society failed to anticipate the political challenges that defined the 1960s.

From its inception, then, sociology has developed in response to challenges to an historically specific social order.

> Sociology emerged as a new approach to politics after the upheavals of the
> French Revolution. It developed and became decisively established as an at-
> tempt to deal with the social, moral and cultural problems of the capitalist eco-
> nomic order. (Therborn, 1976:143)

Sociology is thus historically situated within the capitalist mode of production.
It arose as part of the same social transformation that initiated capitalism, it
matured through ongoing efforts to reconcile order and progress within this
societal form, and it continues to be shaped by periodic challenges to the ex-
pansionary logic and instrumental rationality of the capitalist system. This is
perhaps the only intellectually defensible way in which sociology may be characterized as a "bourgeois science": it was part of the ascendancy of a new social class and a new social order, and the order it has always studied, often supported, and occasionally challenged has been the social order of capitalist
society. The origin, development, and maturation of sociology as a discipline
are thus inseparable from the periodic challenges to modern social order, as the
intersecting paths of social movements and scientific ambitions have profoundly
shaped the sociological enterprise.

CONCLUSIONS

The modern social movement and the discipline of sociology thereby share a
common heritage. Both emerged as products of fundamental, sociohistorical
changes in eighteenth-century Europe that challenged not only the status quo
but the very notion that any status quo had a transcendent foundation. With
the elimination of metasocial guarantees of social order, the social world came
to be seen as a complex but undeniably social construction that represented
one possible social order among a range of alternatives. Throughout the modern era, possible alternatives have been embodied in social movements that have
agitated for the transformation of one socially constructed order into another.
Although such movements rarely achieve immediate or total victories, they often contribute to reform, change, and development in the social order they
challenge. In this sense, contemporary society bears the imprint of numerous
past social struggles that have been inscribed in the contours and institutions
of the modern world.

　　While social movements emerged with the modern world in an attempt to
change it, sociology developed in an attempt to understand it. This meant examining the very social order that movements were in the process of challenging. As defenders of the social order articulated the rationale for their society,
sociology found much of its conceptual and theoretical foundation. As challengers to that social order revived their critique, sociology became enriched
by selectively borrowing from these traditions as well as by elaborating more
extensive theories of social order in the face of new challenges. Thus, just as
the effects of social movements are inscribed in later forms of social organization, their effects have also shaped the development of sociology as a discipline.
It is impossible to understand the shape of the modern world or the evolution

of sociology without according a prominent place to the impact of these movements.

Although sociology has developed through this dialectical relationship with social movements, it has rarely acknowledged the debt. For much of this century, processes of collective action were lost somewhere between broad, sweeping theories of social change that obscured the role of human agency and narrow, specific theories of collective behavior that marginalized the effect of social movements. Neither approach recognized social movements as a fundamental force in the modern world, nor acknowledged what these movements have contributed to the development of the discipline. But this rupture is not irreparable. There are a number of ways that a more self-conscious appreciation of this connection would be beneficial to the ongoing development of sociology.

One benefit would derive from a deeper consideration of Touraine's theory of social movements and their consequences in modern society. Although his conceptual framework is cumbersome and some of his claims are problematic, there is a profound insight in the conception of modern society as increasingly self-produced through the conflicts of various social groups over control of historicity. This theory makes a powerful case that the capacity for self-reflexive action is an increasingly important feature of the modern world. This means that the object of sociological inquiry—society itself—has changed in important ways that sociology must recognize if it is to remain viable as a "science of society." The issue can be framed from other theoretical traditions as well. If one's starting premise is that the world is a social construction, an increasing proportion of action in the world involves intentional, self-reflexive efforts at social reconstruction (with unintended and unanticipated consequences). And in a final twist, these very understandings of the social world are no longer the province of specialized sociological experts, but have increasingly become part of the common understandings of everyday social actors (Giddens, 1984). Sociology needs to locate such processes at the center of its inquiry, and the study of social movements provides an ideal means of doing so. As Melucci has noted, "movements are the social domain which most readily escapes the confines of the inherited, and most perceptibly reveals the manner and locus of the society's self-constructive processes" (Melucci, 1996a:380).

Greater attention to social movements would also shed needed light on some foundational sociological disputes because "movements force us to reflect on the question of how social action . . . constitutes itself in systems" (Melucci, 1996a:380). Among these disputes are questions of structure and agency as well as the relation between macro- and microlevels. Sociology has produced many one-sided theories that privilege one of these poles, but is still searching for a theoretical means of recognizing their dialectical interrelationships. Giddens's structuration theory (1984) is one promising attempt to move beyond these dualities while also recognizing the self-reflexivity of social actors. But it remains a highly abstract approach. Social movements embody these abstractions in particular sociohistorical contexts and concrete social struggles. Because movements are comprised of self-reflexive agents seeking social change, they must wrestle with the very same questions. In effect, their task is to solve the practical puzzle of how microlevel agents can initiate and promote transformation in macrolevel structures that both constrain and facilitate their efforts. Each strategy and tactic is thus a hypothesis that is tested by subsequent practice and thereby informs a movement's theory of social order and change. Examining the relation between movements and contexts would put questions of agency/structure and micro/macro at the center of sociological investigation (Kriesi, 1988), and provide an empirically manageable means of studying what otherwise remain hopelessly abstract and arcane disputes. Commenting on how the study of collective action can help transcend such abstract theoretical dichotomies, Melucci has noted that

> this branch of knowledge and inquiry provides a useful training for those who wish to address the central problem of social theory concerning the relationship between the actor and the system. In no other area of sociology does the dualistic tradition handed down to us from the nineteenth century clash as evidently with the object of study. (Melucci 1996a:381)

Seen in this way, social movements are ongoing experiments that speak to central issues in sociological theory if we can learn to listen to them.

Perhaps the greatest benefit of a renewed appreciation of the role of social movements would be the opportunity to reengage sociological discourse with the fundamental moral, civic, and political questions of the age. Even when some of the classical theorists created intellectual justifications for an emerging capitalist order, they did so out of deep moral and political commitments. This engagement with the world evaporated with the scientization of sociological theory most clearly represented by the ascendancy of Parsonian structural-functionalism (Seidman, 1994). Even though functionalism's theoretical hegemony is long since past, its model of theory—abstract, generalized, universal, objective, deductive, and positivist—has shaped the discipline and its subfields in myriad ways. The price of adopting this model of theory, and of establishing "theory" as a distinct subfield in its own right, has been a profound disengagement from contemporary practical, political, moral, and civic issues; the price has also been the increasing irrelevance of professional sociology to practical questions (Seidman, 1994). Greater attention to the role of social movements—not merely as a specialized subfield but as a constitutive force in shaping the modern world and constructing alternative futures—would help sociology replace its highly abstract and scientized discourse with a renewed engagement with the social world that comprises its subject matter. For all these reasons, a family reunion between the estranged siblings of sociology and social movements is long overdue.

2

Social Movement Theory
A Sociology of Knowledge Analysis

Despite their role in shaping modernity and sociology, social movements have received only intermittent sociological attention. This variability in theorizing about movements is best understood through the sociology of knowledge, which suggests that the "story of social movement theory can be told only together with the story of social movements themselves" (Garner, 1997:1). Indeed, the prevailing view of social movements at a given historical moment reflects not just existing movements but also the larger sociohistorical climate, the dominant sociological paradigms, and the biographies of scholars themselves. From this perspective, the twists and turns in social movement theory reflect societal and disciplinary trends as much as they mirror collective action. Like other subfields in sociology (and other disciplines as well), the history of social movement theory is less the story of cumulative scientific progress than one of paradigm shifts (Kuhn, 1962) that qualitatively redefine the central issues in the field, rendering old questions uninteresting and new ones compelling. The last major paradigm shift in social movement theory occurred in the 1970s, in response to the social activism of the 1960s as well as broader societal trends. What changed was not just the prevailing view of collective action, but also the sociohistorical climate, dominant theoretical paradigms, and typical scholarly biographies. It remains to be seen whether these developments will lead to a more profound reconceptualization of the discipline itself.

This chapter provides a brief sketch of this theoretical history. In some respects, it parallels a recent interpretation of social movement theory by Roberta Garner (1997) that identifies three processes that have contributed to paradigm shifts in social movement theory. Internal imperatives refer to unsolved intellectual puzzles within existing paradigms. External pressures include changes in larger intellectual currents and changes in movement phenomena themselves. Based on these factors, Garner divides the past 50 years of social movement theory into three periods. In the first period (1940s and 1950s), she detects a negative orientation toward movements, a tendency to explain them in terms of social psychology, and a preoccupation with the irrational origins and nature of movements. The second period (1960s and 1970s) brought a more positive orientation toward movements, which were increasingly seen as purposive organizations comprised of rational actors pursuing strategic goals. The third period (1980s and 1990s) brought more ambivalence toward movements, as right-wing countermovements displaced progressive movements and intellectual shifts toward postmodernism undermined the privileged role of movements in a narrative of historical progress (Garner, 1997). Although this account overstates the differences between the second and third periods, it is a very helpful overview of recent changes in social movement theory.

My own version of this history is somewhat different, and it is meant to serve three distinct purposes. First, I want to provide a primer in social movement theory that captures the dominant themes of different conceptual frameworks in successive historical moments. Second, I hope to suggest the plausibility of a sociology of knowledge approach that links these dominant themes to their respective sociohistorical climates and theoretical paradigms. Third, I intend to use this overview of social movement theory as the basis for a critical evaluation of the latest developments in the field and an argument for the approach to be developed in the remainder of this book. Most of the chapter is therefore organized around a fundamental conceptual and historical distinction between classical collective behavior theory and modern social movement theory.

CLASSICAL COLLECTIVE BEHAVIOR THEORY

Classical collective behavior theory rests on several core assumptions. First, collective behavior is a unitary concept that may be manifested in a variety of ways but can ultimately be understood by a single explanatory logic. Panics, crazes, crowds, and movements are thus seen almost as interchangeable manifestations of collective behavior that can be analyzed in the same way. Second, collective behavior is seen as essentially noninstitutional, in sharp contrast to the patterns and rhythms of normal daily life. There is thus a tendency to view this phenomenon as formless, shapeless, unpatterned, and unpredictable. Third, collective behavior is understood as a reaction to societal stress, strain, or breakdown that serves as the fundamental catalyst for such behavior. Such breakdown is presumed to create a state of anomie, which in turn may promote various forms of collective behavior. Fourth, the direct causes of collective behavior are seen as rooted in individuals who are experiencing various forms of discontent or anxiety. By locating primary causation in individuals, the challenge is then to explain the translation of individual discontent into genuinely collective action. Fifth, collective behavior is seen as essentially psychological rather than political in nature. This assumption contains an implicit challenge to the legitimacy of collective behavior by reducing its core elements to the psychological level (McAdam, 1982). Finally, collective behavior is sometimes taken to be a dangerous, threatening, extreme, or irrational form of behavior. This carries another challenge to the legitimacy of collective behavior by preemptively denying the purposive, goal-directed nature of at least some collective behavior.

Although specific theories or schools may not endorse all of these assumptions, they collectively constitute a distinctive theoretical lens for studying collective behavior. Virtually all of these assumptions were ultimately challenged by critics of the collective behavior model. But of all these assumptions, it is the first one (that collective behavior is a unitary concept) that created the greatest difficulties. In the words of one critic, "collective behaviour is too general a container, bringing together under its categorical unity a great multitude of different empirical phenomena ranging from 'spontaneous' panic to planned revolutions" (Melucci, 1996a:19). The insistence that social movements can be analyzed with the same theoretical tools as crowds, panics, and crazes represented a kind of conceptual overreach that took plausible ideas about some types of collective behavior (noninstitutional, psychological, anomic, etc.) and extended them to all types of collective behavior. The emergence of modern social movement theory began with the dissolution of the unitary concept of collective behavior and the insistence that social movements comprise a different phenomenon requiring a different set of theoretical tools. Both the popularity and the retreat of the classical collective behavior model are best understood through the sociology of knowledge. The distinctive assumptions of this model were a direct reflection of the larger theoretical paradigms from which they were developed, the sociohistorical climate of the era, and the biographies of the theorists. Far from mirroring actual collective action in a pure and undistorted way, it was preexisting theoretical investments and social world views that led theorists to see collective behavior through distinct conceptual frameworks.

Collective Behavior Theory I: Symbolic Interactionism

One version of collective behavior theory is closely intertwined with the paradigm of symbolic interaction as synthesized by George Herbert Mead and further developed by Herbert Blumer. This intertwining provides one illustration of a sociology of knowledge approach because this version of collective behavior theory was as much a reflection of symbolic interactionism's core premises as it was a representation of episodes of collective behavior. As a general orientation, symbolic interactionism underscores the importance of fluid and dynamic social processes rather than fixed and static social structures. In so doing, it also emphasizes the active and creative role of individuals in symbolically defining their world and selecting courses of action within that world. In Blumer's classic formulation, the core ideas of the symbolic interactionist tradition can be expressed in the form of three assumptions: that people act toward things on the basis of the meanings the things have for them; that meanings arise out of social interaction; and that meanings are created, sustained, and transformed through an ongoing interpretive process (Blumer, 1969). These specific premises and this general orientation led to a highly distinctive version of collective behavior theory.

For Blumer, collective behavior refers to forms of group activity that are not regulated by social rules or common understandings, but rather are spontaneous, unregulated, and unstructured. Elementary collective behavior is the basic unit of analysis. This behavior is rooted in circular reaction or interstimulation whereby social actors who are copresent react to one another in a way that amplifies and reinforces some initial stimulation or state of arousal. Given the premises of symbolic interaction, it is ironic that Blumer sees this process as nonreflective and mechanistic; at one point he utilizes the metaphor of a herd of cattle in a state of alarm to enliven his description of this process (Blumer, 1951:170). Circular reaction and interstimulation are most likely to occur when there is some disturbance in standard routines and rhythms of everyday life. When circular reaction becomes contagious, it can give rise to social unrest, with elements of randomness, excitability, apprehension, irritability, and increased suggestibility. This social unrest is the crucible out of which new forms of organized activity may eventually emerge, including social movements. The specific mechanisms that produce social unrest are threefold. Milling establishes rapport among actors. Collective excitement elevates emotional arousal and renders people more unstable and irresponsible. Finally, "social contagion refers to the relatively rapid, unwitting, and nonrational dissemination of a mood, impulse, or form of conduct; it is well exemplified by the spread of crazes, manias and fads" (Blumer, 1951:176). Although collective behavior may eventually assume different forms and degrees of organization, it begins with these processes of elementary collective behavior.

Such behavior gives rise to elementary collective groupings of several different types, including acting crowds, expressive crowds, the mass, the public, and social movements. Consistent with this theoretical logic, movements begin as amorphous, poorly organized, and formless, although they may develop into virtual minisocieties with many of the features of complex organizations. General social movements remain vague, indefinite, groping, unorganized manifestations of broad cultural trends, whereas specific social movements consist of well-defined goals, explicit organization, designated leaders, a division of labor, and a distinct we-feeling. Specific social movements develop through distinct mechanisms. Agitation provides arousal and direction by translating inequality or powerlessness into action. The development of *esprit de corps* organizes feelings on behalf of the movement, including a new sense of identity based on in-group–out-group relations, informal fellowship, and ceremonial behaviors that create group enthusiasm. Morale provides persistence and determination to a movement through a set of convictions and a faith in the rightness of the cause or certainty of victory. Group ideology specifies the purpose of the movement, condemns the status quo, and provides justifications of the movement's beliefs and myths. Finally, tactics address how to gain and hold adherents and reach movement objectives. Specific social movements are expected to follow a standard life history through the stages of social unrest, popular excitement, formalization, and institutionalization. In addition to these stages of development, Blumer distinguishes among revolutionary, reform, or expressive movements based on the degree and the locus of the changes they seek in society.

Although Blumer's analysis of social movements sounds quite conventional, it is distinguished from other approaches by his insistence that all forms of collective behavior (including but not limited to social movements) are built up out of the elementary processes described earlier. This same claim may be found in the later work of Turner and Killian, who carried on the Blumerian tradition through three editions of their seminal text *Collective Behavior* (1957, 1972, 1987). Like Blumer, Turner and Killian see collective behavior as the spontaneous development of norms and organization that contradict those of the larger society. Collective behavior is sparked by changes in social organization, and especially by processes of social disintegration, that provoke diverse individual reactions to critical unstructured situations. These diverse responses eventually coalesce around new, emergent norms that develop through collective behavior, but Turner and Killian emphasize that this can happen only if there is some shared image of a better future and some we-feeling in the group. Social contagion is essential to this process as people search for socially sanctioned meaning in a relatively unstructured situation; the search is carried out through milling, which Turner and Killian suggest is best seen as a process of communication. They insist that crowds do not just react to stimuli but rather develop and interpret symbols to orient their action. They see this as an interactive and "rational" process of communication that confers meaning on the environment and on the crowd itself. With these variations, they apply their theory to a wide range of collective behavior, including crowds, masses, and publics.

Turner and Killian's analysis of collective behavior thereby follows Blumer's lead, but with a somewhat greater emphasis on communication and rationality. Emergent norm theory may thus be seen as a more elaborate alternative to Blumer's circular reaction theory (Turner, 1996). Their analysis of social movements is considerably more detailed than Blumer's, however. They define a movement as a collectivity acting with some continuity to promote or resist change. They see movements following standard life cycles, and they acknowledge that movements can become institutionalized when they have an ongoing function to perform and when they continue to provide benefits to members. They provide a somewhat different typology of movements. For instance, value-oriented movements promote a publicly understood program; their success requires promises of social betterment along with immediate benefits, a clear hierarchy of goals, resonance with socially accepted values, and appropriate tactics. Whereas value-oriented movements sound benign, power-oriented movements strike a more ominous chord. These are exemplified by control movements whose main goal is to dominate a larger group; they are often authoritarian in nature and based on a belief that the end justifies the means. Power-oriented movements may also take the form of separatist movements devoted to maintaining some group identity; these typically arise through factionalism within existing movements and can become quite sectarian in nature. The last major category is participation-oriented movements whose main purpose is member satisfaction rather than external goals. Such movements may prepare people for coming changes, provide status to their members, or foster personal goals, and they are especially attractive to marginal or outcast groups seeking validation.

In the most recent edition of their text (Turner and Killian, 1987), the authors propose a theory of social movements based on three distinctive features: a disposition to bypass established structures; the translation of perception, feelings, and ideas into action; and the collectivizing of that action. Bypassing normal channels requires emergent norms within the movement that convey a sense of necessity or obligation to take action. In the most common cases, the emergent norm defines some social practice as unjust, but the question of how and why this definition emerges for some practices and not others remains open. The translation of perceptions, feelings, and ideas into action requires a sense of feasibility and timeliness; the former suggests that it is possible for a situation to be changed whereas the latter conveys a sense of urgency that it must be changed now. Finally, the collectivization of action generally requires membership in some preexisting group of people with cooptable networks that can be redirected to movement purposes as well as a sense of fraternal relative deprivation that defines the problem as collective rather than individual. Although these three elements are described in isolation, they operate as an interactive process in which the timing of the elements is crucial to the actual emergence of collective behavior. The latter is thus best understood through life cycle or interactive spiral models of action that are attentive to the processual nature of collective behavior.

From Blumer's initial formulation to Turner and Killian's last word, this version of collective behavior theory faithfully reflects its roots in the broader perspective of symbolic interactionism. This is a paradigm that emphasizes fluid processes over static structures, creative agency over structural determination, and the symbolic creation and interpretation of meanings as central to human life. It is precisely these concerns that are echoed in this tradition of collective behavior, with its emphasis on spontaneity, contagion, circular reaction, suggestibility, interaction, communication, keynoting, and emergent norms. From a sociology of knowledge approach, it is evident that this theoretical tradition for studying collective behavior is as much a reflection of its broader theoretical heritage of symbolic interactionism as it is a mirror of empirical instances of collective behavior.

Of the three versions of collective behavior theory discussed here, the symbolic interactionist approach remains the most vital and its practitioners continue to make important contributions to the study of collective behavior. This was foreshadowed in Blumer's (1971) later work on social problems as collective behavior, which provides a bridge between classical collective behavior theory and contemporary social constructionism. The productivity of this paradigm is evident in recent work on crowds and crowd behavior (McPhail, 1991;

Snow et al., 1981), on cults (Lofland, 1977), on moral panics (Goode and Ben-Yehuda, 1994), and on the role of emotion in protest (Lofland, 1985); it is also reflected in the continuing centrality of Turner and Killian's (1987) classic text on collective behavior. Scholars in this tradition have also responded effectively to the common charge that collective behavior theory presumes irrational actors by distinguishing between earlier and later work in this tradition and by clarifying the distinction between emotion and irrationality (Killian, 1994; McPhail, 1991; Turner, 1981). Finally, proponents of this tradition have been active participants in the ongoing debate over recent paradigm shifts by identifying the parallel assumptions that can sometimes be found in different approaches and arguing for the ongoing connections between collective behavior and social movements (Aguirre, 1994; Turner, 1981).

Collective Behavior II: Structural-Functionalism

Close connections between a broad theoretical paradigm and a specific theory of collective behavior are also evident in a rather different variant of classical collective behavior theory derived from structural-functionalism. The latter rests on a metaphor between societies and living organisms in which both are seen as complex and bounded wholes consisting of interrelated parts, each of which fulfills some necessary function and thereby contributes to the stability and survival of the larger entity of which it is a part. This venerable tradition received its most elaborate formulation by Talcott Parsons, who conceptualized social order as a series of interrelated action systems in which the social system organizes interaction through status-role complexes, the personality system organizes needs and decision-making capacities, the cultural system provides common, integrative values, and the biological organism provides the prerequisites of intelligent action. When operating smoothly, these four action systems become stable structures that fulfill four essential functional prerequisites of social stability and system survival: adaptation of each system to its broader environment, goal attainment within each system, integration, of the various elements of each system and subsystem, and latent pattern maintenance and tension management of each system (Parsons, 1951).

Because functionalism was centered on problems of social order, it took longer to address collective behavior than some other paradigms. But the challenge to do so was met with the publication of Smelser's *Theory of Collective Behavior* (1962). Firmly grounded in Parsons's elaborate conceptual scheme of society as a social system, Smelser extended this theoretical apparatus to noninstitutional forms of action that served as the defining benchmark of collective behavior. The result was a complex, value-added theory of the emergence of collective behavior through a series of stages. Despite its complexity, the theory was clear about several key points. First, for analytical purposes, social movements were one type of collective behavior alongside others such as panics, crazes, and fads. Linking all these types was the connotation of spontaneous, short-lived, disorganized, and deviant behavior. Second, as with all the other forms of collective behavior, participants in social movements subscribed to fundamentally irrational beliefs that short-circuited appropriate channels of social action. While symbolic interactionism and structural-functionalism are worlds apart in their fundamental theoretical assumptions, there are some remarkable parallels and similarities in their conception of collective behavior. Despite very different theoretical ancestry, both theories partially converge on a view of collective behavior as noninstitutional, spontaneous, short-lived expressions of behavior that rests on shared beliefs and ranges from panic to revolution (Melucci, 1996a:14).

Smelser's version of the theory is distinguished by claims of logical rigor. He proposed that all forms of collective behavior emerged through an identical, value-added process of individually necessary and collectively sufficient steps. The first step is structural conduciveness, which refers to a set of structural conditions that permits or encourages (but does not determine) some form of collective behavior. The less conducive a given set of structural arrangements, the less likely that any form of collective behavior will occur. The second element is structural strain, referring to ambiguities, deprivations, conflicts, and discrepancies. Although Parsonian functionalism had acknowledged social strain, what distinguishes collective behavior from "normal" responses to strain is that it compresses or short-circuits levels of social action, giving collective behavior a crude, excessive, eccentric, impatient quality when compared to routine and institutionalized social action. The existence of social strain alongside structural conduciveness thereby increases the likelihood of collective behavior. The third element is generalized beliefs that supply meaning, motivation, and orientation to potential actors in collective behavior. If strain creates ambiguity, generalized beliefs reduce ambiguity in a short-circuited manner that prepares people for action. The generalized nature of such beliefs refers to their compressing or collapsing of levels and components of social action; as such, generalized beliefs are inherently irrational cognitive responses to structural strain that can nonetheless provide powerful incentives for action. Generalized beliefs can take differing forms, including hysteria, wish-fulfillment, hostility, norm-oriented beliefs, or value-oriented beliefs.

The final three elements of the value-added process receive less explicit attention but are analytically as crucial as the other elements in episodes of collective behavior. The fourth stage involves precipitating factors, which are specific events or actions that provide direct catalysts for collective behavior. Such factors serve to condense prior elements of conduciveness, strain, and generalized beliefs into a potent manifestation of the problem that provokes collective behavior. The fifth stage is the actual mobilization of participants for collective behavior, when all the prior environmental and ideational factors are finally translated into concrete action by those participating in the episode of collective behavior. The sixth stage concerns the operation of social control, which must be at least temporarily absent or disabled if the incipient collective behavior is to manifest itself fully. While identified last, this factor is relevant to every previous stage because various kinds of social control could preclude any of the prior, value-added elements from occurring and adding momentum to the emergence of collective behavior. An episode of collective behavior may thereby be read as signifying the relative absence of various social controls that might have precluded such an episode in a more smoothly functioning social system. Given Smelser's value-added logic, collective behavior emerges only when all six of these elements occur in conjunction with one another; when they do, some form of collective behavior is inevitable.

The same theoretical logic is used to explain five distinct forms of collective behavior: panics, crazes, hostile outbursts, norm-oriented movements, and value-oriented movements. Norm-oriented movements (NOMs) attempt to restore, protect, modify, or create norms in the name of a generalized belief; value-oriented movements (VOMs) attempt to do the same for values. NOMs are more likely to emerge when social structures are conducive to moderate reform movements that allow gradual change to take place; the absence of such possibilities will generate VOMs (if any form of collective behavior emerges). Smelser relies on each of his value-added elements to offer a differential analysis of the emergence of NOMs and VOMs, and emphasizes that in both types of movement the process of mobilization for action is more complex than in the more elementary forms of collective behavior (including relations between leaders and followers, organizational dynamics, and the like). Although his value-added scheme is rather cumbersome, the scope of Smelser's theory is impressive in its ambition to link broad, structural background factors to the dynamics of specific instances of collective behavior. But just as Blumer, Turner, and Killian used collective behavior as a unitary concept that linked movements to elementary collective behavior that could be understood only through the lens of symbolic interactionism, Smelser has his own unitary concept of collective behavior, which places movements on the same analytical plane as panics and crazes and seeks to explain them through the same structural–functional theory of collective behavior.

Mass society theory is an important variant on functionalist approaches to collective behavior that deserves brief mention here as well. Structural-functionalist and mass society approaches both share a common ancestry in the work of the classical French theorist Emile Durkheim. In Durkheim's analysis of modernity (1893), social evolution led from the mechanical solidarity and *conscience collective* of traditional societies to the organic solidarity and division of labor of modern societies. There were distinctive dangers in this process if individualism became too prominent. The problem of anomie referred to a lack of normative regulation in rapidly changing social circumstances, whereas the problem of egoism involved a lack of social integration that would otherwise anchor individuals in groups. Durkheim's diagnosis of the problem of egoism in particular provides a link to modern mass society theory (Kornhauser, 1959). For this perspective, modernity is distinguished by the emergence of large-scale social structures but the disappearance of mid-level groups that would provide social anchors for individuals. With the demise of smaller scale social groups, modern society becomes a mass society in which isolation, depersonalization, and alienation become prevalent. It was the distinctive prediction of mass society theory that the most isolated and alienated individuals would gravitate toward participation in collective behavior because it offered one of the few available social anchors for such individuals. Although this prediction was spectacularly unsuccessful (because isolated actors are no more likely to join collective behavior than any other collective undertaking), the assumptions of the theory echoed those of structural-functionalism: social order normally precludes collective behavior, which must be explained in terms of social strain or breakdown that leads to psychological discontent, irrational ideation, and extreme, deviant, or short-circuited behavioral responses.

Like the structural-functionalism from which it originated, Smelser's theory of collective behavior (and the mass society variant) has come in for heavy criticism. Like the structural-functionalism that was its basis, Smelser's theory incorporates a conservative, status quo bias that privileges existing social structures and defines departures from them as irrational, dangerous, extremist, and deviant. For my purposes, however, the specific criticisms of this theory are less crucial than the manner in which this theory of collective behavior was logically derived from the larger conceptual framework of Parsonian structural-functionalism. Alongside the symbolic interactionist version of collective behavior, we now have two examples of collective behavior theories that analyzed social movements vis-à-vis their larger theoretical assumptions and developed theories whose derivation and content have as much to do with those larger theoretical commitments as with consistent, concrete, empirical instances of social movement activism. This is exactly what a sociology of knowledge approach would lead us to expect, and it is also evident in the final variation on classical collective behavior theory.

Collective Behavior III: Relative Deprivation

A third variant of classical collective behavior theory may be found in approaches that emphasize relative deprivation as the motivating force behind participation in collective behavior. Such approaches rely on a smattering of mainstream sociological concepts with a decidedly social–psychological twist. The tradition of role theory (Merton, 1968; Linton, 1936) and the specific concept of reference groups provide examples here. Reference groups are external groups to whom people refer to judge their own position. When people judge themselves as lacking resources enjoyed by their reference group, relative deprivation may be said to be present. The concept of relative deprivation thus accentuates the role of subjective elements in this process. Indeed, the concept emerged and certainly has functioned to explain cases in which people make judgments that do not necessarily accord with those of neutral observers or objective data. Such judgments are rather based on sentiments, feelings, and perceptions about the reference groups that comprise the foundation for judgments of relative deprivation. Although theorists of relative deprivation do not explicitly describe these processes as irrational, their emphasis on the role of subjectivity and emotional factors implies that these judgments are nonrational. Though arrived at by different means, the resulting social–psychological image of the individual is not that different from that of the other branches of classical collective behavior theory discussed above.

The path by which the concept of relative deprivation entered the field of collective behavior illustrates how it sought to account for nonobvious social situations and conditions. The simplest logic linking motivation to action suggests that the most absolutely deprived groups of people have the greatest incentive to engage in collective behavior to alter their situation. Such a logic would predict that absolutely deprived groups are much more likely to engage in collective behavior than groups that are somewhat better off. It is against this logic that relative deprivation theorists argue that it is not the most absolutely deprived groups that typically revolt or rebel, either because their time and energy must be devoted to sheer survival or because their situation breeds a fatalism and passivity that preclude collective behavior on their behalf. It is precisely the somewhat better-off groups who are historically more likely to engage in such behavior. Since such an occurrence cannot be explained in terms of absolute deprivation, the concept of relative deprivation provides a convenient mechanism for explaining this behavior, and the differential probability that various groups will engage in collective behavior.

The seminal article that linked relative deprivation with collective behavior sought to explain the timing of revolutionary activity (Davies, 1962). Davies describes two preexisting theories that appear contradictory. The "degradation thesis" holds that people's propensity to revolt increases as their condition worsens; the "improvement thesis" claims that as people's situation improves, they are more likely to revolt. Although there is some evidence to support both claims, Davies argues that these factors are best understood as acting in conjunction in a certain historical sequence. His synthesis in the form of the "J-curve" theory predicts that when a prolonged period of economic and social development is followed by a sudden and sharp reversal, rebellion is most likely to occur. The reasoning involves the subjective factor of relative deprivation. That is, people's expectations are shaped by the relatively long period of gradual improvement, and they project these expectations onto a future state of ongoing improvement. When a sudden, sharp reversal occurs after this long history, the result is a substantial gap between what people have come to expect and what they are actually receiving (and expect to receive in the future based on their deteriorating situation). This acute sense of deprivation relative to their expectations (based on a history of gradual improvement) is sufficient to motivate people to participate in collective behavior to alter their situation.

Although the J-curve describes the most acute form, it is by no means the only form that relative deprivation may take. In addition to this "rise and drop" pattern, at least four other patterns of relative deprivation have been identified (Geschwender, 1968). Despite the variations, Geschwender (1968) claims that each rests on the same underlying social–psychological condition of cognitive dissonance. More specifically, each variant of relative deprivation gives rise to the following cognitions. First, there is an image of a state of affairs that the actor believes is possible to attain. Second, there is a belief that the actor is entitled to that state of affairs. Third, there is the knowledge that the actor is not currently enjoying that state of affairs. Cognitive dissonance theory argues that the dissonance between multiple, equally plausible cognitions, perceptions, and beliefs is psychologically painful, and that people will act to reduce this psychological pain. Although there are multiple ways of reducing cognitive dissonance, Geschwender's argument implies that when collective behavior does occur, we are likely to find elements of cognitive dissonance and relative deprivation among the causes of that behavior.

The most elaborate use of the relative deprivation approach may be found in a major study of political violence. Gurr (1969) posits a primary causal sequence in which relative deprivation fosters discontent, which is first politicized and then actualized in political violence. While Gurr recognizes a variety of factors that promote relative deprivation and a diversity of forms of political violence that result from it, it is relative deprivation that provides the crucial link between background conditions and political violence. Relative deprivation, in turn, derives from some rather simplistic psychological assumptions about the connections between frustration and aggression. Thus, even though he seeks to explain phenomena as complex as revolutions, his ultimate explanatory mechanisms are the social–psychological principles of relative deprivation, frustration, threat, and aggression. His emphasis on the subjective elements of how people define a state of relative deprivation implies that it is a nonrational process that flies in the face of objective measures of well-being. Although the tone of his book is that of neutral social science, there is no mistaking the subtext of value judgments that equate collective behavior with political violence and depict both as dangerous, extremist, illegitimate threats to prevailing social order. Indeed, given the sociohistorical climate in which it was written, it is hard not to interpret this as a primer in social control and counterinsurgency. Although the concept of relative deprivation need not lead to these judgments, Gurr's work provides a potent example of the inescapably political subtext of theories about collective behavior.

The Limits of Classical Collective Behavior Theory

Each variant of classical collective behavior theory reflects its respective origins in symbolic interactionism, structural-functionalism, and social psychology. Given the fundamental differences between these broad paradigms, there is remarkable convergence in their imagery of collective behavior. This imagery depicts collective behavior as taking a wide variety of forms, ranging from panics, crazes, and fads to social movements and revolutions. It depicts this behavior as noninstitutional, with the implication that it is spontaneous, unstructured, formless, and short lived. It argues that the structural origins of collective behavior involve social disorganization, strain, disorder, or disruption. And it ultimately argues that the individual's response to strains is the proximate cause of collective behavior, implicitly reducing collective behavior to a social–psychological phenomenon. This focus also paves the way for explicit arguments or implicit suggestions that collective behavior is fundamentally nonrational or irrational behavior that can assume dangerous and extreme forms. Each variant of the theory brings different emphases to these core assumptions, and not every variant is subject to each of the criticisms of the classical model.

But there is enough consensus to warrant evaluating the generic classical model on its own terms.

McAdam (1982) still provides the most concise critique of the classical model of collective behavior; it is directed at several core assumptions of this approach. For example, the claim that social movements are a response to social strain is deeply problematic. It ignores the larger political context in which movements arise and it assumes a mechanistic and linear relationship between macrolevel strain and microlevel behavior. The identification of individual discontent as the proximate cause of social movements constitutes a second problem. In at least some versions of the theory, this presumes an abnormal psychological profile that sharply distinguishes participants from nonparticipants in collective behavior. But aside from this difficulty, the individual level of analysis invoked here can assume away the central social process of translating individual mental states into genuinely collective phenomena. Finally, the individualistic emphasis denies the political dimension of collective behavior by implying that it is nothing more than a "convenient justification for what is at root a psychological phenomenon" (McAdam, 1982:17). When such an assumption guides the analysis, collective behavior is more likely to be perceived through the lens of deviant behavior than political action. Although many other criticisms have been lodged against the classical model, these go to its core by demonstrating how its key assumptions operate as conceptual blinders.

McAdam links his critique of collective behavior theory to the prevalence of pluralism as a political theory. If students of collective behavior adopt a pluralist perspective that presumes the political system is open and accessible to all groups, they will see collective behavior as an unwarranted, illegitimate, "short-circuited" response to problems that are better solved by working through appropriate channels. But there is even more at stake. Although it is true that the assumptions of classical collective behavior theory resonate with a larger set of assumptions defining pluralist political theory, pluralism itself is nested in even larger values that reinforced the plausibility of the classical model of collective behavior. In the postwar "long decade" from the late 1940s to the early 1960s, the social sciences established close links with the dominant institutions of the society. In the guise of value neutrality, many disciplines and their respective conceptual frameworks implicitly adopted a top-down, pro-system world view. Within sociology, it was Parsonian structural-functionalism that most clearly reflected these biases at the same time that it claimed scientific objectivity. It was not surprising that this era culminated with the ultimate ideological claim that we had reached the "end of ideology." The sociology of knowledge suggests that the prevalence of the classical model of collective behavior was not just a reflection of pluralist political philosophy but of a much broader, consensualist, intellectual world view that prevailed during the 1950s.

The sociology of knowledge suggests even more. The foundational assumptions of specific theories are not just related to broader intellectual standpoints. They also resonate with material conditions that define distinct, historically specific, sociopolitical eras. The long decade of the 1950s was variously characterized as one of affluence, progress, and prosperity. The "American celebration" of the "American Century" so trenchantly critiqued by C. Wright Mills (and very few others) typified many of the taken-for-granted assumptions of everyday life for large sectors of the population. In an era in which relations between management and labor appeared harmonious, when race relations had yet to "heat up," when images of marital bliss and familial harmony pervaded gender arrangements, when unprecedented educational and housing opportunities were becoming available to untold millions of Americans, when images of technological progress and material affluence were ubiquitous, and when the United States was the indisputable leader of the "free world," there was simply no room in the American celebration for recognizing deeply rooted, highly politicized conflicts of interest. It was not that there were no enemies, but rather that the enemies were defined as external because such a society could not be seen as generating its own opposition. If the opposition is external, the major threat is infiltration. McCarthyism's hysteria over this prospect and the undermining of the American way of life by communist agents was another expression of the image of America as a place of undisturbed harmony that could be jeopardized only from the outside. It is more than a little ironic that the conceptual tools of collective behavior theory find considerable applicability in the analysis of McCarthyism; the imagery of hysteria rarely found a more congenial home than in the anticommunism of the 1950s.

My purpose in adopting the sociology of knowledge to understand theoretical development is not to mechanistically reduce intellectual production to material conditions. It is rather to point out the resonance between material, social, political, ideological, and intellectual processes that give historically specific periods their unique identities. Both the prominence and the demise of the classical model of collective behavior can be understood only from this perspective. The dominance of the collective behavior paradigm resulted from a complex mix of scientific value, empirical validity, and its fit and resonance with a distinctive intellectual climate and specific sociohistorical conditions. Collective behavior theory was a piece of this larger puzzle that fit snugly because it explained what might otherwise have remained inexplicable. As long as the puzzle remained the same, the piece continued to fit. But when the puzzle of the larger intellectual and sociohistorical climate began to change in a fundamental way, the piece known as collective behavior theory lost its home.

RECENT SOCIAL MOVEMENT THEORY

The social and political activism of the "long decade" of the 1960s made the biggest single contribution to changing the intellectual and sociohistorical climate in which sociology and social movement theory existed. Beginning with civil rights activism in the 1950s, new forms of collective action were eventually taken up by other racial and ethnic groups, by students and youth in general, and by women and gay and lesbian activists. In various ways, these constituencies responded to oppressive discrimination, capitalist intrusions, bureaucratic domination, unrestrained militarism, and environmental devastation.

Although much of this activism had explicit political goals, a great deal of it spilled beyond the polity into a countercultural challenge to the "American way of life." Much of the power of this wave of collective action derived from its multifront character. It was a fundamental political challenge to the legitimacy of the central institutions of the society that dovetailed with a cultural challenge to the hegemony of the core values of the society. Although these movements experienced a combination of successes and defeats on particular issues, their greatest impact was a broader shift in the social, political, and cultural climate evidenced by chronic legitimation deficits and ongoing cultural experimentation. Indeed, the most bittersweet evidence of the extensiveness of the challenge posed by 1960s activism is the depth and power of the conservative and reactionary backlash to it that has dominated the national political scene since 1980 and shaped the "culture wars" of the late 1980s and 1990s.

It was perhaps inevitable that sociology would change in response to these developments, but the parallels between social change and disciplinary change are nevertheless striking. The postwar American celebration found its echo in Parsonian structural-functionalism. The imagery of a social system whose subsystems were smoothly and harmoniously integrated resonated strongly with societal proclamations of an age of affluence and the end of ideology. By the late 1950s, there were modest challenges to this paradigm by analytically oriented conflict theory, but even these challenges did not escape functionalism's foundational assumptions. Not until the social, political, and cultural changes of the 1960s did serious theoretical reexamination occur within sociology. This led to a proliferation of innovative paradigms that directed attention away from the conceptual imagery of functionalism in several ways. At the microlevel, a revival of symbolic interactionism and related perspectives was evident in developments in dramaturgical sociology, social constructionism, phenomenological sociology, and ethnomethodology. Although such developments can hardly be explained in terms of the social movements of the 1960s, their voluntaristic, actor-centered imagery resonated with the ways in which movements were demonstrating the efficacy of individual and collective action. At the macrolevel, the linkages between social change and social theory were certainly stronger. Social activism in society prompted theoretical development in sociology, as a rich diversity of neo-Marxian and neo-Weberian approaches put issues of power, domination, conflict, inequality, and change at the center of sociological theory once again. In these ways, the sibling relationship between social movements and sociology was particularly evident in this era of social and theoretical change.

It was in this context of broad social conflict and related disciplinary development that social movement theory underwent a qualitative change in the 1970s. This change was "cosponsored" by an older generation of scholars who advocated new ideas and a younger generation of sociologists who had been movement activists and subsequently received their professional training during this theoretical turmoil in the discipline. Their efforts to conceptualize the progressive movements of the 1960s challenged the accepted wisdom about collective behavior in at least four ways. First, new theories challenged the subsumption of social movements under collective behavior and suggested that the former were different enough from the latter to warrant their own mode of analysis. Second, social movements were seen as exhibiting enduring, patterned, institutionalized elements, thereby challenging the traditional classification of them as noninstitutional behavior. Third, newer approaches explicitly argued that participants in social movements were, in the words of one theorist, "at least as rational as those who study them" (Schwartz, 1976:135), and this premise of the rational actor became a cornerstone of social movement analysis. Finally, the newer approaches accentuated the political dimension of social movement challenges by conceptualizing them as rooted in collective understandings of group interests; this political interpretation has largely displaced the earlier psychological interpretation of collective behavior. Taken together, these challenges constituted a fundamental paradigm shift in the sociological analysis of social movements. At the broadest level, this shift can be understood only through a sociology of knowledge attentive to the interplay of sociohistorical change, disciplinary development, and historically situated biographies.

The theoretical strands that constituted these challenges came to be known as resource mobilization theory, and this has been the dominant paradigm guiding social movement analysis since the late 1970s. Although it has been the target of some important criticisms, resource mobilization theory has fundamentally altered the terrain for studying social movements by establishing this topic as an independent domain of social analysis. The divorce between collective behavior and social movements has not gone completely uncontested, however, as some have called for a rapprochement between the symbolic interactionist approach to collective behavior and the resource mobilization approach to social movements (Marx and McAdam, 1994). This case has been most effectively made by one of the major rivals to resource mobilization theory known as social constructionism. At the very least, this rivalry has restored some appreciation of the socially constructed aspects of social movements that resource mobilization theory tended to ignore. The other major rival to resource mobilization theory has come from the European tradition of new social movement theory. Although sharing some premises with social constructionism, new social movement theory has sought to reintroduce a macrolevel, sociohistorical dimension to the analysis of social movements. In what follows, I offer a brief, critical overview of each of these perspectives. The goals of this overview are to provide a concise summary of each approach, to assess the state of the art in social movement theory, and to suggest how this theory might evolve most productively in the future.

The Resource Mobilization Paradigm

Resource mobilization theory emerged in the 1970s as a distinctively new approach to the study of social movements. According to this perspective, social movements are an extension of politics by other means, and can be analyzed in terms of conflicts of interest just like other forms of political struggle. Movements are also seen as structured and patterned, so that they can be analyzed in terms of organizational dynamics just like other forms of institutionalized action (Oberschall, 1973; McCarthy and Zald, 1977, 1973; Tilly, 1978). In sharp contrast to the collective behavior tradition, resource mobilization theory views social movements as normal, rational, institutionally rooted, political challenges by aggrieved groups. The border between conventional politics and social movements thus becomes blurred, but does not disappear altogether. Whereas established special-interest groups have routine, low-cost access to powerful decision makers, social movements must pay higher costs to gain a comparable degree of influence within the polity. Resource mobilization theory thereby redefined the study of collective action from an example of deviance and social disorganization to a case study in political and organizational sociology.

Resource mobilization theory also takes a distinct position on questions of recruitment, motivation, and participation. Based on a rational actor model, individuals are viewed as weighing the relative costs and benefits of movement participation and opting for participation when the potential benefits outweigh the anticipated costs (McCarthy and Zald, 1977). When movement goals take the form of public goods that cannot be denied to nonparticipants, the free-rider dilemma is created because it is individually rational for each actor to let others win the goal and then share the benefits without the costs. In response to the free-rider dilemma, organizations may offer selective incentives for active participants that can be withheld from nonparticipants (Olson, 1965). This logic has been criticized as economistic by those who argue that collective, moral, purposive, or solidary incentives often motivate people to join movements even if they could theoretically "ride free" on the efforts of others (Fireman and Gamson, 1979). The role of different incentives remains a subject of debate, but the debate assumes rational actors on the individual level just as it assumes the normality of movements on the collective level.

Resource mobilization theory may be roughly divided into two camps. McCarthy and Zald (1977, 1973) are the originators and major practitioners of the entrepreneurial version of the theory, whereas Tilly (1978) and McAdam (1982) provide examples of the political version of the theory. The entrepreneurial model entered social movement theory through a distinctive critical wedge by arguing that grievances had little if any explanatory value in accounting for movement origins. The standard argument was that many groups in many times and places have had grievances but have not created social movements; hence, grievances cannot be the critical factor in generating social movements. What has been more variable, and more closely correlated with collective action, is group access to and control over the various resources necessary for effective social movement activism. The assumption of constant or ubiquitous grievances thereby made the variable factor of resources the central explanatory mechanism of social movement activity. Thus, the first principle of this approach is that the aggregation of resources is crucial to social movement activity. Resource aggregation, in turn, requires some minimal form of movement organization without which protest will not occur. A third principle is that the role of outside groups is often crucial in determining the flow of re-

sources toward or away from a given protest group. More broadly, it is principles of supply and demand that influence the flow of resources toward or
away from a given social movement organization. And finally, the involvement
of both individuals and organizations in protest is best explained in terms of
the balance of costs and rewards (McCarthy and Zald, 1977).

The entrepreneurial version of resource mobilization theory thereby blends
economic and organizational theory to understand collective action. The basic
concepts reflect this emphasis. Social movements (SMs) are defined simply as
opinions or beliefs that represent preferences for change in society, thereby
putting the premium on social movement organizations (SMOs), which are
complex or formal organizations that identify their goals with the preferences
of a social movement. These SMOs, in turn, are grouped into social movement
industries (SMIs) that include all the SMOs with overlapping goals that reflect
the same SM. All SMIs, in turn, comprise the social movement sector (SMS)
of society, implying that collective action has become a permanent and institutionalized part of modern, complex societies. In this model, SMOs operate
like small businesses competing for resources and followers. Because survival is
dependent on resource acquisition, the accent falls on the role of external resources from government, foundations, wealthy elites, or conscience constituents who bankroll movement activities. For the same reason, the role of
leaders and entrepreneurs is critical because they often function as fundraisers
seeking to create a sustained flow of resources into the SMO. These tasks have
in turn promoted a high degree of professionalization in the leadership of
SMOs; many leaders essentially have entire careers as professional organizers or
entrepreneurial leaders of SMOs (McCarthy and Zald, 1977). The entrepreneurial version of resource mobilization theory thereby brings a very distinctive economic and organizational spin to the general premises of the theory,
and it has much to tell us about a number of moderate, reform-oriented movements with a middle-class base. It is less informative about informally organized movement forms such as social movement communities (Buechler, 1990)
or loosely structured collective action (Oberschall, 1993), but these formations
are somewhat better handled by the other version of resource mobilization
theory.

If economic relationships provide the guiding metaphor for the entrepreneurial version of the theory, power struggles are the guiding metaphor of the
political version of the theory. One example is provided by the work of Tilly
(1978), whose core assumptions are conveniently summarized in two models
of collective action. The polity model describes a bounded population such as
a nation-state that is internally divided between polity members and challengers.
The former have routine, low-cost access to powerholders, whereas the latter
must engage in collective action to have any influence. This model serves as a
critique of pluralist images of power and also underscores the importance of
alliances between polity members and challengers. The mobilization model
identifies the key elements involved in collective action. The first element consists of group interests, conceptualized as the gains and losses for a group resulting from its interaction with other groups. The second element is organi-

zation, involving the intersection of categories and networks of people so that the highest degree of organization occurs when people of similar status interact intensively with one another. The third element consists of mobilization, which is a function of both the resources under group control and the probability that they will actually be delivered in an episode of collective action. The fourth element is opportunity, which is subdivided into three components identified as repression/facilitation, power, and opportunity/threat (Tilly, 1978). Although Tilly relies on some economic logic, the dominant imagery here is one of tactical, strategic, and instrumental power struggles among competing groups. The result is a model that adheres to the core assumptions of resource mobilization theory, but with a very different spin on those assumptions from that of the entrepreneurial model.

Another example of this political version is provided by McAdam's political process model (1982). Although he offers this as an alternative to resource mobilization theory, his real foil is the entrepreneurial version of the theory; his alternative is best seen as another illustration of the political version of resource mobilization theory. McAdam is critical of the entrepreneurial version for overstating the role of elites, underemphasizing the importance of the mass base, and oversimplifying the nature of grievances. In McAdam's model, the essential elements of collective action begin with the structure of political opportunities. Although this is an external factor not under the direct control of activists, it nevertheless shapes their potential for success. Political opportunities improve when the power discrepancy between authorities and challengers is reduced and the bargaining position of challengers improves. The second factor shaping collective action is indigenous organizational strength. This internal factor is largely under the control of activists, and it is a product of the interaction between members, leaders, incentives, and communication. The third element involves what McAdam calls cognitive liberation. This subjective factor refers to a change in group consciousness whereby potential protesters see the existing social order not only as illegitimate, but also as subject to change through their own direct efforts. It is the interaction of the these three factors that shapes the emergence of social movements; their persistence, in turn, is a function of processes that sustain organizational strength and the social control responses of authorities. As with Tilly's model, the dominant imagery here is more of political struggle than economic entrepreneurship, illustrating again the diverse interpretations that have been placed on the core assumptions of resource mobilization theory.

These diverse interpretations have promoted some important debates between the two versions of resource mobilization theory about the role of entrepreneurial leaders, the value of external resources, and the variability of movement grievances (McAdam, 1982; Morris, 1984). The same issues have provided targets for critics of the resource mobilization paradigm as a whole. Perhaps the most common criticism is that the theory oversimplifies the role of grievances and downplays the role of ideational factors in general. The theory has also been criticized for overstating the importance of formal organizational structures as opposed to informal or decentralized networks. The model of the rational actor has attracted criticism for its hyperrational assumptions about movement participants and for its individualistic orientation to what is essentially a collective process. For the same reason, resource mobilization has been inattentive to the role of collective identity in movements, and it has done little to acknowledge the internal diversity of many movement groups. In the broadest theoretical terms, the resource mobilization framework emphasizes instrumental action oriented to political and economic domains and ignores the cultural and symbolic life world that necessarily underpins such strategic action (Habermas, 1987, 1984). Put differently, resource mobilization's concern with resources and organization leads it to ignore the role of culture in collective action. If we take culture to refer to symbolic systems of meaning construction, it encapsulates many of the specific criticisms already discussed. Given this, it is no accident that both social constructionism and new social movement theory have sought to bring cultural processes back into social movement analysis [see Buechler (1993) for a more detailed discussion of these criticisms of the resource mobilization paradigm].

Although these criticisms have become widely known, less critical attention has been directed to the level of analysis at which resource mobilization theory operates. Research within this tradition initially focused on the mesolevel to the relative exclusion of both macro- and microlevels of collective action. This is a logical extension of resource mobilization's emphasis on the role of organization and the mobilization of resources as central to understanding such action. Given an historical context of sociological theories that traditionally approached collective behavior as a microlevel phenomenon to be explained in social–psychological terms or as the manifestation of macrolevel social disorganization and breakdown, the establishment of the mesolevel of analysis was an important step forward. However, there was a tendency within this framework to focus so exclusively on the mesolevel of organizational analysis that larger questions of social structure and historical change and smaller issues of individual motivation and social interaction received scant attention. The result was an image of movement organizations as disembodied and reified social actors detached from larger structural constraints and historical contexts as they engaged in collective action. In the last decade, however, much work has been done on bridging the meso- and microlevels of collective action through various studies of micromobilization.

Although there has been a sustained effort to move from the mesolevel to the microlevel, much less attention has been paid to the macrolevel (Mueller, 1992). Research in the organizational tradition may give fleeting attention to the macrolevel to explain movement origins through changes in the availability of resources, but the subsequent analysis typically ignores this level. Research in the political tradition is somewhat more attentive to how macrolevel change alters political opportunity structures for collective action, but once again the subsequent analysis tends to focus on the mesolevel. Despite a difference in degree, both versions of the theory take an eclectic, ad hoc approach to structural issues, and neither offers any systematic theory of how macrolevel organization affects movements (and vice versa) beyond resource availability or opportunity structures. Systemic power relations and structural inequality thus tend to be ignored by this approach (Canel, 1992; Mueller, 1992). Without such a macrosociological theory, the resource mobilization framework can say little about how group interests, the stakes of conflicts, or even resources themselves are defined prior to collective action; such accounts can quickly become tautological as a result (Kitschelt, 1991). Since these processes can be theoretically understood only over significant periods of historical time, insensitivity to the macrolevel results in a distinctly ahistorical approach to the study of social movements as well. The consistent tendency of the resource mobilization framework to ignore macrostructural, historical contexts has limited its analysis of collective action.

There has been no major effort to resolve this problem and theorize the macro–meso link in the way that some have theorized the meso–micro link. A rare exception to this claim is a highly atypical article on the "Political Economy of Social Movement Sectors" (Garner and Zald, 1987) that situates social movements in a context of class structure, dual labor markets, a consumer economy, and a global system. This article may be read as an open invitation for scholars to integrate the macrolevel into social movement analysis, but the subsequent literature suggests that few have taken the invitation seriously. Five years later, Zald identified resource mobilization theory's strengths at the meso- and meso–micro levels and acknowledged that the theory had not done enough to analyze class structure, epochal cultural crises, or macrotheories of change (Zald, 1992). This inattentiveness to the macrolevel is particularly curious because contemporary social theory offers several promising approaches to the macrolevel and to addressing multiple levels of analysis (Ritzer, 1996; Collins, 1988; Giddens, 1984). Social movement theory is a particularly fruitful area for such work because movements are microcosms of individual action embedded in larger, sociohistorical contexts. The fact that resource mobilization theory has not made these moves to date suggests the outer limits of this perspective, as well as the inherently partial nature of all theoretical perspectives. It remains a sharp tool for certain questions, but it is also a very blunt instrument for other questions about social activism.

In retrospect, the rise to prominence of resource mobilization theory seems almost overdetermined. New social conflicts were rapidly emerging across the social landscape; the classical model of collective behavior seemed unable to account for the most distinctive features of these conflicts; social theory in general had shifted away from a dominant concern with stability to new interests in conflict, power, and struggle; and many young sociologists who helped develop this approach were former activists themselves. It was this historically specific conjuncture of forces that not only precipitated a crisis for the older paradigm of the classical model, but also made the newer paradigm of resource mobilization appear as a compelling alternative. Just as the collective behavior tradition fit the sociohistorical puzzle of the 1950s, resource mobilization theory was an equally good fit for a later sociohistorical puzzle. For almost a decade, resource mobilization theory was so compelling that it virtually crowded out other explanations of collective action. By the late 1980s, however, two other perspectives began to establish themselves.

Social Constructionist Theory

Although social constructionism is presented here as an alternative to the resource mobilization paradigm, it also signifies a revival of the symbolic interactionist version of collective behavior theory that predated the rise of the resource mobilization paradigm. There is a certain irony in the fact that although symbolic interactionism is often criticized for being inattentive to power dynamics, this theoretical tradition has itself been engaged in a decades-long struggle against structuralist approaches in sociology. Although the demise of functionalism in the 1960s created more space for symbolic interactionism, some of that space was filled by newer structuralist approaches (both Marxist and mainstream) that continued to deny the central premises of symbolic interaction. This general theoretical battle also occurred in the specific domain of social movement theory. Even during the prominence of the classical model of collective behavior, the symbolic interactionist version was at loggerheads with functionalist versions as well as relative deprivation approaches. With the rise of resource mobilization theory, there was a tendency for all of the versions of the classical model to be collapsed, critiqued, and rejected; this tendency ignored the different theoretical underpinnings of these models and obliterated their subtleties and nuances. But of the three versions, the symbolic interactionist one has the most resiliency, as indicated by the prevalence of its key premises in contemporary social constructionism (Gusfield, 1994).

Symbolic interactionism's premises also ground criticisms of other approaches to collective action. For example, the insistence on interaction as the appropriate unit of analysis is said to avoid problems of psychological reductionism, structural determination, and reification. If interaction is the appropriate unit of analysis, the most important process that occurs on that level is the use of symbols. Whether construed as meanings, interpretations, definitions, or identities, symbols are central to the communication processes and interaction networks that comprise society in general and collective action in particular. Such premises link symbolic interactionism, its classical model of collective behavior, and social constructionism. Despite this common heritage, there are some differences between the latter two approaches. Contemporary social constructionism is more attentive to social movements than to elementary forms of collective behavior; it recognizes that collective action can be sustained over time and patterned in its organization; it is more attuned to the cognitive dimensions of motivation and recruitment into social movements; and it places more emphasis on the role of networks and organizations as conduits of collective action. Although these premises locate social constructionism at some distance from the collective behavior tradition and in some proximity to the resource mobilization approach, social constructionism remains insistent that every aspect of collective action must be understood as an interactive, symbolically defined and negotiated process among participants, opponents, and bystanders. These emphases are evident in the seminal contributions of this paradigm.

Some of the central concerns of social constructionism were foreshadowed by the concept of cognitive liberation (Piven and Cloward, 1977; McAdam, 1982) and calls for a new social psychology of collective action (Klandermans, 1997, 1984). These issues recur in the social constructionist concept of framing, borrowed from Goffman (1974). Framing means focusing attention on some bounded phenomenon by imparting meaning and significance to elements within the frame and setting them apart from what is outside the frame. In the context of social movements, framing refers to the interactive, collective ways that movement actors assign meanings to their activities in the conduct of social movement activism. The concept of framing is designed for discussing the social construction of grievances as a fluid and variable process of social interaction—and hence a much more important explanatory tool than resource mobilization theory had maintained. Grievances are framed in at least three ways (Snow and Benford, 1988). Diagnostic framing identifies a problem, including attributions of blame or causality so that the movement has a target for its actions. Prognostic framing suggests possible solutions and remedies, often including tactics and strategies that are appropriate to the target identified. Taken together, these accomplish consensus mobilization (Klandermans, 1988) by creating the mobilization pool from which movements recruit; such pools are socially constructed rather than structurally guaranteed. Activating mobilization pools requires motivational framing that issues a call to arms and a rationale for action by providing a vocabulary of motives that compels people to act (Benford, 1993b). In sum, successful framing translates vaguely felt dissatisfactions into well-defined grievances and compels people to join the movement to do something about those grievances.

Although motivational framing may supply a sense of urgency, movements must engage in additional frame alignment processes to maximize recruitment efforts. Frame alignment refers to linking together the interpretive orientations of individuals and social movement organizations, so that individual interests, values, and beliefs are congruent with the activities, goals, and ideologies of social movement organizations (Snow et al., 1986). This further specification of how movements achieve both consensus and action mobilization involves four distinct frame alignment processes. Frame bridging is the most minimal process; it involves movement organizations reaching people who already share their orientation to the world through publicity efforts and organizational outreach to let people know that there already exists a group that shares their views on a given issue. Frame amplification appeals to deeply held values and beliefs in the general population and links those values and beliefs to movement issues; in this way, people's preexisting value commitments provide a "hook" that can be used to recruit them into the movement. Frame extension involves enlarging the boundaries of an initial frame to include issues of importance to potential participants, positioning the movement as a logical response to preexisting concerns of some segment of the population. The most elaborate process is frame transformation, in which the creation and nurturance of new values, beliefs, and meanings induce movement participation by redefining activities, events, and biographies as requiring people to become involved in collective action. Although not all movements engage in all frame alignment processes, virtually every movement engages in at least some of these tactics to define grievances and recruit participants. This conceptual repertoire thereby provides a powerful language for analyzing the social construction of collective action. At the same time, frame alignment tends to be a top-down perspective on the relation between leaders and followers. In the words of one critic, "we are never told how the potential audience reacts to the marketing pitch of social movement organizations, and how this reaction affects the interpretative process" (Aguirre, 1994:268).

As the concepts of individual and collective identity became more central in social movement theory with the rise of new social movement theory, practitioners of the framing perspective demonstrated its applicability to questions of identity as well (Hunt et al., 1994). For example, protagonist framing involves a fundamental distinction between an in-group and an out-group that identifies the allies of the movement and helps to maintain its solidarity. Antagonist framing identifies the enemies of the movement by specifying the source of the problem and villainizing the people framed as responsible for the problem that the movement is addressing. Finally, audience framing identifies the relevant bystanders to a given conflict and their potential for joining either the movement or its opposition. Audience framing may also involve strategies for recruiting support or neutralizing opposition. The framing processes involved in defining grievances, recruiting participants, and shaping identities are obviously intertwined in the ongoing daily activities of social movements, but the conceptual distinctions are nonetheless important in underscoring the socially constructed nature of these processes in collective action.

Although most of these concepts are couched in terms of interpersonal interaction at the micro- and mesolevels, the concept of master frames addresses general ideological trends at the macrolevel of social order (Snow and Benford, 1992). Master frames refer to the broadest structures of meaning in social movements that define grievances in terms of oppression, injustice, or exploitation and call for liberation, fairness, or equity. Their generality is what allows master frames to be adopted by more than one constituency; multiple groups can find a home under the broad symbolic canopy of a master frame. Because of this feature, Snow and Benford (1992) see master frames as intimately related to cycles of protest. Thus, such cycles may originate with the creation of a new master frame that galvanizes a number of aggrieved groups in ways that were not possible earlier. Movements that appear earlier in a cycle of protest may pave the way for later movements that adopt the same frame, but those same path-breaking efforts may constrain the options or effectiveness of later movements using the same master frame. Master frames thereby influence the goals, tactics, strategies, coalitions, and resources of entire social movement industries. For these reasons, the concept provides a potential bridge between the largely microlevel focus of the framing perspective and macrolevel, ideological questions about public, political, and media discourse.

One model for analyzing multiple social levels is provided by Klanderman's (1992) analysis of the social construction of protest. He proposes that we analyze transformations in collective consciousness as involving public discourse at the societal level, persuasive communication at the interactive level, and consciousness raising at the individual level. Each level is interdependent with the others, as they shape collective beliefs about movement grievances and success expectations. Public discourse and media discourse can create, sustain, or dissolve a collective definition of a situation and the collective identities associated with that definition. Persuasive communication is a form of contestatory symbolic politics that interacts with media discourse to create consensus mobilization or frame alignment. Consciousness raising is often less a predecessor of collective action than an emergent by-product of that action if the appropriate frames are available. This analysis provides an important reminder that the social construction of protest always operates through several interacting levels of social reality.

These interacting levels may be understood as comprising a political culture that provides people with meaning systems and cultural themes for talking about political objects (Gamson, 1988). Political culture relies on interpretive packages that are internally structured by frames that make sense of relevant events; as such, they are critical to successful collective action. Media discourse is one site at which such packages are constructed and disseminated to audiences; this discourse promotes multiple packages, but they all bear the imprint of prevailing media sponsors and practices. Public opinion represents a parallel system for constructing meaning that is shaped but not determined by media discourse since the former admits of personal experience and recognizes people as active creators of meaning. Alongside media discourse and public opinion, personal experience constitutes another basic source of information. Indeed, the most robust collective action frames combine media discourse and experiential knowledge to speak to themes of injustice, agency, and identity; such framings anchor grievances in daily life (Gamson, 1995). The social construction of collective action occurs within this preexisting political culture, as movements borrow, modify, or create frames to advance their goals. One of Gamson's most compelling examples concerns the differential framing of nuclear disasters. The political and cultural climate of the late 1970s made it relatively easy to define events at Three Mile Island as a technological catastrophe. Thirteen years earlier, by contrast, an arguably more serious partial meltdown at the Fermi reactor caused no political fallout in the absence of antinuclear packages that did not emerge until the 1970s (Gamson, 1988; Gamson and Modigliani, 1989). The historical contrast nicely illustrates how people act toward things on the basis of the meanings things have for them, and how those meanings emerge from political culture, including social activism.

Because Gamson has done more than anyone else to extend the social constructionist perspective to the macrolevel context of media discourse and public communication, it is all the more significant that in a major programmatic statement he has argued that the "frontiers of social movement theory are in social psychological territory" (Gamson, 1992:74). This theme permeates a broad ranging discussion of some central concepts of social movement analysis. Thus, collective identity is posed as an expansion of personal identity in a collective setting. Solidarity is described as a linking of individual and social levels. Consciousness raising is represented as the mesh between individual cognition and sense making on the one hand and cultural world views, schemata, and scripts on the other hand. Micromobilization is viewed as connecting these processes to collective action by organizing the lines of action of multiple actors in similar fashion. In each case, a central concept in the analysis of collective action is presented in a social–psychological frame that pulls attention back down from the macrolevel to the microlevel and to micro–mesolevel linkages. Although Gamson is surely correct in arguing that social constructionism has greatly improved earlier social–psychological premises in the collective behavior tradition, his valorization of social psychology as the new frontier of social movement theory leaves little space for a theory of social movements that is attentive to macrolevel social structures and to historical specificity in the analysis of collective action.

As this brief overview suggests, social constructionism has made a number of important contributions to social movement theory since its emergence in the mid-1980s. These contributions have established the paradigm as a major contender in the study of collective action. Despite this newly won status, "no critical review of this approach has been published to date" (Benford, 1997:410). This observation introduces Benford's own "insider's critique" of the social constructionist perspective. His assessment underscores a schism whereby the perspective as a whole has neglected empirical work in favor of conceptual development, but the empirical work that has been done suffers from a descriptive bias (and a proliferation of terms for various frames) that has prevented it from being theoretically grounded. Other problems include static tendencies in the formulation of theoretical concepts and a tendency toward reification that neglects human agency and emotions and anthropomorphizes nonhuman entities. Still other studies fall into the opposite error of reductionism by psychologizing the sociological level of interaction and offering individual-level explanations of social action. An additional problem (not unique to this perspective) is an elite bias that focuses more attention on framing by elites than by rank-and-file members. Most generally, Benford summarizes these problems as monolithic tendencies that oversimplify collective action and neglect "the multi-layered complexities of frames and framing activities" (Benford, 1997:422). Benford's remedies clarify his critique as not only an insider's but also an internalist critique. By this I mean that his criticisms do not challenge the foundational premises of social constructionism as much as they reveal the gap between the potential of those premises and work done to date; his remedies would not move beyond social constructionism as much as they would develop it more fully.

The sociology of knowledge can suggest why social constructionism has attracted relatively little critical assessment. The amount of criticism directed at a theoretical perspective reflects not only its inherent strengths and weaknesses but also its position in a field of competing theoretical frameworks. Dominant frameworks attract extensive critical attention (perhaps far out of proportion to their actual shortcomings) as a function of their dominance and the resulting lack of theoretical space for alternatives. This is what happened to the classical model of collective behavior when resource mobilization theory came on the scene, and to a lesser extent resource mobilization theory has begun to attract the level and type of criticism often reserved for dominant perspectives. Challenging frameworks, on the other hand, receive less critical attention (perhaps again out of proportion to their actual limitations) simply because they are challengers fighting for theoretical space against dominant theories. There is also a more specific factor at work here. Social constructionism has not presented itself as a totalizing, universal paradigm for understanding collective action as much as it has claimed to offer partial, perspectival contributions toward a more holistic understanding of collective action. This was certainly the spirit expressed in much of the social constructionist literature from the mid-1980s to the mid-1990s, which argued not that resource mobilization theory was fundamentally flawed but rather that it left certain explanatory gaps that social constructionism was well prepared to fill. Both general and specific factors thereby combine to suggest why social constructionism has attracted relatively little critical attention to date.

My goal here is not to offer such a critique, but rather to underscore social constructionism's impact on the directionality of social movement theory. The classical collective behavior tradition was primarily a microlevel, social–psychological approach to its subject matter (with the partial exception of Smelser's theory that acknowledged structural conduciveness and strain). Resource mobilization theory established the mesolevel of organizational analysis that had been previously lacking in social movement theory. The impact of social constructionism as an alternative to resource mobilization theory has been to valorize the linkages between micro- and mesolevels of analysis and to (in Gamson's words) redefine social psychology as representing the real frontier of social movement theory. The other contribution of social constructionism has been to reinforce a certain style of theorizing in social movement analysis. For all its differences with resource mobilization theory, both paradigms seek increasingly abstract and generalizable theoretical concepts removed from the historically specific contexts in which social movements arise. The combined effect of both approaches has been to direct attention away from historically specific aspects of macrolevel social structures and their impact on collective action. These moves perpetuated gaps in social movement theory that new social movement theory claims to fill. It is to this perspective that we now turn.

New Social Movement Theory

Whereas social constructionism emerged as a "national" rival to resource mobilization theory, new social movement theory appeared as an "international" challenger rooted in continental European traditions of social theory and political philosophy (Cohen, 1985; Klandermans, 1991; Klandermans and Tarrow, 1988; Larana et al., 1994; Pichardo, 1997). This approach is, in large part, a response to the economic reductionism of classical Marxism that pre-vented it from adequately grasping contemporary forms of collective action (Canel, 1992). These premises have led Marxists to privilege proletarian revo-lution rooted in the sphere of production and to marginalize any other form of social protest. New social movement theorists, by contrast, have looked to other logics of action (based in politics, ideology, and culture) and other sources of identity (such as ethnicity, gender, and sexuality) as the sources of collec-tive action. The term "new social movements" thus refers to a diverse array of collective actions that has presumably displaced the old social movement of proletarian revolution. Even though new social movement theory is a critical reaction to classical Marxism, some new social movement theorists seek to up-date and revise conventional Marxist assumptions whereas others seek to dis-place and transcend them. Indeed, despite the now common usage of the term "new social movement theory," it is a misnomer if it implies widespread agree-ment among a range of theorists on a number of core premises. It would be more accurate to speak of "new social movement theories," with the implica-tion that there are many variations on a general approach to something called new social movements (Buechler, 1995).

As a first approximation to this general approach, however, it is possible to identify a number of themes that are prominent in most if not all versions of new social movement theories. First and foremost, most versions of these theories operate with some model of a societal totality that provides the con-text for the emergence of collective action. Although theorists differ on the na-ture of this societal totality, the attempt to theorize a historically specific social formation as the structural backdrop for contemporary forms of collective ac-tion is perhaps the most distinctive feature of new social movement theories. This restoration of the macrolevel in social movement theory distinguishes new social movement theories from both social constructionism and resource mo-bilization approaches. A second theme in most new social movement approaches is a causal claim that links these new movements to this societal totality; this often means seeing new social movements as responses to modernity or post-modernity. If modern or postmodern societal totalities are defined by capital-ist markets, bureaucratic states, scientized relationships, and instrumental ra-tionality, new social movements are historically specific responses to these features of the modern and postmodern condition. These characterizations of-ten emphasize the extent to which large, anonymous social institutions have become especially intrusive and invasive in the late twentieth century; these "colonizing efforts" (Habermas, 1987, 1984) have prompted many social movement actions in response to the invasive and controlling aspects of social life in late modernity.

A third theme concerns the diffuse social base of new social movements. Some analysts see these movements as rooted in some fraction of the (new) middle classes (Eder, 1993; Kriesi, 1989; Offe, 1985). Others have argued that these movements are no longer rooted in the class structure, but rather in other statuses such as race, ethnicity, gender, sexual orientation, age, or citizenship that are central in mobilizing new social movements (Dalton et al., 1990). Still others have argued that even these statuses are less important than ideological consensus over movement values and beliefs. For all these reasons, the social base of these movements is presumed to be more complex than in older and more conventional class-based activism (Buechler, 1995). This leads to a fourth theme concerning the centrality of collective identity in social protest (Hunt et al., 1994; Johnston et al., 1994; Klandermans, 1994; Melucci, 1996a, 1989; Stoecker, 1995). This theme reflects the uncoupling of activism from the class structure as well as the fluidity and multiplicity of identities in late modernity; hence the ability of people to engage in collective action is increasingly tied to their ability to define an identity in the first place (Melucci, 1996a, 1989). This places a premium on the social construction of collective identity as an essential part of contemporary social activism, and it has led to a belated appreciation of how even "old" class-based movements were not structurally determined as much as they were socially constructed in the mobilization process itself (Thompson, 1963).

A fifth theme involves the politicization of everyday life as the "relation between the individual and the collective is blurred" (Johnston et al., 1994:7) and formerly intimate and private aspects of social life become politicized. The equation of the personal and the political fosters not only identity politics but a life-style politics in which everyday life becomes a major arena of political action. Like many aspects of these movements, this characteristic cannot be understood apart from the social context. For new social movement activists (and most theorists of such activism), it is late modernity that has blurred the lines between the political and the personal through invasive technologies; movements are thus responses to a systemic politicization of life rather than the initiators of such politicization. A sixth theme concerns the values said to typify new social movements. Although some have argued that the sheer pluralism of values and ideas is their defining hallmark (Johnston et al., 1994), others have focused on the centrality of postmaterialist values (Inglehart, 1990; Dalton et al., 1990) in such activism. Whereas materialist values involve redistributive struggles in the conventional political sphere, postmaterialist values emphasize the quality rather than the quantity of life (Habermas, 1987, 1984). Rather than seeking power, control, or economic gain, such movements are more inclined to seek autonomy and democratization (Rucht, 1988). Although the aptness of the "postmaterialist" designation can be challenged, such a focus does make movements less susceptible to traditional forms of social control and cooptation by the conventional political system.

A seventh theme involves the role of cultural and symbolic forms of resistance alongside or in place of more conventional political forms of contestation (Cohen, 1985). For many movements, this embodies their philosophical or spiritual rejection of the instrumental rationality of advanced capitalist society and its systems of social control and cooptation. This cultural emphasis rejects conventional goals, tactics, and strategies in favor of the exploration of new identities, meanings, signs, and symbols. Although some have criticized this orientation as apolitical, such criticisms may ignore the importance of cultural forms of social power. As Nancy Whittier (1995) has argued, if hegemony is an important form of social power, the culturally oriented, antihegemonic politics of many new movements is a valid form of resistance. The ability to envision and symbolically enact new and different ways of organizing social relationships can itself be a potent challenge to dominant social arrangements (Melucci, 1996a, 1989). A final theme in new social movement activism is a preference for organizational forms that are decentralized, egalitarian, participatory, prefigurative, and ad hoc (Melucci, 1989; Gusfield, 1994; Mueller, 1994). For these movements, organization is less a strategic tool than a symbolic expression of movement values and member identities. New social movements function less as standing armies than as cultural laboratories that vacillate between latency and visibility (Melucci, 1996a, 1989) as they episodically organize for specific battles and then revert to politicized subcultures that sustain movement visions and values for the next round of explicitly organized activism.

Although these themes distinguish new social movement theories from other approaches, it is also possible to internally distinguish a "political" and a "cultural" version of such theories. The political version draws on the most promising neo-Marxist scholarship to argue that the central societal totality is advanced capitalism and that there are strong connections between advanced capitalism and the emergence of new social movements. The political version of new social movement theory is macro oriented in general and state oriented in particular. It retains a concern with strategic questions and instrumental action as the ultimate goals of social movements while recognizing the importance of identity formation, grievance definition, and interest articulation as intermediate steps in the process of movement activism. It recognizes a role for new constituencies in social activism based on race, gender, nationality, or other characteristics, but it does not jettison the potential for class-based or worker-based movements alongside these groups. It emphasizes the potential for proactive, progressive change if appropriate alliances and coalitions between class-based and nonclass-based movements can be forged. The political version tends to be somewhat critical of the "apolitical" nature of more culturally oriented new social movements because it limits their potential for producing meaningful social change. And finally, this perspective identifies the social base of new social movements in class terms by analyzing the complexity of contemporary class structure and its contradictory locations as the backdrop for social activism.

The cultural version of new social movement theory is post-Marxist in presuming a more radical break between past and present societal types and movement forms. The cultural version identifies the societal totality in cultural or semiotic terms as an information society whose administrative codes conceal forms of domination. It emphasizes the decentralized nature of both power and resistance, so it is not particularly macro oriented or state centered but rather focuses on everyday life, civil society, and the creation of free spaces between state and civil society. The cultural version eschews strategic questions and instrumental action as pitfalls to be avoided, while emphasizing symbolic expressions that challenge the instrumental logic of systemic domination. The cultural version not only recognizes new social constituencies but also argues that the old worker-based constituencies for social activism have been transcended along with industrial capitalism. The cultural version views activism as a defensive reaction to domination that can potentially challenge systemic imperatives, but it eschews the language of "progressive" movements as invoking an unwarranted metaphysics of history. This approach also rejects the apolitical label often attached to culturalist movements by arguing that political movements are the most easily coopted and that cultural movements fighting on symbolic terrain can do more to expose contemporary forms of power than more conventionally political movements. And finally, this version is more likely to identify the social base of new social movements in nonclass terms that identify other statuses or distinctive values and ideologies that define movement constituencies. This typology is no more than an ideal-typical sensitizing device, but it helps to organize a variety of issues into two relatively coherent positions with a fair degree of internal consistency (Buechler, 1995).

Whereas social constructionism has received remarkably little critical attention, the same cannot be said for new social movement theory. The sociology of knowledge suggests a common thread in the reception of both theories, however. Just as the gentle reception for social constructionism reflects its modest positioning as a partial, complementary orientation in the field of social movement theory, the harsher response to new social movement theories reflects their much grander claims about the changing nature of society and social movements. In some cases, these claims are totalizing narratives that seek to displace rather than complement existing perspectives. This was obscured for a time by the cliche that resource mobilization theory explained the "how" of movement mobilization whereas new social movement theory explained the "why" of such mobilization (Klandermans and Tarrow, 1988). The implication that because they answered different questions they could somehow be combined was simplistic and optimistic at best. The subsequent work of American sociologists suggests that although they continue to utilize resource mobilization theory to understand how movements operate, the question of why is at best secondary and new social movement theory is at best a poor relation of resource mobilization theory. As the comparison with social constructionism suggests, however, the chilly reception of new social movement theory reflects its style of theorizing and its positioning relative to dominant perspectives as much as it reflects its intrinsic theoretical merit.

If the style of theorizing made this perspective suspect, the claim of "newness" provided an explicit target for critics. The argument that there is a defensible category of "new" movements sufficiently like each other and demonstrably different from "old" movements to be the foundation of a whole new theoretical approach to social movements has drawn the most criticism. The "newness" of new social movements has been challenged by criticisms that the category overstates their novelty (Plotke, 1990), ignores their organizational predecessors (Tarrow, 1991), mistakes an early position in a cycle of protest for a new type of protest (Tarrow, 1991), ignores long-standing historical cycles of cultural critique (Brandt, 1990), and misinterprets a generational phenomenon as a categorical shift in collective action (Johnston et al., 1994). The most injurious critiques have come from historical studies of nineteenth-century labor movements (the quintessential "old" movement) that reveal them to possess most of the supposedly distinctive features of "new" social movements (Calhoun, 1993; Tucker, 1991). Although defenders have attempted to specify the newness of new social movements (Cohen, 1983; Dalton and Kuechler, 1990; Eder, 1993; Offe, 1990), many concede that there is more continuity between supposedly old and new movements than this terminology implies (Johnston et al., 1994; Johnston, 1994; Larana, 1994; Shin, 1994; Taylor, 1989). The combination of a grandiose theoretical style and a dubious categorical foundation has thereby made new social movement theory an easy target for its critics.

Like many criticisms, however, these rest on certain interpretations of the claims of new social movement theorists in the first place. Given the multiplicity of theorists and claims, interpretations can quickly become misinterpretations of the paradigm as a whole. Melucci's response to critics is instructive in this regard. As an early advocate of new social movement theory, Melucci was always careful to present the concept as nothing more than a fluid, sensitizing device for exploring contemporary forms of protest. Despite this, most critics and some practitioners of new social movement theory have imputed much more to this category by reifying, ontologizing, and essentializing the term into a fundamental category of analysis that then becomes subject to all the critiques mentioned above (Melucci, 1996a, 1995a, 1989). Although Melucci's response to critics has become well known, there is another (mis)interpretation of new social movement theory that has received less attention. This is the widespread tendency to divorce new social movements from the social structures that generate them and to analyze (or criticize) them in isolation. In my view, the most distinctive feature of new social movement theories is their attempt to identify the links between (new) social structures or societal totalities and (new) forms of collective action. Hence, the newness that is the focus of the theories is not so much a quality of movements in isolation as it is a quality of the social structures to which movements respond, and which they inevitably reflect. To whatever extent this is correct, many standard critiques of new social movement theory misconstrue the theory and ignore this relationship between collective action and its social environment.

There are several noteworthy examples of new social movement theories for which the connections between societal totalities and social movements are crucial. For Melucci (1996a, 1989), the emphasis falls on the semiotic aspects of a postmodern information society and the numerous ways in which these elements are reflected in contemporary activism. For Castells (1983), it is the capitalist transformation of urban space alongside the state's role in collective consumption that provokes important forms of collective action. For Habermas (1987, 1984), it is the tendency in advanced capitalism for a systemic political economy to instrumentally dominate and colonize a communicative life world that provokes new forms of social resistance. For Touraine (1985, 1981), the nature of postindustrial, programmed society is at the root of contemporary collective action as movements challenge authorities for control of what Touraine calls "historicity." Each of these rather different theories makes reference to "new social movements," but the newness and distinctiveness of these movements cannot be understood apart from the equally new, historically specific, social structures to which they respond. It is precisely these connections that are often ignored by critics, and even by sympathetic interpreters of new social movement theories. It is instructive that in the introduction to their oft-cited reader on new social movements, Larana et al. (1994) identify eight characteristics of such movements; none makes any reference to the historically specific societal totalities that these movements inhabit. The resulting interpretation of new social movement theories filters out the macrolevel claims of the theories to focus on symbols, values, and identities. Although these are important elements of new social movement theories, this is a very selective reading; it is as if new social movement theories were being viewed through a social constructionist lens for an American audience.

A fuller consideration of the holistic nature of new social movement theories would not save them from criticism. All of them are problematic in a variety of ways, and some of them seem especially susceptible to criticism. Touraine's work is instructive here for its brilliance in analyzing contemporary society and social activism alongside very dubious claims about how each social formation contains one central contradiction and thereby generates one predominant social movement that responds to this contradiction. Such essentialism seems to preserve the worst of the Marxist tradition, with its designation of the proletariat as the universal class and inevitable gravediggers of industrial capitalism. Although some holistic versions of new social movement theory are admittedly difficult to defend, this does not warrant eliminating an entire level of social analysis from social movement theory. It would seem more promising to explore more flexible versions of the insight that there are connections between historically specific societal totalities and forms of collective action, and that as the former change so do the latter. This is the task that I will undertake in the second part of this book. In so doing, I regard new social movement theories as highly provocative but deeply flawed preliminary efforts to locate social movements within historically specific societal totalities.

The State of the Art

Contemporary social movement theory is characterized by a proliferation of perspectives. Whereas market forces like pressure on young academics to produce something "new" may help explain the number of approaches (Lofland, 1993), their specific content and historical trajectory require a more subtle analysis. The period from the late 1970s to the mid-1980s was dominated by resource mobilization theory, exemplified by the political (Oberschall, 1973; Tilly, 1978) and the entrepreneurial (McCarthy and Zald, 1977) versions of the theory as well as the political process variant (McAdam, 1982). By the mid-1980s, two very different challengers appeared, and they were very much in evidence by 1990. Social constructionism and the framing perspective (Snow et al., 1986) was both a revival of the symbolic interactionist version of collective behavior theory and a fresh challenge to some of the premises of resource mobilization theory. As such, it represented the main "domestic" rival to resource mobilization theory. At about the same time, new social movement theory appeared as the main "international" rival to resource mobilization theory, as more and more of the work done by European theorists became accessible to U.S. scholars. Compared with many other theoretical disputes, this one initially appeared quite productive because practitioners of different approaches seemed willing to reexamine their premises and entertain the claims of rival paradigms. Many resource mobilization theorists acknowledged the complexity of grievances and the role of framing that were central to the social constructionist perspective. They also seemed receptive to the European import of new social movement theory. Klandermans and Tarrow (1988) were especially instrumental in initiating a transatlantic dialogue around the notion that resource mobilization theory explained the "how" and new social movement theory explained the "why" of mobilization.

By the early 1990s, the rival perspectives of social constructionism and new social movement theory provided a major culturalist challenge to resource mobilization theory. In rather different ways, both questioned the instrumental, political, rationalist cast of resource mobilization theory by underscoring the expressive, symbolic, socially constructed, and prefigurative dimensions of much of contemporary social activism. For a time, it appeared that studies of resources, organization, and mobilization had all but disappeared in favor of frames, discourses, and signs, leading some to comment that "[t]he pendulum of Kuhn's normal science now seems to swing toward culture, gathering speed in what may well be a paradigmatic shift" (Johnston and Klandermans, 1995a:3). This remark introduced a reader on *Social Movements and Culture* (Johnston and Klandermans, 1995b) that contains papers presented at a 1992 conference on the same theme; both the conference and the volume conveniently symbolize the culturalist challenge in social movement theory that typified the early 1990s. Whereas the "old guard" of resource mobilization theorists may have temporarily been put on the defensive by the "young Turks" of the culturalist challenge, there has also been much talk of the value of cross-fertilization and synergistic advances toward a possible new synthesis in social movement theory based on these developments.

By the mid-1990s, there had been a fair amount of cross-fertilization (and a great amount of cross-citation), but there was no grand synthesis emerging. Indeed, an impressionistic survey of recent literature suggests rather different tendencies. One is a reassertion of mainline resource mobilization approaches that is striking against the extensive attention paid to cultural questions in the early 1990s. Several examples illustrate this trend. McCarthy and Wolfson (1996) explored the factors that influence the types and amounts of resources mobilized by collective actors in the movement against drunk driving. Their investigation of agency, strategy, and organizational structure is classic resource mobilization analysis with no hint of competing paradigms or premises. Cress and Snow (1996) analyzed similar questions for a different movement by examining distinct resource configurations among homeless social movement organizations and their differential consequences for organizational viability. This is also classic resource mobilization theory; it is perhaps all the more remarkable that David Snow (a leading social constructionist) is co-author of this mainline resource mobilization article. Meyer and Staggenborg (1996) examined the interaction of movements and countermovements as a function of shifting political opportunities and the intervention of the state in social movement dynamics. This mesolevel organizational analysis typifies the resource mobilization approach and responds to an earlier plea from Zald and Useem (1987) for more exploration of countermovements within the resource mobilization approach. Finally, Robnett (1996) used the concept of micromobilization to examine the role of African-American women as an intermediate layer of leadership in the civil rights movement, offering an analysis that falls clearly within mainstream resource mobilization theory. It is striking that all of these articles appeared in the same year in either *American Sociological Review* or *American Journal of Sociology*, and that they are all classic resource mobilization analyses without a trace of competing paradigms. These articles collectively testify to a resurgence of mainline resource mobilization theory that does not easily fit proclamations of a synthesis in social movement theory.

Although it is not difficult to find mainline resource mobilization analyses, this is perhaps not the dominant trend. Even more prevalent are articles that explicitly address more than one theoretical framework, but do so in a fashion that might be called "conceptual poaching." Whereas genuine theoretical synthesis implies moving beyond preexisting paradigms to create something new, conceptual poaching means appropriating the language and issues of a different paradigm and incorporating them as a minor theme in a preexisting paradigm that undergoes no fundamental change in the process. Such poaching is evident in several directions across various theories. Diani's (1996) study of regional populism in Italy acknowledges the interaction of political opportunities and mobilization frames, but opportunity structures carry the weight of the argument whereas framing activities are seen as altering the effectiveness of resources in preexisting opportunity structures. Gamson and Meyer (1996) fire a salvo in the opposite direction by arguing that the concept of political opportunity structure is deeply problematic because it is used in so many differing ways; their solution is to recognize that opportunity is itself a function of framing and that opportunities are as much a matter of intersubjective definition as objective reality. Another poach is evident in Williams's (1995) argument that movement rhetoric about the public good often functions as a cultural resource with instrumental and strategic value to movements that deploy such rhetorical strategies; seemingly expressive or cultural elements of movements can thereby be accommodated to the resource mobilization perspective after all. A similar argument is implicitly made in Bernstein's (1997) study of "identity deployment" as a form of strategic collective action in the lesbian and gay movement. A final example is provided by the poach of the concept of identity by Hunt et al. (1994). They acknowledge the role of new social movement theory in making the concept of identity central in social movement analysis, but they proceed to critique such treatments of identity and argue for the superiority of framing approaches to identity. Without denying the value of this work or the possibility of genuine synthesis, these examples collectively suggest not theoretical synthesis but rather conceptual poaching in which practitioners of established paradigms selectively incorporate the concerns of competing paradigms with little fundamental change in the original theoretical model.

The results of this three-way theoretical contest are becoming clear. Resource mobilization theory has survived a major challenge to its theoretical dominance and is now reasserting itself, with ritual nods to rival contenders. Social constructionism has carved out a solid if subordinate niche that suggests it will persist for some time as the legitimate "alternative" approach in the analysis of social movements. New social movement theory, on the other hand, has been relegated to the sidelines of the contest. Although elements of this approach (e.g., the concept of collective identity) have become common in social movement analysis, they have also been detached from the core assumptions of new social movement theory to become welded to other approaches in piecemeal fashion. Against this backdrop, claims of an emerging synthesis across perspectives must be evaluated with some care. One of the most coherent such claims may be found in the argument of McAdam et al. (1996a) about an emerging synthesis in social movement theory around the concepts of political opportunities, mobilizing structures, and framing processes. There is an implication that these three concepts represent the input of new social movement theory, resource mobilization theory, and social constructionist theory, respectively, and an additional implication that this synthesis represents the macro-, meso-, and microlevels of analysis. But as the authors acknowledge, the concept of political opportunity derives more from resource mobilization theory than from new social movement theory (although the concept has recently been the focus of research by new social movement theorists). In addition, the distinctive claims of new social movement theory about the links between societal totalities and collective action are entirely absent from this synthesis; the macrolevel is solely represented by a limited notion of the political opportunity structure. The resulting "synthesis" is really revived resource mobilization theory complemented by social constructionism (Giugni, 1998b:373); the analysis remains primarily oriented to the mesolevel of mobilization and organizational dynamics as well as meso-micro links where the role of framing plays a more prominent role.

The difficulties in arriving at a genuine synthesis in social movement theory are formidable. Much of the talk about the possibility of synthesizing theories rests on a somewhat facile and oversimplified understanding of theories and their domain assumptions. Thus, theories are sometimes portrayed as merely addressing different levels of analysis or abstraction (Klandermans, 1997: Chapter 8), with the implication that they are therefore compatible candidates for synthesis because they address different problems through a theoretical division of labor. To take another example, theoretical disputes are sometimes portrayed merely as a focus on different variables, in another version of the argument that we are dealing more with a division of labor than with theoretical contestation

(Lofland, 1996:372–373). Although Lofland's (1993) call for "answer-improving" over "theory-bashing" is welcome, and although he would doubtless regard this analysis as a prime example of "theory-bashing," my contention is that there are more than different variables or levels of analysis at stake in these theoretical disputes. My own view of the theories at issue is that they are holistic, organically related entities, and that their power comes precisely from these features. Even when theories do not explicitly address a given variable or level of analysis, there is usually an implicit stance toward that variable or level of analysis within the theory. In addition, the fact that a variable or level of analysis is ignored or marginalized is itself a theoretical statement on its importance. Finally, different theories often subscribe to different metatheoretical orientations, ranging from positivist explanation to interpretive understanding to critical analysis to textual deconstruction. If synthesis means nothing more than detaching elements from differing organic theoretical frameworks and lumping them together, the resulting "synthesis" is likely to be of very limited value.

In any case, the trajectory of social movement theory in the United States is not surprising from a sociology of knowledge perspective. The staying power of resource mobilization theory reflects its style of theorizing and its domain assumptions. The style of theorizing involves the development of middle-range theory through hypothesis testing and empirical generalization (Kitschelt, 1991); as such, resource mobilization theory reflects mainstream sociological theory more generally. This theoretical style is accompanied by an empiricist bent that

> has also tended to restrict the American horizon to those aspects of social movements that can most easily be observed and measured: large, professional social movement organizations rather than more diffuse activities, networks or subcultures; individual attitudes as expressed in surveys rather than structural cleavages, ideologies, or collective identities. (Kriesi et al., 1995:239)

Despite this empiricist bent, the ultimate goal of this style of theorizing is generalizable, social-scientific, law-like statements about the causes and consequences of social activism; this also reflects the paradigm's roots in the instrumental, utilitarian, natural science tradition (Mueller, 1992). Each step toward generalization, however, is also a step away from historical specificity. At best, it produces a type of knowledge that is broad but thin. At worst,

> [t]he content of such work tends to assume a movement so lacking connection to a particular time and place that its existence may well be doubted. This movement *sui generis* tends to be scrutinized as if it can be understood without much reference to its particular social roots or its distinctive goals but instead by utilizing an array of generic concepts. (Darnovsky et al., 1995:xv)

The longevity of this perspective also reflects certain domain assumptions. Even though resource mobilization theory is a middle range theory, it contains implicit assumptions about the macrolevel context in which activism occurs. These assumptions reflect the historical and national specificity of U.S. social movements and their distinctive political environment. This is an environment that is shaped by powerful elites but nevertheless provides numerous opportunities for open, pluralistic, single-issue, interest-group activism in which the entire population of citizens provides a potential mobilization pool. In short, the domain assumptions of resource mobilization theory mirror the liberal, formally democratic political environment of social activism in the United States (Mayer, 1995). It is no small irony that resource mobilization theory really is an (unacknowledged and implicitly) historically specific theory of social activism at the same time that it explicitly seeks to develop abstracted empirical generalizations applicable to all times and places. Although both factors limit the utility of resource mobilization theory, they simultaneously help to explain its ongoing theoretical predominance in the United States.

The same factors that produced a congenial fit between resource mobilization theory, U.S. sociology, and U.S. society have permitted an accommodation with social constructionism while deflecting the distinctive claims of new social movement theory. The accommodation with social constructionism within social movement theory mirrors the larger accommodation with symbolic interactionism in sociological theory more generally: it provides an agency-centered, processual, pragmatic, interactive counterweight to theoretical tendencies toward reification and determinism. And finally, the deflection of new social movement theory is another reflection of styles of theorizing and domain assumptions in sociological theory here and abroad. New social movement theory derives from broader traditions of continental social theory that tend to be holistic, philosophical, and critical in precisely those places in which American social theory has historically been elementarist, empirical, and objective. Such a theoretical style does not bode well for either acceptance or genuine synthesis within a U.S. context. The same may be said for the domain assumptions of new social movement theory. In the words of one practitioner,

> [t]he main focus of the European tradition is on broad social-structural changes.... Within the European debate, the concept of "new social movements" occupies a central place. Typically, these movements are seen as carriers of a new political paradigm and heralds of a new era labeled postindustrial, postmaterialist, postmodern or postfordist.... In the United States, on the other hand, not even the concept of "new social movements" has been able to gain currency, and little attention has been paid to the macrodevelopements that are central to the European discussion. (Kriesi et al., 1995:238)

This remarkable observation from a major new social movement theorist underscores the distance remaining before this theory becomes part of any genuine theoretical synthesis in U.S. social movement theory.

The sociology of knowledge is no substitute for theoretical debate and empirical investigation across different theoretical perspectives. My use of this perspective is not intended to obscure the strengths of resource mobilization theory or the problems with new social movement theories. But the sociology of knowledge is a powerful tool for understanding the extrascientific factors—political, cultural, epistemological, and disciplinary—that shape distinct theoretical traditions in specific sociohistorical contexts. As I have argued throughout this chapter, the sociology of knowledge helps explain both the rise and the persistence of resource mobilization theory in the United States. But this theoretical dominance has exacted a price by confining social movement analysis to a certain theoretical style and particular sets of questions. My goal in the remainder of this book is to open up social movement analysis to a different theoretical style and a broader set of questions.

Part II

Sociohistorical Structures and Collective Action

3

Global Structures and Social Movements

The World-Capitalist System

Modern social movements have a history as old as that of sociology itself. Indeed, as indicated in Chapter 1, the histories of these two phenomena share an important family resemblance in the premise that society is a social construction to be transformed or explained. Despite this lineage, sociology has been only intermittently attentive to social movements, and its periodic attention has reflected sociohistorical and intellectual climates as much as collective action itself. Nevertheless, the past 25 years have been one of the most productive and intensive periods in the history of social movement theory. My goal in Part II of this book is to consolidate, build on, and contribute to this revival of social movement theory by developing a structural approach to social movements. Based on the premise that social movements are rooted in multiple, historically specific levels of social structure, this approach explores the myriad linkages between these types of social structure and the nature of social movements. This structural approach is briefly described in the next section. The remainder of this chapter then explores the global level of sociohistorical structure; subsequent chapters take up the national, regional, and local levels of sociohistorical structure.

A STRUCTURAL APPROACH TO SOCIAL MOVEMENTS

Our understanding of social activism today is seriously hampered by the lack of a broader theory of society. To paraphrase Mills's discussion of the sociological imagination (1959), the promise of such a theory is the ability to interpret social activism by locating it in the larger contexts of social structure and historical location. It is these linkages that are the least developed aspect of contemporary social movement theory. The style of theorizing I am advocating has become suspect of late in the social sciences, and not without good reason. Some theories of society quickly become hopelessly abstract, sterile, and ahistorical, thereby creating more problems than they solve. Other forms of this theorizing lead to the kind of totalizing, grand metanarratives that have attracted the critical attention of postmodern scholars who prefer to emphasize the unavoidable partiality, relativity, and discontinuity of reading the social world as a text (Rosenau, 1992). But the problems of existing theories and the pitfalls of this type of theorizing should not preclude reasonable attempts to identify the links between forms of societal organization and modes of social activism. We should rather take our cue from these critiques and realize that any plausible theory of society will inevitably be selective and partial in its characterization. Within these broad constraints, there is much work to be done.

A useful beginning is a conception of society as consisting of multiple, overlapping, and intersecting levels of social reality that may be designated as global, national, "regional," and local structures. This structural conception of society is guided by several basic principles. First, the various levels of social structure are best seen as nested or embedded within each other at varying levels of abstraction. Second, at each of these levels, what I mean by "structure" is best captured by Giddens's (1984) notion of structuration in which social patterns do not exist apart from the actors who continually recreate (and sometimes transform) them. Third, also following Giddens's lead, structure (or structuration processes) should be seen as simultaneously enabling and constraining various lines of social action. Fourth, I do not intend to ascribe any necessary primacy to structure over agency or to the macro- over the microlevel because these are best seen as dialectically interrelated and mutually constituting one another. Fifth, all structures have an historically specific character that requires us to locate them in terms of ongoing patterns of social change and continuity. Given these principles, the term "structural approach" is hardly sufficient to convey what is in fact an "historical–dialectical–structurational" analysis of social movements. Nonetheless, I have retained the more succinct term "structure" (with all the appropriate caveats) to accentuate the dimension that I feel is least theorized in current approaches and most in need of elaboration in future approaches to the study of social activism.

The historical dimension of this structural conception deserves particular emphasis because the elaboration of these multiple levels of structure as well as their particular articulation in late modernity is itself an historical product. In a profound sense, modernity has involved the establishment of national and global levels of sociohistorical structure as human agents have created systems that encompass greater and greater expanses of social time and space. If modernity witnessed the creation of these systems, the technical capacities of late modernity have fostered and accelerated the interconnection of these systems. Thus, as observers as diverse as Giddens (1984), Habermas (1987, 1984), and Melucci (1996a) have noted, late modernity has forged historically new connections between global, planetary social systems and personal, intersubjective life worlds. As Giddens (1984) has also argued, an awareness of these connections is increasingly finding its ways into the practical consciousness of everyday social agents. This simultaneous elaboration and interpenetration of multiple levels of social structure is the historical trajectory of modern society and a defining characteristic of late modernity. Among other things, they constitute the sociohistorical environment in which social movements mobilize.

Given these structural and historical realities, it follows that reference to any single level of sociohistorical structure inevitably involves an abstraction of that level from a more complex ensemble of multiple levels of sociohistorical structures. Nonetheless, theoretical exposition and analysis require that each level of structure be presented on its own terms. At the global level of sociohistorical structure, my topic will be the intertwining of world-capitalist and nation-state systems, with a particular focus on how the location and trajectory of the United States within this system has shaped the agendas, issues, and ideologies of social movements. At the national level of sociohistorical structure, my topic is the nature of advanced capitalist social formations with distinct crisis tendencies, colonization dynamics, and post-Fordist transitions; my particular focus will be on how these national characteristics have alternately politicized and depoliticized various arenas of social conflict. At the "regional" level of sociohistorical structure, my topic is the multiple structures of power rooted in the past and present dynamics of class, race, and gender relations; my particular focus will be on how these structures of power have shaped specific social movements and how a comparison across these movements can enhance our understanding of each of them. At the "local" level of sociohistorical structure, my topic is the ministructures of everyday life and the microphysics of interpersonal power; my particular focus will be on how these dynamics have become additional sites of conflict and social activism in modern society. The remainder of this chapter addresses the global level of sociohistorical structure and its implications for social movements; subsequent chapters will address national, regional, and local structures and their relationship to collective action. These chapters have a parallel structure. In the first part of each chapter, I discuss the most promising strands of theoretical work for conceptualizing each respective level of sociohistorical structure; in the second part of each chapter, I explore the implications of this work for our understanding of social movement activism.

THE GLOBAL LEVEL OF SOCIOHISTORICAL STRUCTURE

Studies of social movements in less-developed countries typically emphasize the location of the society in a global economic and political structure as a key variable. When attention is turned to movements in more-developed countries, however, this global awareness generally disappears and the movement is treated as if it existed in a social vacuum. This is one way our understanding of social movements is decontextualized and distorted by ignoring the larger structural setting in which it occurs. One thesis of this book is that global structures are often essential in defining the arenas within which social conflicts and social movements unfold. Although it may be easy to appreciate this point for movements in less-developed countries, it has equal validity for understanding movements in more-developed countries. One useful approach for capturing this reality is provided by world-system theory (Wallerstein, 1989, 1980, 1974). This is not the place to enter into the more arcane disputes that characterize this theoretical viewpoint. My goals are rather to selectively borrow some features of this approach, to sketch the broad outlines of the world system, and to suggest the importance of a social movement's relative location within this structure. The following summation of world-system theory is heavily indebted to Thomas Shannon's (1989) useful overview of this perspective.

World-System Theory

World-system theorists argue that a cohesive and coherent international economic system that transcends national boundaries has existed for several centuries. This system is comprised of a single economy and a global division of labor that incorporates numerous cultures and nation-states. This economic system is quintessentially capitalist in nature, and it organizes global activities through the institution of private property, the process of commodification, and the practice of exploitation. Although this form of economic organization is unitary and global, it nevertheless includes distinct economic zones that comprise the world system. Core states are the economically and politically dominant nations that function as leaders of the world system. They tend to utilize the most advanced means of production and the most sophisticated technologies to engage in capital-intensive, high wage forms of economic production. Peripheral states are much less powerful economically and politically and tend to use less advanced means of production to engage in labor-intensive, low wage forms of production. Semiperipheral countries are located between the core and periphery and exhibit some combination of the elements of each of these two regions.

Whereas the world system exhibits a unitary economic organization subdivided into these three zones, the political organization of the world system is more fragmented through an interstate system of competing, sovereign nation-states. Like capitalism itself, the nation-state system is an historical development that has now encompassed every region of the globe. As might be expected, the state structures of core states are generally more powerful than those of peripheral states, and they are often one tool by which the core extends and maintains its power over peripheral regions. World-system theory also proposes a distinctive view of social class relations. Because capitalism is a world system, it logically follows that the fundamental classes of capitalism— capitalists and workers—are international in scope. Hence, world-system theorists do not curtail their class analysis at national boundaries, but rather underscore the international dimensions of class interest, organization, consciousness, and struggle. In terms of class formation, it is increasingly evident that the capitalist class is an international group that seeks to maximize the extraction of surplus value without regard to national boundaries. The working class is also an international class whose labor power is exchanged on a global market. In terms of class formation in this case, world-system theory underscores an array of national, cultural, and linguistic barriers that stand in the way of international working-class mobilization. Despite these difficulties, this analysis implies that organization within a single nation-state is not sufficient because it will play into capitalist strategies of dividing and conquering workers by playing different national groups off against one another. As a world system, capitalism thereby combines a single, global, economic system and class structure with multiple, diverse nation-states and status groups based on culture, language, and citizenship.

According to world-system theory, there are several essential relationships and processes that unfold within this world system and provide its *raison d'être*. The "engine" that drives the system is the process of capital accumulation whereby owners of private property seek to maximize profits under pain of losing their capital through competition with other capitalists. Profits are made through the exploitation of labor power and the extraction of surplus value. Since capitalism is a world system, these processes are increasingly acted out on a global stage, and the result is the systematic flow of surplus value or wealth from peripheral areas to core areas. This fundamental relationship had aided the development of core areas and retarded the modernization of peripheral areas, reflecting a fundamental conflict of interest rooted in economic practices that is now overlaid by complex relationships between nation-states and status groups. Indeed, these economically driven processes are typically mediated and reinforced through political organizations and processes. Like capitalists, states compete with one another for predominance in a global interstate system. The result is often a symbiotic relationship between state managers and national capitalists in core countries in which each group pursues its own interests by facilitating those of the other group. Thus, the structural division between a unitary global economy and a diverse international polity is continually recreated through the processes by which capitalists and state managers pursue their goals within this world system.

This system of global economic and political relationships has been in place for approximately 500 years, with different regions and areas playing different roles over time. In the contemporary period, the core of the system includes the United States, most Western European nations, and Japan. As advanced capitalist societies, these regions are economically wealthy, politically dominant, and relatively stable. At the same time, they exhibit substantial internal inequalities and conflicts that are both the cause and the effect of systemic crisis tendencies. These dynamics will be analyzed more closely in the next section on the national level of sociohistorical structure. The periphery of the system in the contemporary period includes much of Africa and South Asia as well as parts of Latin America. Peripheral states are still dominated by a history of colonialism and by lingering forms of neocolonialism that continue to shape their economic and political systems. Peripheral areas exhibit extreme economic inequality, weak and unstable states, and a number of competing national elites seeking to control the local state in keeping with their particular class interests. These states thereby tend to be relatively unstable, with frequent turnovers in political leadership despite their continuing role in the capitalist world system. The remainder of the globe is classified as the semiperiphery of the world system, including much of Latin America, some of Africa and the Middle East, scattered sections of East Asia, and the former Soviet Union and its satellites. The semiperiphery is perhaps the most diverse economic zone of the world system, including newly industrializing countries with rapid rates of growth as well as some relatively stagnant economies. In broad outline, the semiperiphery resembles the periphery more than the core, but it can still be distinguished from the former because semiperipheral states are able to establish their own exploitative relations with peripheral countries even as they remain exploited by core countries.

World-System Dynamics

Some of the most intriguing elements of the world system concern its dynamics of change over time. There is considerable evidence for cycles of economic expansion that alternate with periods of decline. The longest cycles are known as logistics, in which periods of growth and decline may each run as long as 75 years. Within these are Kondratieff waves of growth and decline in alternating cycles of approximately 25 years. These cycles are at least loosely correlated with changes and turnover within the core states of the world system. These may be conceptualized as cycles of hegemony. During relatively rare periods of full hegemony, a single core state will have major economic advantages over the others in the areas of production, commerce, and finance. World-system theorists generally recognize three such periods of full hegemony by a single country: Holland in the mid-1600s, Great Britain in the mid-1800s, and the United States in the mid-1900s. More typically, no single state can monopolize all these forms of economic power, and they are shared among a small number of core states that nevertheless maintain their dominance over the remainder of the world system.

In the ascending phase of a hegemonic cycle, the rising state typically takes advantage of some new set of economic opportunities in the world system for which it is better positioned than any of its rivals. Building on new technologies or organizational forms, this country achieves a productive advantage that accumulates the resources necessary to extend its power into commercial and financial privileges. In the usual case, these rising powers have been characterized by strong states that were nevertheless under the control of capitalists associated with new productive techniques and organizational forms who prevailed on the state to act in their interests. This growing economic power in the context of a strong state also leads to the development of major and often dominant military power. The decline of a hegemonic power typically follows a similar sequence, in that it loses its productive advantage first, creating a downward spiral in which commercial, financial, and military power also erode over time. The initial loss of productive advantage occurs as competitors copy the productive techniques initially monopolized by the hegemonic power, as dominant producers lose their competitive edge, and as the costs of militarism drain off productive resources. Although there have been extended periods during which there was not a single hegemonic power, eventually a new ascending core state presumably rises to a position of dominance and experiences the same cycle of hegemony as its predecessors.

The relative position of a core state in a cycle of hegemony has important implications for domestic stability. World-system theorists suggest that during prosperous periods of hegemonic maturity, economic growth should blunt class conflict and encourage moderate and gradual social reform. In a relatively open and permissive political climate, the viewpoints of various groups may be afforded a hearing and many may achieve partial victories in struggles for rights and resources. In a context of domestic prosperity and global dominance, a consensus on foreign policy should be relatively easy to forge, and many may join in the celebration of the nation's international stature. This political climate may be expected to change with the transition from hegemonic maturity to hegemonic decline, particularly if it corresponds to a shift in a Kondratieff wave from growth to stagnation. Such a period is typically characterized by increasing economic and political inequality and greater state repressiveness in the context of a stagnant or declining pool of available economic resources. The range of viable political options is likely to narrow to only those policies that strengthen the hands of a declining and beleaguered national capitalist class. The state is likely to cut expenditures that do not fit this narrowly defined procapitalist logic, undermining the living standards of substantial portions of the population. As the state attempts to foster accumulation in a time of increasing stagnation and cyclical decline, oppositional political forces are likely to find their options restricted by these structural forces rooted in the world system.

The cycles of hegemony that define such very different political climates have been identified in even greater detail by world-system theorists, and the history of the United States provides one rich illustration of these theoretical claims. Like preceding hegemonic states in the world system, the United States has now experienced all four of the specific stages associated with the rise and fall of a hegemonic power. In the initial phase of ascending hegemony (1897–1913/1920 in the United States), there was an ongoing conflict between rival powers in which a new contender challenged a previously hegemonic state. In the next phase of hegemonic victory (1913/1920–1945 in the United States), the rising state consolidated a productive and military advantage over rival core states and surpassed the declining hegemonic power. In the next phase of hegemonic maturity (1945–1967 in the United States), the dominant state exercised full hegemony in all the major spheres of economic and military power, and there were no comparable rival powers to be found within the world system. In the final stage of declining hegemony (1967–? in the United States), a formerly dominant state sees the erosion of its military and economic advantages amid the appearance of strong rivals and challengers for the role of hegemonic power. These cycles of hegemony appear to be correlated with the larger logistic cycles and Kondratieff waves that presumably create the opportunities and constraints that contribute to the rise and fall of differing core states.

The changing international position of the United States thereby corresponds to the expectations of world-system theory for a hegemonic power in decline. The same may be said for the altered domestic political climate in the United States over the past 25 years. Since the early 1970s, the U.S. economy has been plagued by a variety of domestic economic crises while seeing challenges to its international predominance as well. The results have included increasing inequality and poverty, accelerated concentration of capital assets (though with no proportional increase in productive capacity), direct and indirect attacks on the wages and living standards of workers and welfare recipients, and generalized pressure on government to cut expenditures and reduce tax burdens on corporations. World-system theory would predict a reversal in the near future, as a new Kondratieff wave of expansion replaces the stagnation of the past 25 years. If such a wave results, however, it could underscore the decline of the United States as a hegemonic power if the United States is no longer organized or positioned to take full advantage of such an upswing. World-system theorists argue that the United States has already lost the critical productive competitive advantage that is the key to gaining and maintaining hegemonic power. Although decline in commercial and financial power is less evident, the long-term erosion of investment in social capital such as education and research is expected to further weaken the long-term competitive position of the United States. The long and gradual decline of Great Britain from its position as a hegemonic power to a relatively minor role among other core states thus offers one long-term possibility for the trajectory of the United States in the world system.

Some proponents of world-system theory present these arguments as if they conclusively demonstrate the causal primacy of a totalistic global system whose inexorable laws are pushing toward predetermined outcomes. In so doing, they reach far beyond the available evidence and run the risk of offering precisely the sort of grand theory or metanarrative that has been appropriately criticized from various directions. My recourse to world-system theory is grounded in the much more modest goal of finding a partial, tentative, and fluid set of concepts for thinking about the most general sociohistorical backdrop in which various forms of social activism are embedded. Although there may be no direct correlations between the world system and social movements, there are numerous more complex and dialectically mediated connections between systemic dynamics and many aspects of social movements.

A related issue concerns the continuing validity of world-system theory in an era of heightened globalization. This theory was formulated in the 1970s in the context of a superpower rivalry, and it remains to be seen whether the dissolution of the Soviet bloc and the increasing pace of globalization will alter the fundamental dynamics of the world system. For the foreseeable future, however, the world system remains a fundamental structuring force in the genesis of a diverse range of social movements. In contrast to some commentators who describe globalization through vague metaphors of leveling or equalizing, globalization is better seen as a tighter integration of social spaces into a hierarchical structure in which the center maintains important controls over the periphery. This hierarchical relation between center and periphery is one of the distinguishing feature of world-system theory, and globalization has done little to alter these power dynamics. As a major theorist of globalization, Melucci has posed the issue of whether transnational entities are superseding older nation states (Melucci, 1996a:193), but he has also conceded the general importance of ongoing conflict between the center and periphery and the specific reality of new nationalist conflicts with the passing of Soviet control over Eastern Europe (Melucci, 1996a:153ff). Finally, globalization may actually heighten and sharpen the connections between location in the world system and social movement dynamics, precisely because globalization allows distant powers to impact daily life instantaneously while also providing the means for ever-more rapid diffusion of social movement activism throughout the world system (Giugni, 1998a). Globalization may thus actually accentuate the links between structural location and social activism. These connections now warrant further attention.

GLOBAL STRUCTURES AND SOCIAL MOVEMENTS

The claim that social movement theory has been inattentive to questions of social structure is perhaps strongest with reference to the most macrolevel, sociohistorical structures associated with approaches like world-system theory. With few exceptions, this is a vastly undertheorized area in the study of social movements. The exceptions include both classic and recent theories of revolutions, which are so obviously played out on a global stage that it is impossible to ignore this level of structure. But for the most part, social movement theory has been inattentive to structure in general and to global structure in particular—even though such structures are a ubiquitous backdrop enabling and constraining virtually all forms of collective action (McAdam, 1996). In an era defined by the globalization of social processes, this represents a major gap in our understanding of the dynamics of social activism (McAdam et al., 1996). Hence, "the analysis of contemporary movements must today take a systemic, global point of view" (Melucci, 1996a:191).

Two steps in this direction may be briefly noted. Even these steps, however, do not focus on social movements in advanced capitalist core countries but rather on the world system as a whole or on movements in peripheral nations. The first contribution is by Wallerstein (1990), and it features the same sweeping historical and geographical generalizations that characterize world-system theory itself. He argues that "antisystemic movements" were a major social invention of the nineteenth century as collective actors consciously sought to realize and expand the goals of the French Revolution. These forms of activism ultimately developed into both social(ist) and national(ist) movements in many areas of the globe, and in most instances they achieved at least partial success. In fact, these movements achieved enough success to become institutionalized, and thereby to become new targets of a renewed wave of social activism in the present era. Wallerstein's schematic categorization of these movements is based on the three zones of the world capitalist system. In the core countries, social-democratic parties have come to at least partially represent the interests of workers in forming state policy. In semiperipheral countries, communist parties positioned themselves as the embodiment of working-class interests. Finally, in peripheral countries, nationalist groups have come to power in the wake of anticolonial struggles. On one hand, then, Wallerstein reminds us that current powerholders are often the beneficiaries of prior social movement struggles that took historically specific forms in different sectors of the world system. On the other hand, as these leaders have become institutionalized and entrenched, they have acquired vested interests in existing forms of social organization that have prompted new waves of social activism on behalf of excluded groups or newly defined interests. In the core states, this has taken the form of new social movements that represent those nonworkers left out of the social-democratic coalition. In the semiperipheral states, the opposition has taken the form of antibureaucratic efforts to resist the privileges that have accrued to new elites. In the peripheral states, this has taken the form of a renewed resistance to Westernization and the collusion of an older generation of nationalist leaders with these social dynamics. Wallerstein (1990) thereby envisions six varieties of antisystemic movements that have appeared in two historic waves to challenge the logic and trajectory of the world capitalist system.

Several objections may be raised against this characterization, including the familiar problems of social-scientific typologies as well as Wallerstein's political agenda of interpreting all these movements as responses to global capitalism. Perhaps most important, the claim that any single theory—however complex—can accommodate the diversity of social activism in this fashion is certainly problematic. But despite these problems, it is the scope of theorizing and the level of analysis that are most instructive in this instance. Thinking about social activism against the broadest possible backdrop of geographical space and historical time can suggest unexpected similarities, intriguing contrasts, and fruitful hypotheses about the structural roots of social activism across many different specific contexts. Such theorizing also underscores how dominant institutions in the contemporary world are inscribed with the imprints of past struggles and conflicts. When movements enjoy even partial success, they create changes that tend to become institutionalized over time. Even when movements fail, they often leave institutional traces because of how the prevailing social order responded to the movement before its demise. Hence, the contours of the world-capitalist and nation-state systems reflect a heritage of conflict and struggle played out over several centuries. It is this scope of theorizing that is lacking in current social movement theory. Attentiveness to the global structures of social activism can offer new analytical leverage in our understanding of these movements and their social contexts.

The other major exception to the lack of global theorizing in social movement analysis calls attention to "global social movements" with the premise that "in an age of globalization of economic and political structures it is no longer appropriate to analyze social movements solely at the level of nationally defined space" (Ray, 1993:xvii). Drawing on Habermas, Ray argues that social movements may be seen as carriers of alternative forms of modernity that are released during crises of global regulation; in such cases, cultural reserves of cognitive and moral learning may be selectively incorporated into the dynamics of national development in the form of defensive or offensive social movements. Whereas Habermas developed this argument with reference to advanced capitalist societies, Ray transplants it to developing societies in the late twentieth century. This leads him to focus on legitimation in peripheral states in which state managers (rather than a national bourgeoisie) have been the main agents of partial modernization. These dynamics have often created authoritarian statist regimes dependent on political clientelism and prone to corruption, scandal, and crises of legitimation. It is in this specific context that social movements may arise that carry different potentials for modernization and that often build on issues of national identity and autonomy for their focus. Although these movements may take dramatically different forms (offensive and progressive or defensive and reactionary), it is the theory of globalization that provides the necessary backdrop for closer analyses of the variations that actually occur in social movements in developing societies. Examples may be found in the crisis of state socialism, the role of "Islamic Jacobins," and the dynamics of race and regulation in South Africa (Ray, 1993).

As with Wallerstein, it is possible to challenge Ray's analysis on several grounds. Not everyone will be convinced that a theory developed in the context of advanced capitalist societies can be transplanted to such a different context. Specialists will doubtless challenge the details of his case studies. But it is the scope of theorizing that is once again most important in this work. At the most general level, Ray's argument is that the location of a society in time and place (as structured by the world-capitalist system and its associated nation-state system) is critical in shaping the dynamics of social activism in that society—and that the resulting forms of collective action are often equally important in sustaining and transforming the structures that gave rise to them. Unlike Wallerstein and Ray, my goal is to apply this insight to the United States as an advanced capitalist society and a core country in the world-capitalist system. The lack of such approaches to date may reflect not only an antithesis to (global) structural analysis, but also a kind of theoretical arrogance associated with positions of relative privilege in any system of power. Thus, just as dominant groups often tend to think that only subordinate groups have race, gender, or class characteristics, it may be assumed that peripheral countries are shaped by their location in a global system but that this rule does not apply to core countries. But just as dominant groups do have race, gender, and class characteristics, so too does the (privileged) location of a society in a global system influence its forms of collective action.

Social Movements in Core Countries: The U.S. Case

Bringing all these considerations to bear on the case of the United States, it will be helpful to distinguish static and dynamic aspects of this nation's location in the world-capitalist system. From a relatively static standpoint, the United States has been a member of the core of the world-capitalist system for a very long time, and that tenure has had important consequences for social movement activism. One obvious example is that as a core country (and, for a time, as the undisputed leader of the world-capitalist system), the United States has played a major role in global affairs for much of the twentieth century. The involvements associated with this role have served as the flash point for a good deal of social movement activism. This is perhaps clearest in the case of military engagements, which have provoked pacifist, anti-interventionist, and anti-war movements throughout the twentieth century. In the most recent and divisive case, movement resistance to U.S. involvement in Vietnam created an ongoing anti-interventionist movement subculture that resurfaced in response to Central American politics in the 1980s and that shaped the conduct of the Persian Gulf war in 1991. These involvements and movements have also sparked sporadic countermovements of jingoistic and chauvinistic nationalism that have provided "Americans" with a rare and fleeting sense of national solidarity. Although most citizens do not become deeply involved in such movements (on either side), they have nevertheless provided important sources of political identity for several generations and thus have defined some major axes in the political culture of the United States.

Although militarism provides the most vivid example, other roles and obligations associated with the status of a core country in the world system have also shaped social movement activism within the United States. The economic, commercial, and financial power of the United States, and its impact on other peoples and societies, has attracted considerable movement opposition at various points in our history. The Cold War conflict with the former Soviet Union defined the international political landscape for almost half a century, and it provided the major reference point for a variety of movements addressing themselves to the superpower struggle. Another family of movements reflects a consciousness of the relatively privileged status of the United States in their calls for philanthropy, aid, and assistance to peripheral states. The status of the United States makes it a desirable destination for many immigrant groups, and there have been periodic episodes of social movement activism surrounding the issue of immigration. Finally, the impact of U.S. production, marketing, and consumerism on a global scale has become a major focus of several strands of the environmental movement, for whom national boundaries are a chimera superimposed on a holistic but endangered ecosystem. In all these ways, the position of the United States as a core country in the world-capitalist system has promoted actions, policies, and consequences that in turn have provided the themes for a good deal of collective action. Although there are constituencies in other sectors of the world system that have also responded to these issues, the activism in core countries has a distinctive flavor because of activists' claim that it is their own nation or government that is responsible for the problem, and that they have a particular responsibility as citizens to control the actions of their own government.

The overall level of societal development in core nations has also had important consequences for movement mobilization. On balance, such nations enjoy a relatively greater abundance of material resources that creates political opportunities and lowers mobilization costs for many different groups. As a result, much social movement activism in core countries derives not from the most disadvantaged sectors but rather from groups and classes who enjoy some resources and privileges and use them to pursue others. As a core nation, the United States has also acquired a rich ideological repertoire that has supported a variety of social movements positioning themselves in republican, democratic, socialist, feminist, or populist traditions. There is ample evidence from contemporary versions of these forms of activism that their own history can be a kind of movement resource, and ideology is a crucial bridge between that past history and present efforts. Much the same can be said for the organizational forms that are a crucial underpinning of any successful movement. The long history of social activism in the United States as a core country has witnessed considerable exploration of different organizational styles, their strengths and weaknesses, and the ways in which they can or cannot be combined for more effective results. One outcome of the kinds of resources available in a core country such as the United States is that it becomes possible to create movement cultures and subcultures that survive and persist even through periods of relative inactivity. When opportunities improve, these ongoing movement cultures can be important facilitators for new rounds of activism. The concept of a social movement sector (McCarthy and Zald, 1977) is one way of summarizing these developments. The term is meant to refer to a patterned, permanent, and quasi-institutionalized arena of social movement contention, and such sectors are most well established in core countries with the characteristics described above. Although none of these aspects is unique to the United States (or even to core countries), the combination and extensiveness of these characteristics create a distinctive climate for social movement activism that may be broadly attributed to the role of the United States as a core country in the global system.

There are other characteristics of the United States as a core country that have double-edged implications for social activism. The role of individualism as a cultural value and a social fact provides an example. There is a venerable sociological tradition linking this phenomenon to the breakdown of traditional communities, the fragmentation of the social fabric, and the rise of anomie and alienation (Durkheim, 1897; Bellah et al., 1985). Although these dire conclusions are often overplayed, it remains true that with the emergence of individualism and the fragmentation of community, much of the social glue necessary for successful activism is no longer built into the social relations of modern society. Thus, the preexisting social organization that resource mobilization theory has demonstrated to be critical to mobilization has become a variable rather than a constant in a (post)modern world of extensive individualism and shifting identities. Although these trends have made it more difficult to mobilize some movements, they have facilitated the emergence of other movements in which issues of individual and collective identity are central and whose goals are as much expressive as instrumental. Alongside individualism, another significant but double-edged characteristic of (post)modern society is the extensive role of mediated forms of communication. On the one hand, this has promoted the massification and commodification of virtually all aspects of social life in ways that can impede the formulation of grievances and the imagining of alternatives. On the other hand, movements have a long history of creating or appropriating media forms for their own ends, so it would be a mistake to view such media simply as an obstacle to movement aims. These aspects of the United States as a core country—material resources, ideological diversity, organizational alternatives, movement subcultures, individualistic milieux, and mass media—collectively shape a distinctive set of opportunities and constraints that distinguishes the range of social movements in core countries such as the United States from those in other parts of the global system.

World-System Dynamics and U.S. Movements

Although these generalities apply to social activism in core countries over a period of decades, a more finely grained analysis requires consideration of how the position of the United States has changed over time within the world-capitalist system. As detailed above, the United States has experienced the first three stages of a hegemonic power and arguably entered the fourth stage of hegemonic decline. The general expectation of world-system theory is that in a period of hegemonic maturity, economic growth should blunt class conflict and promote moderate and gradual social reform. In a period of hegemonic decline, the expectation is for increasing economic and political inequality, declining resources, greater state repressiveness, and a narrowing of political options. There is at least a reasonable fit between these theoretical expectations and the political situation of the United States over the past 50 years. The period of hegemonic maturity (from approximately 1945 to 1967) was defined by a strong U.S. economy that lent some credence to the notion that this was an age of affluence witnessing the end of ideology. In this context, management and labor reached a class compromise that brought relative stability and social harmony. The subsequent period of hegemonic decline has seen a reversal in fortune as economic indicators worsened and social policy became more restrictive. These tendencies were evident throughout the 1970s and dominated the 1980s. Thus, soon after taking office, the Reagan administration reignited the class war with labor and initiated a new class war (Piven and Cloward, 1982) directed at social welfare programs. The contrast between the sociopolitical climate of the 1960s and the 1980s suggests the importance of contextualizing social activism against the backdrop of a rapid change in the trajectory of the United States within the global system.

The most obvious lesson of mapping the recent history of social activism onto the reversal of hegemonic fortune in the United States is that the wave of "60s activism" (which really occurred in the late 1960s and early 1970s) was a kind of marker of the end of hegemonic maturity and the beginning of hegemonic decline. As such, this cycle of social activism was fatefully intertwined with the other major marker of this turnaround: U.S. involvement and eventual defeat in the Vietnam War. Although the general dynamics of the world-capitalist system cannot explain such an historically specific event as U.S. involvement in this particular conflict, this action nevertheless symbolized the ambitions of a hegemonic power to control events throughout the global system (as well as the limits on such power that doomed this effort to failure). A dynamic reading of the world system thereby underscores the historically situated and specific nature of the activism we associate with "the 60s." The hegemonic maturity of the United States underwrote the relative prosperity and opportunity on which these movements were based, but they were also fueled by the perception that as a great power, the United States was falling short of its promises to its own citizens. It was this perception that made the early civil rights movement (which originated in the 1950s and thereby significantly preceded "60s" activism) such a powerful indictment of the dominant society for many liberal whites. By the early 1960s, various strands of social activism were emerging on the basis of available structural opportunities and the example of the civil rights movement. But with the exception of the latter, it required the Vietnam War to convert these early efforts into truly mass movements. If the Vietnam War makes sense only in the context of the ambitions of a global hegemonic power, and if the movements of the 1960s make sense only in the context of the Vietnam War, then the salience of global structures of power such as the world-capitalist system for understanding social movement activism is readily apparent.

A further example of the significance of a shifting location in the world-capitalist system is provided by the recent history of the labor movement and working-class politics. As noted above, the period of relative prosperity associated with the hegemonic maturity of the 1950s allowed organized labor to gain significant concessions from capital in a time of overall economic growth and prosperity. But these outcomes were heavily dependent on a degree of U.S. dominance of the global economy that proved to be short lived. As other core countries began to reemerge as viable economic competitors in an increasingly global marketplace, U.S. capital responded by dismantling much of the social contract between management and labor that had prevailed throughout the post–World War II period. The combined result of deregulation, restructuring, deindustrialization, and capital flight has been to reduce the role of labor as a significant actor on the political scene. In the eyes of some, this decline in organized labor has undermined the viability of any form of working-class politics, with the ironic result that even though this society remains a capitalist one, the role of class as a structuring principle of political contention and social activism has receded into the background (Aronowitz, 1994). These developments, in turn, have created something of a vacuum that has been increasingly filled by social movements more likely to be rooted in identity politics. These arguments will be examined more closely in subsequent chapters, but they have important roots in the changing fortunes of the United States and the erosion of its position of unrivaled dominance in the world-capitalist system.

Aronowitz's analysis of the changing fortunes of various movements is part of a larger debate on the left about which movements and coalitions are most likely to promote a newly viable form of progressive politics. But the search for progressive movements should not obscure the possibility that as the United States loses its position of unrivaled dominance in the core of the global system, this raises the specter of a new wave of reactionary movements in response to this relative decline. It is a truism of political sociology that societies in decline (and middle classes in decline in particular) will often turn to leaders who offer nationalist, chauvinist, racist, or fascist policies and solutions to what appear to be intractable problems. Building on status anxiety, class resentment, and the dynamics of scapegoating, such movements can be directed at numerous target groups both domestically and internationally. The classic case is Germany between the world wars, but there are numerous contemporary examples of nativist, anti-immigrant, racist, and anti-Semitic mobilizations throughout Western Europe. These reactionary responses to the relative decline of European dominance within the world system may foreshadow one potential future for the United States as well. Even the most extreme versions of the politics of resentment are certainly nothing new in the context of U.S. politics, but there is considerable evidence from the 1980s and 1990s that a reactionary revival is well underway. The theoretical issue is whether the relative decline of the United States in the world-capitalist system will continue to provide an impetus to the mobilization of both moderate and extremist reactionary groups. Once again, a structural theory of social movements provides no simple answers, but it does suggest the folly of trying to answer such a question without recognizing the global parameters that condition the prospects for domestic social activism.

Perhaps the most ambitious question to be raised about the relation between global structures and social movements concerns the cyclicity of both phenomena. The world-capitalist system appears to follow cycles of differing durations that have been identified as logistics, Kondratieff waves, and hegemonic cycles. Social movement activism also appears to occur in cycles of protest (Tarrow, 1991, 1994). The question of whether there is any relationship between these cycles bears further examination. As we have seen, the most recent wave of major social activism in the United States corresponded to the end of a period of hegemonic maturity and the beginning of hegemonic decline. The protest cycle of the 1930s occurred roughly in the middle of the period of hegemonic victory (1913/1920–1945), whereas a prior cycle of activism in the early 1900s also occurred roughly in the middle of the period of ascending hegemony (1897–1913/1920). Although the timing of these protest cycles obviously reflects idiosyncratic factors, careful cross-national comparisons might nevertheless reveal some systematic relationships between the location and trajectory of a particular nation in the world-capitalist system and the timing and cyclicity of social movement activism in that nation. As the resource mobilization tradition has emphasized, one crucial intervening variable is likely to be changing political opportunity structures that may wax and wane with world-system cycles and, in turn, shape more specific cycles of protest and activism.

Transnational Social Movements

To this point, I have emphasized how social movement activism is conditioned by its specific location in the world-capitalist system. This system, however, is undergoing increasing integration through communication and transportation networks that have dramatically shrunk spatial, temporal, and interactive distances between various arenas of social activism. The result is that some movements are increasingly able to transcend the limitations of a particular location in the world system by reliance on these mechanisms of global integration. One manifestation of this process is the diffusion of social movement ideas, themes, and forms across national boundaries. Although the initial diffusion of movement ideas may still require interpersonal contacts, their subsequent spread may occur largely through secondary channels of transmission ranging from mass media to newly emerging interactive modes of communication (McAdam and Rucht, 1993). Although cultural diffusion has always been an important social movement process, the opportunities for such diffusion are qualitatively greater now, and they afford the possibility of coordinating social activism across national boundaries to an unprecedented degree.

Such coordination is evident in the emergence of a relatively new development that has been designated as the transnational social movement, and corresponding transnational social movement organizations (Smith, 1995). The emergence of these movement forms in many ways replicates the emergence of the national social movement in an earlier era. Just as nation-states provided resources, targets, grievances, and opportunities for the mobilization of national social movements in the past, global social structures are now providing similar incentives for the mobilization of transnational social movements. Such movements are particularly likely to coalesce around issues that inherently transcend national boundaries and borders. Thus, the human rights movement appears to be the largest, whereas the environmental movement is the most rapidly growing transnational social movement (Smith, 1994). This global arena of social activism brings distinctive opportunities for, as well as constraints to, effective mobilization. On the opportunity side, transnational social movements may appeal to multiple governments as well as nongovernmental organizations to exert pressure on a particular nation or group of nations. On the constraint side, cultural differences and political fragmentation can pose severe obstacles to cross-national coordination of social movement efforts (Smith and Pagnucco, 1995).

Despite these obstacles, the emergence of a transnational social movement sector signifies a new form of social activism with the potential to challenge various aspects of the world-capitalist system. Thus, during the height of the Cold War, "sister city" programs that linked localities in the United States and the former Soviet Union posed an important symbolic challenge to the imagery of rival and competing superpowers. Human rights activism seeks to establish universal standards of behavior by appealing to a notion of global citizenship that transcends allegiance to any one nation-state. Environmental movements dramatize the fact that ecological processes do not follow national boundaries and cannot be solved by national policies alone. Peace and justice groups challenge the logic of domination at varying levels of the world-capitalist system by calling for solidarity across national borders. Although the term "identity politics" has come to refer to a style of politics and social activism that tends to fragment and divide people into particularistic identities, transnational movements promote a different type of identity politics. In these movements, attempts to build bridges across groups promote an identity as global or planetary citizens that transcends the bonds of any one collectivity, organization, or place. To the extent that the world-capitalist and nation-state systems utilize social differences to reinforce patterns of domination, transnational movements and global identities can pose an important symbolic challenge to long-standing practices of divide and conquer that have bolstered such structures of power.

The emergence of transnational movements has occurred in tandem with a relative decline in the power of nation-states within the world-capitalist system. As economic and technological developments have increasingly been organized on a planetary scale, the abilities of even the most powerful nation-states to control and direct such processes have been curtailed. Although this has opened up new possibilities for global social activism in the form of transnational social movements, these possibilities are not all sanguine. As Tarrow (1994) recently argued, the globalization of social protest may signify a shift from intermittent cycles of protest to a permanently mobilized global society in which movements spread and diffuse around the world at the speed of modern telecommunications. The dire side of these developments may be that such mobilizations can no longer be contained or constrained by state-mediated forms of conflict because the nation-state has lost its former centrality in these movement dynamics. As social movements become "ex-prisoners of the state" (Tarrow, 1994:195), the potential for more violent and unregulated forms of social contention may well increase.

As suggestive as all these hypotheses may be, there will always remain a major explanatory gap between even the most sophisticated understanding of the global dynamics of the world-capitalist system and the most careful mappings of specific instances of movement mobilization in various locales. There are simply too many intervening factors, intermediate structures, and historically specific processes to ever permit any straightforward, deterministic global theory of social activism. This does not mean that global dynamics are unimportant; it simply means that their importance is mediated by other factors. What all the diverse approaches analyzed in this chapter share, however, is the premise that contemporary social movement activism can be understood only in a global frame of reference. This premise has been sorely lacking in prevailing social movement theories, and they will remain impoverished until they can incorporate the diverse and subtle ways in which global dynamics and structures both enable and constrain the opportunities for social movement mobilization in different times and places. This task is all the more pressing given the globalization of all social processes as world society enters the twenty-first century.

4

National Structures and Social Movements
Crisis, Colonization, and Post-Fordism

Despite the growing role of global dynamics in modern society, the bulk of collective action still occurs within nationally defined contexts in which the state plays a critical role. Thus, any workable theory of society must have a means of conceptualizing the national level of sociohistorical structure as a crucial backdrop of social movement activism. There has been no shortage of sociological attempts to identify and describe the leading features of modern society, but I believe the most useful of these attempts characterize the United States as an advanced capitalist social formation. Such a designation has several advantages. For one, it provides a thread of continuity between our understanding of global and national structures by placing the economic dynamics of capitalism at the center of the analysis. For another, it underscores the fact that capitalism is a changing system that has evolved from earlier forms to "advanced" forms in a process of social transformation that altered many other societal dynamics as well. Finally, although such a conception draws heavily on the Marxist tradition (as does world-system theory), the most useful theorists of advanced capitalism propose a complex and tentative theory of an open system that eschews the dogmatism and orthodoxy that have sometimes plagued such approaches. Just as the work of Wallerstein and other world-system theorists served as a useful guide for understanding the global level of structure, I will rely on the work of Jurgen Habermas, along with several theorists of "post-Fordism," to orient us to advanced capitalism. Once again, there is a voluminous literature of critique and commentary that is beyond the scope of this discussion; my goal is rather to selectively borrow those features of this theoretical work that offer the best angle of vision for theorizing collective action.

THE NATIONAL LEVEL OF
SOCIOHISTORICAL STRUCTURE

Crisis Tendencies

A concept of advanced capitalism that emphasizes its crisis tendencies (Habermas, 1975) has great promise for analyzing the structural context of social movement activism. In advanced capitalism (as in other societies), a genuine social crisis involves threats to two independent levels of societal integration. System integration refers to the technical challenge of meeting material needs of survival and social reproduction through work and production. Social integration refers to the practical challenge of providing normative order, stable social identities, and symbolic meaning and purpose in the life world. Because these two types of integration are independent of one another, a genuine social crisis will not occur until there is some combination of objective breakdowns in technical adaptation to an external environment and subjective breakdowns in the cultural traditions that typically provide normative frameworks and stable identities through socialization. In such a situation, a full-blown societal crisis may be said to occur. The liberal capitalism of the nineteenth century was particularly crisis prone because the market was central to both types of integration, and market disturbances could simultaneously jeopardize both levels of integration and precipitate a society-wide crisis (Habermas, 1975).

Whereas Marx anticipated that such a crisis would undermine capitalism altogether, the outcome instead was a transition to a new stage of capitalism. The distinguishing characteristics of advanced capitalism are a pronounced concentration of capital coupled with an extensive degree of state intervention into the economy. These adaptations, both planned and unplanned, allowed capitalism to survive and transcend the crisis tendencies of liberal capitalism and to assume a form that is arguably no longer susceptible to the same crisis dynamics. In descriptive terms, advanced capitalism consists of four systems. The economic system is subdivided into three sectors: a private, monopoly, corporate, capital-intensive sector; a private, competitive, small business, labor-intensive sector; and a public, monopoly, state-controlled sector. The administrative system involves a strong national state that intervenes into the economy to engage in economic planning, investment channeling, and market-supplementing activities. These forms of state intervention mean that the market can no longer play the same legitimating function it did in liberal capitalism. Hence, advanced capitalism requires a separate legitimation system consisting of formal democracy to elicit diffuse support, technocratic ideologies to legitimize decision making by experts, and a syndrome of civic privatism evidenced by political abstinence and a narrow focus on family, career, leisure, and consumption in place of the traditional obligations of informed citizenship in the public sphere. Finally, advanced capitalism generates a distinctive class structure that amounts to a partial class compromise between capital and labor characterized by politicized wage bargaining, a partial breakdown of class identity, and the fragmentation of class consciousness (Habermas, 1975).

A central question about advanced capitalism is whether and how it is subject to chronic crisis tendencies. It would appear that although advanced capitalism is less subject to a straightforward economic crisis, it has become vulnerable to a range of other crisis tendencies that result precisely from the means by which it has forestalled economic crises. Put differently, advanced capitalism has managed to displace its crisis tendencies from the economy to other sectors of the society. Although there are still underlying economic dynamics that could result in an economic crisis, state intervention has become so extensive that it has effectively precluded a full-blown economic crisis from occurring within advanced capitalism. Through this intervention, the state has partially displaced the market as a steering mechanism; it has altered the way surplus value is produced by underwriting the costs of education, research, and development; and it has politicized the wage structure through its involvement in collective bargaining. Such actions may have permanently altered capitalism's susceptibility to a purely economic crisis, but not without other costs.

The most significant of these costs is that the very same state intervention that forestalls an economic crisis sows the seeds of a rationality crisis evidenced by chronic problems in public finances and the state's inability to generate and deploy sufficient federal revenue to fully offset the economic crisis cycle. This occurs as the state takes on more and more responsibility for providing unprofitable goods and services, maintaining the economic infrastructure, sustaining social consumption, meeting social welfare obligations, responding to environmental problems, and the like. State action is thus subject to several contradictions that limit its effectiveness. It must intervene extensively to offset an economic crisis, but doing so requires more revenue than it can effectively generate. It must engage in long-term planning and regulation, but it has no real authority over the critical variable of capital investment. It must respond to a wider range of societal needs, but each effort to do so creates higher expectations and invites further demands on its already limited resources. These dynamics combine so that even in the best of circumstances (from the perspective of crisis management), the most the state can do is to displace crisis dynamics from the economy to the state, substituting a rationality crisis for an economic crisis.

Economic and rationality crises occur on the level of system integration, but they sow the seeds of crisis tendencies on the level of social integration as well. With state intervention into the market, the latter no longer appears as a quasi-natural phenomenon beyond human control. By virtue of its intervention, the state thereby acquires greater accountability for economic performance. Hence, state intervention increases the need for legitimation while undermining older forms of legitimation. This combination creates the chronic possibility of a legitimation crisis in which people withdraw their support and legitimacy from the state. In response to this danger, the state may use several strategies of depoliticization to reduce the need for legitimation. These include separating administration from legitimation by appealing to expertise rather than popular decision making, relying on civic privatism to preoccupy people and preclude political involvement, and using formal democratic structures to

channel political impulses in the relatively harmless direction of electoral politics. Finally, a highly productive society may be able to substitute material rewards for legitimacy and thereby avoid a legitimation crisis. These strategies of
crisis avoidance have two limits, however. First, demands for material rewards
(as a legitimation trade-off) may exceed their availability, as exemplified by the
increasingly prohibitive costs of housing and education even for middle-class
families. Second, some demands cannot be met in a commodified fashion (clean
air, meaningful work), and represent political impulses that the state may not
be able to contain. The more difficulty the state has in effectively meeting its
multiple obligations (evidenced as a rationality crisis), the greater the likelihood
that these difficulties will promote a legitimation crisis, and hence a full-blown
societal crisis.

A fourth and final crisis tendency in advanced capitalism involves tensions
between the systemic requirements of the political economy and the identities
emerging out of the cultural sphere. A motivation crisis refers to the possibility that the goals, motives, values, and needs of recently socialized actors will
not mesh with the imperatives of the occupational system and the bureaucratic
state. To oversimplify greatly, this tension involves a clash between socialization patterns promoting autonomy and self-direction on the one hand, and institutional requirements of compliance and obedience on the other hand. Put
differently, modern culture and socialization create the potential for a nonalienated existence, only to have this potential denied by the instrumental, commodified, and bureaucratic imperatives that prevail at the level of system integration. However powerful the economic system may have become in advanced
capitalism, it cannot supply the meaning, purpose, and motivation that have
traditionally come from cultural belief systems. With modernization, however,
the religious belief systems that have historically provided this cultural foundation are displaced by more secular orientations that do not have the same capacity to supply meaning. With advanced capitalism, even the motivational syndromes of liberal capitalism (as exemplified by the Protestant ethic's fusing of
religious and economic concerns) are weakened, precipitating a crisis of meaning. Motivation crises thus arise from the interplay between the modern crisis
of meaning (with its profound potential for both alienation and autonomy) and
the instrumental demands of the system, which precisely require actors who are
perfectly comfortable in a condition of meaninglessness (Habermas, 1975).

In summary, advanced capitalism is a complex, crisis-prone social formation. Although there are still underlying, economically rooted crisis tendencies,
they have been more or less effectively contained through the mechanism of
state intervention into the economy. The effect of this state intervention has
been to prevent the outbreak of a major economic crisis at the expense of dis-
placing these crisis tendencies from the economy to the state, hence, the historically new potential for a rationality crisis. Through this same intervention,
the state increases its need for and decreases its supply of legitimation because
the market loses the quasi-natural status it was accorded in liberal capitalism.
If the state cannot meet the need for legitimation or reduce the level of needed
legitimation through various strategies of crisis management, advanced capi-

talism becomes subject to a legitimation crisis in which increasing numbers of citizens come to question the authority of the state and the normative validity of the social formation of advanced capitalism. These tendencies may be reinforced from the cultural sphere to the extent that social actors experience and respond to the crisis of meaning in a politicized fashion that reinforces the legitimation problems of the state. These various crisis tendencies coalesce around the possibility of a legitimation crisis; when this develops in the context of an ongoing rationality crisis, a full-blown, society-wide crisis is in the making (Habermas, 1975). This crisis theory provides one promising means of theorizing the connections between sociohistorical structures at the national level and forms of social activism.

Colonization Dynamics

Before turning to this question, the role of colonization dynamics also merits attention for how it deepens this characterization of advanced capitalism. The theory of communicative action (Habermas, 1987, 1984) characterizes modern society as the product of social evolution and rationalization along two major trajectories. The development of instrumental rationality has given rise to a system level concerned with production and survival and characterized by rational-calculative capitalism and bureaucratic state organization. The development of communicative rationality has shaped an increasingly distinct life world concerned with meaning and identity and characterized by socialization practices and cultural norms. The distinction between system and life world thus mirrors the earlier distinction between system integration and social integration. Whereas most theories of rationalization have treated instrumental rationality as the whole of reason, this theory emphasizes communicative rationality as an even more fundamental form of reason subject to its own developmental dynamic. Because communicative action is geared to reaching agreement and mutual understanding, it becomes rational to the extent that people give reasons for their positions and defend them against criticism. Communicative action is thus rationalized to the extent that it is free from domination, coercion, or external authority. In the modern world, normative and value questions are increasingly subject to discourse, and validity claims must be defended in unconstrained, consensus-building, argumentative speech. Such communicative action is most evident in the life world where such rationalization has largely replaced normatively ascribed agreement with communicatively achieved understanding. Whereas rationalization in the system is measured by increased steering capacity in response to technical tasks, rationalization in the life world is measured by an increasing reliance on discourse and communicative action for justifying social norms and cultural practices (Habermas, 1987, 1984).

In this model of social evolution, both system and life world become more internally complex at the same time that they are uncoupled from one another. This evolutionary uncoupling of system and life world means that system actions are no longer coordinated by linguistic communication; the subsystems of economy and polity become coordinated through generalized media of exchange (money and power) that act as steering mechanisms and decision-making principles. Although money and power are special derivative languages for coordinating action, as generalized media they become norm-free structures detached from their roots in the life world, thereby separating these media from the responsibility, accountability, and discursive consensus that characterize communicative action in the modern life world. As generalized media, money and power "predecide" courses of action, removing them from any grounding in normative consensus and discursive procedures. Even though these generalized media are derivative languages, with the rise of capitalism they come to dominate not only the system and its technical tasks, but also the life world and its practical tasks. This process represents a kind of colonization of the life world by the logic of the system; it is a form of domination in which money and power displace communicative action as the basis for reaching decisions and coordinating actions within the life world. Such colonization of the life world means that the open debates that might otherwise occur in the public sphere as one expression of communicative rationality are squeezed out by the role of money and power that intrudes on this sphere. It also means that experts using economic and administrative rationality play an increasingly predominant role in the life world, gaining control over the practical tasks of cultural transmission, social integration, and personality development (Habermas, 1987, 1984).

The metaphor of colonization enriches and deepens the earlier analysis of crisis tendencies in advanced capitalism; it is precisely these colonization efforts that manifest themselves as crisis tendencies because of the inability of instrumental rationality to completely colonize and control the life world. Put differently, crisis tendencies and colonization dynamics reflect an indissoluble tension between capitalism and democracy. That is, in keeping with the imperatives of capitalism, political leaders must secure the trust of private investors toward the goal of accumulation; in keeping with the imperatives of democracy, they must also garner the support of the masses to legitimate their decision making and policy implementation. However, genuine participatory democracy might question the capitalist priorities of the system, so what elites really seek is diffuse mass loyalty uncoupled from real decision-making processes. In this way, colonization efforts, however imperfectly realized, serve the interests of elites because the instrumental logic of the system becomes a form of domination that seeks to channel all political behavior in terms of systemic steering media. These issues coalesce around the role of the welfare state, which serves as a prime example of the colonization of the life world through the monetarization and bureaucratization of people's legitimate needs and aspirations. With the welfare state, efforts to meet the practical tasks of social integration through communicative discourse are replaced by monetary-bureaucratic forms of control.

The prime objective of the welfare state in advanced capitalism is therefore to control the extent and the type of public spending so as to fit dominant steering mechanisms of money and power. These conflicts are most evident at the links between the system (with its subsystems of economy and state) and the life world (with its public and private spheres); corresponding to these links are the roles of employee, consumer, citizen, and client. The mass democracy of the welfare state helps neutralize traditional class antagonisms so that alienated labor and alienated political power (embodied in employee and citizen roles) lose their oppositional potential; the traditional Marxist problematic of false consciousness is replaced by the newer problematic of fragmented consciousness. As a result, the roles of employee and citizen no longer serve as conduits through which the life world might influence the system. With these changes, the conflict potentials in advanced capitalism shift to the roles of consumer and client, which bear the full brunt of colonization dynamics as they become the conduits by which system imperatives are channeled into the life world. It is here that new potentials for protest can be expected in response to colonization dynamics. Such action may range from defending the life world against the encroachment of economic and administrative subsystems to progressive political action to reestablish a public sphere in which citizens can engage in dialogue, debate, and a process of rational will formation based in communicative rationality. Such a process would not only reject the imposition of instrumental rationality onto the life world, but would also provide a foundation for challenging the imperatives of money and power in the system itself (Habermas, 1987, 1984).

This analysis of advanced capitalism from the related angles of crisis tendencies and colonization dynamics provides an incisive characterization of the national level of sociohistorical structure confronted by many social movements. As such, it provides a conceptual language that embraces the observations of many social movement theorists about the nature of the society to which social movements respond. Thus, Touraine (1977) argued that with the evolutionary decline of metaphysical warrants for social order, their replacement by forms of what he calls historicity has granted powerholders a new capacity for manipulation that has simultaneously provoked new levels of cultural resistance in programmed, postindustrial society. Melucci (1996a, 1989) argued that contemporary society involves new social controls and conformity pressures as power intrudes on social relationships, symbolic systems, and the constitution of identities and needs, and that this intertwining of material and cultural realms creates a new field of possibilities for social movement activism. Offe (1985) argued that late capitalism involves a deepening and broadening of the forms of domination in which publicly constituted authority intrudes more fully into private life, thereby politicizing new domains of social life as well as expanding the range of forms of social activism that resist these tendencies. Although these authors proceed from diverse theoretical traditions, they arrive at similar conclusions about some of the distinctive features of contemporary society and the corresponding forms of social activism they are likely to provoke. One virtue of Habermas's theory is that he provides the most global and inclusive set of theoretical concepts for locating these claims and exploring their implications for social activism.

Post-Fordist Transitions

Despite these strengths, this approach contains its own shortcomings and blind spots. Habermas's account of advanced capitalism is somewhat abstract and ahistorical, and it deemphasizes the prospects for ongoing, economically rooted social activism. In addition, this analysis completely ignores how advanced capitalist societies are embedded in the global system of world capitalism that was the focus of the previous chapter. It is therefore necessary to complement this model of advanced capitalism with the work of various theorists of "post-Fordism" who have been particularly attentive to each of the areas in which Habermas's work is weakest. Whereas Habermas proposes a sweeping chronological distinction between liberal capitalism and advanced capitalism, theorists of post-Fordism offer a more finely grained distinction between substages within advanced capitalism. One of the more detailed accounts distinguishes between the Fordist structure of U.S. capitalism that emerged after World War I, the "high Fordist" period that coalesced after World War II, and the transition to "post-Fordism" that occurred in the late 1960s and early 1970s (Antonio and Bonanno, 1996). Such theories merit attention because they provide the historical specificity, economic analysis, and sensitivity to global events that are lacking in Habermas's more general model of advanced capitalism.

The term "Fordism" was coined by Antonio Gramsci (1971) in the 1920s to refer to a particular structure of capitalist accumulation that was becoming predominant in the United States and subsequently spread to other core capitalist countries. Fordism was rooted in the mass production assembly-line techniques introduced by Henry Ford to manufacture automobiles, but it ushered in a distinctive type of capitalist society that involved far more than production techniques. Mass production required mass consumption to be economically viable, and mass consumption in turn required the development of extensive advertising and public relations to promote a consumerist ethic and life-style throughout the society. Fordism also required relatively high wages in return for high productivity so that workers had adequate purchasing power to fulfill their role as consumers. Finally, Fordism would have been impossible without a vastly expanded role for the state, which became a veritable third partner in industrial production and thereby foreshadowed corporatist arrangements linking the inputs of capital, labor, and the state. The interventionist state increasingly underwrote the Fordist structure of accumulation at the very time the United States was consolidating its hegemonic victory in the world capitalist system between the two world wars (Steinmetz, 1994).

World War II marked the transition from hegemonic victory to hegemonic maturity in the United States, and it also marked the transition to "high Fordism" (Antonio and Bonnano, 1996). This period witnessed a qualitatively greater development of Fordist trends, underwritten by an historically specific situation of uncontested global dominance for U.S. capital in the wake of the destruction of rival capitalist powers in the Second World War. High Fordism involved the development of highly rationalized, centralized, and vertically integrated firms alongside highly bureaucratized unions and a greatly expanded state. The combination of these organizational forms and this historical climate led to unprecedented levels of mass production and mass consumption, resting on steady accumulation, Keynesian policies, and enhanced legitimacy (Antonio and Bonnano, 1996). The prevailing ideological themes of high Fordism stressed affluence, material abundance, the "end of ideology," and the coming of postindustrial society. Dominant cultural motifs included the homogenization, conformity, and commodification that underwrote the affluence of high Fordism, and that would soon attract the attention of a new wave of cultural and political activism. High Fordism thus rested on a unique confluence of economic, political, social, and cultural developments that sharply distinguished this historical era.

Just as high Fordism reflected the period of hegemonic maturity in the United States, the transition to post-Fordism corresponded to the beginning of declining hegemony for the United States that may be dated from the later 1960s. By the mid-1970s, it was evident that international competition and the relatively high cost of U.S. labor were creating new problems of accumulation for U.S. capital, and the response was a ragged but progressive dismantling of the Fordist structure of accumulation and its replacement with a newer, post-Fordist, relatively unregulated mode of accumulation (Aronowitz, 1992). This transition occurred amid much talk about the dangers of big government, the problem of rigidities and barriers to accumulation, and the excesses of democracy. Its material manifestations included deindustrialization, plant relocation, capital flight, the rise of a service economy, and declining rates of unionization. This transition to "post-Fordism" has resulted in more decentralized forms of production to maximize flexibility and respond to distinct market niches, the spatial and temporal compression of economic activity, the dissolution of earlier political alignments, and major transformations in the quality and nature of work. Although post-Fordism has actually intensified class inequalities, it has also obscured them through social and spatial fragmentation that has undermined workers, fragmented communities, and destabilized families (Antonio and Bonnano, 1996). By its very nature, post-Fordism does not have the same degree of unity and integration as the preceding structure of Fordism. These concepts nevertheless provide powerful analytical tools for mapping major changes in the national level of sociohistorical structure and corresponding forms of social activism.

Before proceeding to those forms of activism, the links between global and national levels of sociohistorical structure merit a summation. Unfortunately, practitioners of world-system theory rarely address the internal dynamics of core countries in detail, and critical theorists whose focus is advanced capitalism have been even less likely to locate these societies in a broader global framework. Despite the almost mutual exclusivity of these approaches, it is obvious that developments in global and national structures will have profound connections. This is one reason theories of post-Fordism are helpful: they are more attentive than either world-system theory or critical theory to the connections between global and national levels of structure. Perhaps the most obvious link concerns the timing of long waves and hegemonic cycles in the global economy and the waxing and waning of crisis tendencies in many advanced capitalist countries. By superimposing these two levels of analysis, a number of promising hypotheses emerge about how changes in national structures may be synchronized with upswings and downturns in long waves and a nation's particular location in a hegemonic cycle. In the context of the United States, the late 1960s and early 1970s were thus a unique historical conjuncture when a long wave of prosperity was giving way to a long wave of stagnation, when the United States was shifting from hegemonic maturity to hegemonic decline, when high Fordism was giving way to post-Fordism, and when the national political scene witnessed a potent combination of rationality and legitimation crises. The cycle of protest associated with this period may be seen as both cause and consequence of these sociohistorical dynamics, but it cannot be understood apart from them.

NATIONAL STRUCTURES AND SOCIAL MOVEMENTS

While global structures define the broadest constraints and opportunities for social movement activism, their effects are filtered through national structures that have an even more obvious salience for most forms of social activism. The national structures most central to social movement mobilization involve the domestic political economy. In the case of core countries such as the United States, these structures are defined by the nature of advanced capitalism as a social formation oriented to the ongoing accumulation of capital in a corporate-dominated economy with the assistance of an interventionist state. As we have seen, this social formation has been subject to major crisis tendencies, colonization dynamics, and post-Fordist transitions. It remains to explore the relationship between this structure and social activism.

Crisis Tendencies and Social Activism: A Dialectical Relation

Although little work has been done on this issue, the operation of crisis tendencies in advanced capitalism (Habermas, 1975) is central to a structural understanding of social movement dynamics. Indeed, advanced capitalism cannot be adequately understood without according a significant role to past social movements that have shaped the contours of this society. In the transition from liberal to advanced capitalism, social activism in the form of class struggle played an essential part. Liberal capitalism was especially prone to crisis because the market provided both system and social integration. In this social formation, economic disturbances as mediated by the market sparked social activism in the form of class struggle as workers sought to defend themselves against the ravages of economic crises. But the causality also ran the other way, as class struggle that challenged social integration was mediated by the market and contributed to economic disturbances. Liberal capitalism was thus a social formation in which at least one type of social activism—working-class struggle—was a central dynamic of social change. Such struggle contributed to the transition from liberal to advanced capitalism, particularly in the form of an interventionist state and a Fordist mode of accumulation. Thus, the structures of existing capitalist society bear the imprint of past resistance to earlier forms of capitalism, just as these structures continue to provoke new forms of resistance.

With the consolidation of advanced capitalism, however, the role of social activism—at least in the traditional mold of working-class struggle—became much less pronounced in theories about the operation of the society. This was evident in the earlier Frankfurt School's profound pessimism about the prospects for progressive social change in modern society; once faith in the inevitability of proletarian struggle was abandoned, it became much more difficult to locate sources of resistance to modern capitalism. Although Habermas does not share this pessimism, his early work nevertheless shares a reluctance or an inability to theorize contemporary forms of resistance to social domination. But the theory of crisis tendencies is amenable to revisions that explicitly acknowledge the ongoing role of social activism and its interweaving with crisis tendencies as both cause and effect. My immediate goal is to suggest the direction such revisions might take with reference to each of the four crisis tendencies.

Although economic crisis tendencies persist in advanced capitalism, they do not provoke direct resistance as dramatically as they did in liberal capitalism. This is because such crises are generally less severe as a result of state intervention, and because the state has partially replaced the market as a steering mechanism. As noted above, however, these realities are themselves the product of past struggles that altered the dynamics of current economic crisis tendencies. The state intervention that has moderated economic crises was in large part a response to the economic breakdown and social turmoil of the Great Depression. Without the challenge of both employed and unemployed workers in a variety of 1930s social movements, state intervention would not have been as extensive nor as responsive to working-class interests. Collective resistance was central in several specific changes in the logic of economic crisis tendencies. These include recognition of labor's right to unionize, the role of the state in legitimating and mediating collective bargaining between capital and labor, and the subsequent politicization of the wage structure. Although it is possible to interpret these changes as top-down, procapitalist initiatives, this reading exaggerates both the power and the foresight of capitalist interests while minimizing the role of working-class struggle (Piven and Cloward, 1977).

Although the responses to economic crisis tendencies may not be as dramatic as in earlier decades, it would be a mistake to underestimate the ongoing potential of economic crises for provoking collective action. For all the theoretical attention being paid to the new forms of capitalism, this remains an economic system dedicated to capital accumulation. In the context of an increasingly global economy, this often translates into capital flight, plant relocations, deindustrialization, and declining wages that jeopardize the economic well-being of millions of U.S. workers. Although the 1970s and 1980s provide relatively few stories of successful resistance to these developments, the role of economic crises continues to provide a fundamental source of grievances. But several factors have made the translation of grievances into collective action more difficult. For one, the interventionist state has shifted the most severe grievances to the least powerful segments of the work force while providing partial benefits to the more powerful segments—a particularly effective tactic during high Fordism. For another, the transition to post-Fordism has undermined traditional bases of mobilization and strategic opportunities for collective action. Finally, the interventionist state has complicated the strategic question of who the target of economically motivated action ought to be. As the interventionist state has become more prominent in advanced capitalism, even economically driven movements whose immediate targets are employers, businesses, and corporations are increasingly likely to put pressure on the state as an indirect means of applying strategic leverage against those targets. The fact that even these movements look primarily to the state is compelling testimony to how state intervention has altered the landscape of social activism in advanced capitalism.

State intervention in advanced capitalism is thereby overdetermined. On one hand, it represents procapitalist initiatives to foster accumulation, lower costs, and maximize profits. On the other hand, it represents a belated and imperfect response to social movement pressure that may partially redress grievances, but as part of a larger effort to maintain the viability of advanced capitalist society. Whatever the ultimate mix of motives, the outcome of state intervention is a vastly increased role for government in the economy and the society as a whole. As the state acquires new obligations in areas such as public goods, industrial infrastructure, social consumption, health care, public education, social welfare, and environmental management, the potential for a rationality crisis increases. The crisis emerges when the state is unable to formulate coherent policies and generate sufficient revenue to meet these obligations. Once again, there is a two-way relationship between these structural realities and the mobilization of social movements. Reading the causality one way, social movements play a profound role in exacerbating rationality crises by raising demands that overload the system. Reading the causality the other way, rationality crises shape the context and opportunities for social movement mobilization, often with contradictory effects on the prospects for movement success.

In the former case of movement effects on rationality crises, there is an increasing tendency for movements that arise in all arenas to direct their demands to the state since the state has publicly proclaimed its commitment to sustaining the social viability of advanced capitalist society. The interventionist state is a veritable invitation to formulate grievances, mobilize resources, seize opportunities, and frame demands in ways that are amenable to state response. This is particularly obvious when some groups that have mobilized achieve partial success, thereby creating precedents and opportunities for similar groups to follow the same path toward state redress of grievances. Even without such precedents, however, the fact that the state has assumed such a wide range of obligations and commitments in advanced capitalism makes it difficult to draw a meaningful line that excludes any particular set of initiatives and policies that might be the goal of particular movements. When growing numbers of diverse needs, demands, and interests are placed at the state's doorstep in this fashion, it is not surprising that they outstrip state resources (even if the state is favorably disposed to such demands). In this way, a high level of social activism in the context of an interventionist state increases the likelihood and the severity of a rationality crisis, as evidenced by the state's inability to redeem its various promises.

The fact that the interventionist state is open to more social movement initiatives does not mean that movements necessarily enjoy a higher rate of success, however. This is primarily so because the state is most open to the interests of corporate capital in accumulation and profitability. As the social movement wisdom has it, the rich and powerful "march on Washington" every day in the form of lobbyists, consultants, and campaign contributions. Thus, when there is a rather clear conflict of interests between the goals of a particular social movement constituency and the goals of the corporate community, social movements will have a very difficult battle to prevail even in the arena of the interventionist state. In such cases, the state often functions as a kind of filter such that progressive demands may go into the filter but what comes out is typically a procapitalist or progovernment version of those demands (at best). State intervention has thus increased opportunities for movement mobilization without necessarily improving their chances for success.

The other side of this dialectical circle concerns the impact of rationality crises on social movement activism. When rationality crises become severe, state managers come under intense pressure to reduce expenditures and eliminate programs. In theory, all state expenditures contribute equally to the deficits and debts that have become one hallmark of a rationality crisis. But the reduction of expenditures typically follows a procapitalist logic in which corporate interests are protected while general social interests (in health, education, welfare, environmental protection, etc.) experience the greatest cuts and reductions. When such governmental reductions are sustained and systematic, it can heighten grievances while also increasing the costs of movement mobilization, with mixed effects on movement opportunities. On balance, however, severe rationality crises that trigger major reductions in state expenditures work against the prospects for social activism by undermining one major resource base for social activism. Such changes in state policy are often accompanied by ideological counteroffensives stressing the limits of governmental power and the need for individual responsibility. In one version or another, this has been the conservative reaction to the politics and movements of the 1960s and early 1970s. This reaction first appeared as a concern about the "crisis of democracy" in the mid-1970s when it was argued that too many different groups were gaining too much input into governmental decision making. The reaction continued in the 1980s as the Reagan administration gave official backing to the ideological thrust of the conservative reaction. When Reagan left office, the rationality crisis (at least as measured by the federal debt) was worse, but federal spending had been reallocated in ways that substantially altered the availability of resources for social movement activism. The interventionist state that typifies advanced capitalism has thereby created a kind of dialectical circuitry between rationality crises and social activism in which each component transfers energy to the other, with complex and contradictory effects on the outcomes of collective action.

Every social movement conveys an implicit challenge to the legitimacy of prevailing authority systems by seeking goals through unconventional means. Legitimation problems are thus central to all of the various crisis tendencies and forms of social movement activism. However, legitimation crises have their own specific relationship to social activism. As we have seen, advanced capitalism is prone to a legitimation gap because the need for legitimation increases with state intervention at the same time that older forms of legitimation (e.g., market-based ideologies) lose their viability precisely because of that intervention. This legitimation gap may be filled by various forms of depoliticization that could preclude a legitimation crisis. These include separating administration from legitimation by appealing to the need for expertise, using formal democratic structures to channel political action into electoral politics, relying on civic privatism to preclude political involvement, and substituting material rewards for legitimation (Habermas, 1975). To the extent that such depoliticization occurs, a society may experience technical problems of system integration (evidenced by economic and rationality crises) and nevertheless avoid a legitimation crisis and the social movement activism that is its political expression. From the perspective of social movements, this analysis of legitimation and depoliticization maps the terrain on which movements arise and the challenges they face in mobilizing.

Translating this verbose formulation into a more colloquial form, the issues here are "who decides?" and "why bother?" The question of who decides encompasses the viability of electoral politics and the role of experts in decision making. The populist position of many movements has been that everyone affected by a particular decision should have meaningful input into that decision. At the other extreme, the technocratic position of many powerholders has been that only those with expert credentials should decide. Representative democracy occupies a middle ground, granting the populace some control over those who will make decisions on their behalf. The ideological appeal of many movements in the United States has been based on a rejection of the technocratic position and a deep suspicion of representative decision making. Such movements can pose a radical challenge to the status quo while also aligning themselves with long-standing American traditions of democratic free expression; the combination can be a potent political force. In the long run, however, movements have had great difficulty resisting the cooptation of elections and experts. On the one hand, the system of electoral politics has demonstrated a tremendous ability to absorb antisystemic initiatives and ultimately channel them into relatively harmless reforms. On the other hand, an increasing number of decisions are being relegated to experts. As the colonization of the life world suggests, this expertise now extends to basic decisions about health, education, spirituality, emotional life, and the like—potentially taking "private" as well as "public" decision making out of individual hands. One fundamental battleground for social movement activism thereby involves the determination of who will make vitally important societal decisions and the conditions under which legitimation will be granted to or withheld from such decision makers.

The issue of "why bother" raises the possibility that civic privatism and material rewards will preclude social movement activism. Although these arguments raise fundamental questions about human motivation, they can be posed more practically as potential obstacles to the mobilization of participants in social activism. The thesis that material rewards will preclude social activism obscures the very unequal distribution of those rewards throughout the social order. For substantial numbers of people, it is precisely the lack of material rewards that defines an oppressive daily reality that may foster either fatalism or activism, depending on how such a reality is framed. For those who enjoy such rewards, the impact on their propensity for social activism turns on the constancy and future prospects of receiving such rewards as well as the symbolic meaning and importance of such rewards to the actors involved. There is no straightforward relation here, because the availability of a certain level of material resources may facilitate movement mobilization toward the gaining of other resources, and it may also underwrite nonmaterial movement struggles in which status, symbols, signs, and identities are central to social activism.

A similar indeterminacy applies to the argument that civic privatism will preclude political activism. If civic privatism is defined as an apolitical orientation to work, home, and family, this claim is tautologically true. Once again, however, this thesis contains certain biases in presuming that a particular mix of career, domestic, and familial arrangements is the norm in society. In point of fact, the life-style presumed by this syndrome is not available to many members of society. It is possible that this life-style may inspire social activism by those seeking to achieve it, but the approved cultural script has historically called for individual effort rather than collective action to achieve the American dream. What may have changed is that this syndrome has become less attainable for increasing numbers of people as material standards of living have become less dependent on individual action and more implicated in the public provision of needed resources—which in turn could invite new forms of social activism and play back into the dynamics of rationality crises. In sum, if the potential for a legitimation crisis turns on responses to the questions of who decides and why bother, it is these same issues that define the terrain on which movements must mobilize members and resources for social action. When they are able to do so, we can expect a mutually reinforcing relationship between legitimation crises and social movement activism.

As with the other crisis tendencies, there is a dialectical relation between legitimation crises and social movements. The appearance of movements can be a causal factor initiating or exacerbating a broader questioning of authority structures throughout society. Alternatively, a preexisting situation of delegitimation can be a causal factor in creating opportunities for new movements to emerge. As these dynamics unfold, movements encounter another dialectic of legitimacy. Just as movements must decide how to challenge the legitimacy of external authorities, they must also establish the internal legitimacy of their own decision-making procedures and leaders. This dual question of legitimacy can be fateful for movements; one potent combination is the movement that is seeking greater societal democratization while maintaining hierarchical movement structures. This combination will appear as a contradiction to many movement members, touching off efforts to reform the internal structure of the movement or promoting schisms and factions. The ideal that there should be consistency between these levels is captured in the notion of prefigurative politics, i.e., that movements should be organized as microcosms that foreshadow the macrolevel social order that they are seeking.

As minisocial systems, it is therefore possible that movements themselves will experience a legitimation crisis when there is discord about the structure of authority and patterns of decision making within them. By virtue of their ideological critique of the larger society, however, movements have the potential to adopt a self-reflexive stance toward their own procedures, to recognize them as social conventions, and to engage in argumentative debate over various alternatives. Those movements that allow democratic debate on these issues can thus engage in collective learning experiences that speak both to internal movement organization and external movement goals. Those societies that tolerate a multiplicity of such movements (and the political traditions of advanced capitalism in the United States support such tolerance up to a point) witness numerous, ongoing experiments in participatory decision making whose ultimate goal is a parallel democratization of the larger society. In the most promising cases, movements function as "free spaces" (Evans and Boyte, 1986) of democratic decision making while also seeking to legitimate public spaces in which similar forms of decision making can be cultivated on a societal-wide basis. In the case of legitimation problems, there is thus a double dialectic that links both external and internal legitimation crises to the potential for social activism.

Just as there is a logic linking economic and rationality crises as manifestations of system integration problems, there is a parallel logic linking legitimation and motivation crises as symptoms of social integration problems. Indeed, the fundamental questions of "who decides?" and "why bother?" that are central to legitimation crises reappear in motivation crises. The latter reflect the contemporary condition of meaninglessness and anomie that emerged as modernity eroded traditional answers to questions about meaning, purpose, and identity. A more promising interpretation of motivation difficulties, however, views them as a mismatch between modern socialization patterns that value autonomy and self-direction and systemic requirements of obedience and compliance. Seen in this way, motivation crises involve a contradiction between the needs of the occupational system and the aspirations of recently socialized actors (Habermas, 1975). The positive potential here is that the erosion of traditional bases of meaning, purpose, and identity need not imply an inevitable descent into meaninglessness and anomie, but can rather clear the way for a new normative order grounded not in unquestioned tradition but rather in a discursive process of rational will formation. In such a world, the norms governing social life would be collectively decided through rational arguments rather than blindly accepted (or rejected) on the basis of tradition.

Despite this positive potential, it is likely that most actors who experience a motivation crisis do not respond by joining social movements seeking greater democratization of society. It seems more likely that motivation crises will promote a variety of antisocial expressions of the anomie and meaninglessness that define this condition. At first glance, this form of crisis may thus have more direct relevance for the explanation of deviance than for the critical concerns that typify social movements. The implications for social movements become clearer with a slight reframing of the question. Rather than asking about all the possible consequences of motivation crises, a better question is under what conditions actors experiencing a motivation crisis will act on the modern socialization values of autonomy and self-direction and engage in the discursive processes described above. The earlier depiction of social movements as laboratories of reflexive debate and collective learning suggests one answer to this question. Although movements do not provide concrete answers to the existential questions that comprise a motivation crisis, they can provide a forum in which personalities imbued with the values of autonomy and self-direction can act on those values in the processes of collective decision making about the meaning and role of the movement. My argument is not that motivation crises lead people into social movements, but rather that (some) social movements provide a forum for realizing the positive potential of motivation crises by offering social settings in which people can move from autonomous personalities to reflection on society and collective processes of self-definition. If this occurs, social movements can provide a vital link between motivation and legitimation crises because movement involvement can turn potentially anomic individuals toward a reflexive consciousness that critically examines the foundations of social authority and seeks a rational grounding for social values and movement orientations.

The foregoing logic applies to all movements that permit the relatively democratic exploration and formulation of movement goals, tactics, and strategies. The more politically oriented such a movement is, the more effectively it may serve as a kind of lightning rod converting motivational syndromes into legitimation crises. The dynamics of motivation crises have an even more direct applicability to certain other kinds of movements. New social movements have been described as emphasizing symbolic, expressive, postmaterialist, identity-oriented values and themes in contrast to "old social movements" addressing the distribution of material resources. As such, the concerns of new social movements resonate with the syndrome of motivation crises to a remarkable degree. The link here is not so much political (at least in the narrow sense) as it is cultural. If motivation crises involve a cultural malaise of anomie, new social movements offer spaces to explore (counter)cultural remedies through the collective construction of new signs, symbols, values, and identities. In such settings, the instrumental, goal-oriented issues of traditional social movements become marginal to the social activity of movement members. More relevant are the social bonds and cultural creativity involved in processes of collective self-definition and the pursuit of a distinctive set of values and norms. Whether such movements are, or can become, "political" is a difficult question to be addressed later. For now, the point is that there is a close correlation between whatever it is that is supposedly "new" in new social movements and the cultural dynamics of motivation crises. This suggests that like all of the other crisis tendencies, there is a dialectical relation between motivation crisis tendencies and social movements. On the one hand, such existential questioning can lead actors into social movements as one way of responding to these questions; on the other hand, participation in such movements may promote the questioning that typifies motivational crisis tendencies.

In sum, Habermas's earlier work (1975) proposed that advanced capitalism constitutes a distinctive social formation susceptible to four interrelated crisis tendencies. A genuine societal crisis is said to occur when problems of system integration (economic and rationality crises) occur alongside problems of social integration (legitimation and motivation crises). Whereas Habermas was silent about the role of social activism in this theory, I have proposed that social movements are vitally implicated in the dynamics of each of these crisis tendencies, and that they often provide the connecting links between crisis tendencies. In each case, there appears to be a dialectical relation between a given crisis tendency and the role of social movements. In different ways, economic, rationality, legitimation, and motivation crises can promote the mobilization of social movements just as the activity of existing movements can create or intensify the dynamics of each type of crisis. Movements also act as cultural translators that can reframe grievances across different types of crisis tendencies. In this way, movements can function as collective learning experiences that focus the vague discontents associated with social problems and bring them to bear on the viability and legitimacy of the social order as a whole. Although there are too many social forces at work to allow deterministic predictions, the value of the theory of crisis tendencies for analyzing contemporary social movement activism seems evident.

Colonization Dynamics and Social Movements: A Critical Appraisal

It is in his later work that Habermas (1987, 1984) turns more explicitly to the role of social movements in modern society, but this account is not without problems. This analysis posits a pattern of social evolution in which system and life world become more differentiated as the system develops instrumental rationality and the life world sees the emergence of communicative rationality. With the rise of capitalism, the systemic media of money and power become norm-free structures for coordinating action; with the full development of capitalism, these system imperatives intrude on the life world, threatening to displace communicative rationality as the basis for value choices and courses of action. Reframing the theory of crisis tendencies, the results are now conceptualized as an indissoluble tension between capitalism and democracy in which state managers must gain diffuse mass loyalty to maintain systemic legitimacy while also responding to the imperatives of capital accumulation.

The welfare state is the prime example of colonization as people's needs are "monetarized" and bureaucratized to reconcile public spending and capital accumulation. It is in this context that protest potentials may be evaluated in terms of four roles that link system and life world. According to the theory, the roles of employee and citizen have lost much of their oppositional potential because the mass democracy and diffuse legitimacy of this social formation have neutralized these historical bases of resistance to capitalist encroachment. As a result, these roles no longer offer a pathway for the life world to influence the system. This conclusion appears to be a retreat from the theory of crisis tendencies and the potential for legitimation crises; as such, it seems a premature judgment that flies in the face of contemporary dissatisfactions with both work roles and electoral politics and their potential for promoting social activism. The colonization thesis privileges two other roles (consumers and clients) as major conduits for life world colonization and as offering the greatest potential for resistance to that colonization. At a minimum such resistance will defend the life world against further depersonalization; beyond this, such resistance could restore a genuine public sphere in which the role of the citizen in collective decision making can be revitalized.

Following this logic, the protest potentials of greatest interest do not involve struggles over material reproduction, have not been channeled into existing political structures, and can no longer be allayed by material compensation. The new conflicts revolve rather around life world concerns that cannot be coopted by the media of money and power. This shift suggests the utility of a distinction between an "old politics" concerned with material security and a "new politics" whose themes include the "quality of life, equal rights, individual self-realization, participation, and human rights" (Habermas, 1987:392). This new politics is associated with youth, the new middle class, and those with extensive formal education. These supporters are distinct from the industrial core of direct producers associated with "old politics," and because they are located on the periphery of industrial production they are particularly sensitized to the destructive consequences of unrestricted capitalist growth. These heterogeneous groups are linked by their ideological critique of growth; these movements thereby resemble the social romantic protests of early industrialism more than either bourgeois emancipation efforts or organized labor movements.

A critical issue concerns how to distinguish movements with emancipatory potential from those more oriented to resistance and withdrawal. Only the feminist movement is characterized as an offensive, emancipatory, liberation movement. The other new movements fit the mold of resistance and withdrawal. Within this category, another distinction is drawn between movements that defend traditional bases of social order and property (e.g., middle-class tax revolts) and those that express a new conflict potential that "operates on the basis of a rationalized lifeworld and tries out new ways of cooperating and living together" (Habermas, 1987:394). The latter are exemplified by "youth and alternative movements for which a critique of growth sparked by themes of ecology and peace is the common focus" (Habermas, 1987:394). It is the latter category of resistance movements that symbolizes counteroffensives against the colonization of the life world and attempts to establish alternative social spaces in which communicative rationality can become an organizing principle of social life. This is expressed in environmental movements concerned with standards of livability, in movements against the excessive complexity of the system and its overshadowing of the life world, and in movements to nurture subcultural communities and collective identities in the face of impersonal administrative domination. In diverse ways, these movements arising along the seams between system and life world explore alternative ways of organizing social relations that challenge the monetarization and bureaucratization of social life resulting from the colonization of the life world. When successful, these movements can establish counterinstitutions in which communicative rationality takes precedence over system imperatives.

There is a voluminous literature on the theory of communicative action that is beyond the scope of this analysis, but several examples merit attention for evaluating the utility of this theory for the study of social movements in advanced capitalism. Critical commentaries may be divided into two categories: those that address the larger theory of system and life world and those that address the specific suggestions regarding social movements. Concerning the former, Habermas's work has long been criticized for relying on a false and misleading dualism between system and life world. Despite his insistence that these are merely differing perspectives on society, his writing often reifies these categories and obscures the communicative foundations of the system and the material dimensions of the life world. This problem appears in especially sharp focus in Fraser's (1989) feminist critique of Habermas's theory. She points out that this account ignores the ways in which gender and patriarchal power are interwoven in both the system and life world. This leads him to ignore the patriarchal norms of economic and administrative subsystems that shape the role of money and power as generalized media of exchange. It also leads him to ignore the material foundations of the life world and the role of power in the family by collapsing these complexities into a notion of a life world under siege. It finally leads him to ignore the way in which all the major roles he discusses—employee, citizen, consumer, and client—are gendered roles in advanced capitalism that cannot be fully understood from the gender-blind categories employed by Habermas. Fraser concludes that women's struggles "are not adequately clarified by a theory that draws the basic battle line between system and lifeworld institutions. From a feminist perspective, there is a more basic battle line between the forms of male dominance linking 'system' to 'lifeworld' *and us"* (Fraser, 1989:137, italics in original).

Fraser's critique has direct relevance to the analysis of gender and the role of feminist movements—both of which have long been marginalized in Frankfurt School critical theory. But her critique also speaks to problems that affect other identities and movements as well. If she (and others) are correct that Habermas reifies the distinction between system and life world, the colonization argument itself is jeopardized and hence the notion that new social movements are responses to this colonization. Although this may be one root of some movements, it should not blind us to other roots of other forms of protest and activism. Thus, struggles for workplace democracy occur within the economic subsystem through the employee role that Habermas marginalizes in postindustrial advanced capitalism. And yet, because the system also rests on a communicative foundation, this can be an important arena of struggles to extend communicative rationality and argumentative discourse into the system. This does not mean that workers can talk bosses into doing what they want; it does mean that discursive challenges to the structure of authority at work can enlarge the sphere of worker control when successful and can feed into legitimation crises when they fail—perhaps sparking further mobilization.

Conversely, struggles against forms of domination within the life world are also more important than Habermas appears to recognize because the life world is not simply a sphere of traditionally or communicatively secured action but is also a site of domination and power. Feminist analyses of the various ways in which patriarchal power is privatized within the family (and resisted by women in the family) testifies to the importance of this form of activism. Thus, the danger in Habermas's argument is that by exaggerating the dualism of system and life world as a way of identifying colonization dynamics and resistance, other patterns of domination and resistance within each sphere are obscured. And because there are elements of material power and normative foundations in both spheres, resistance within each sphere has the potential to advance communicative rationality and democratization every bit as much as resistance to the colonization dynamics between system and life world. Hence, there is no solid foundation for privileging the specific mobilizations cited by Habermas over others that may in fact be moving toward the same ends.

Habermas's analysis can also be challenged for its more specific claims about new forms of social activism. Among these criticisms are that the novelty of new social movements has been exaggerated, that the distinction between identity politics and interest politics is overdrawn, that this approach privileges middle-class social movements over others, and that the emphasis on symbolic aspects obscures the grievance base of many new social movements (Ray, 1993). The danger in exaggerating the newness of these movements and the distinction between interest and identity politics is that it obscures the continuities between older and newer forms of social activism and the ways in which "new" social movements may really be expanding the sphere of the political to include cultural or private aspects of life. Habermas is also unclear about exactly how colonization dynamics engender social movement responses. Against his implicit reliance on social–psychological models of strain and anomie, we need to recognize how all social protest is socially constructed; against his tendency to valorize any and all identity-based struggles, we need greater sensitivity to how the increasingly fluid boundaries between public and private can coopt movements by privatizing public issues and diverting potential protest into life-style politics or consumerism (Ray, 1993). Perhaps the greatest challenge to the Habermasian approach concerns its ambiguity over the directionality of the protests engendered by colonization processes. The central unanswered question here is how to identify the circumstances that lead to offensive, emancipatory movements rather than defensive, reactionary ones (Ray, 1993).

Many of these issues are part of a larger debate about the role of new social movements that extends far beyond Habermas's specific contributions. But

Habermas's framework could respond more effectively to these concerns with the following modifications. First, the earlier theory of multiple and related crisis tendencies concerning both system and social integration needs to be maintained to understand multiple points of grievance and resistance to structures of domination in advanced capitalism. Second, the dialectical relation of crisis tendencies and social movements needs to be recognized: crises may provoke social activism, but social activism is also a constituent element in crises themselves. With reference to the categories of system and life world, there is a parallel need to recognize the dialectical relation between these spheres to offset the monolithic imagery of an omnipotent system. As Fraser (1989:137) notes, "the channels of influence between system and lifeworld institutions are multidirectional." Third, we need a less reified conception of system and life world that recognizes the normative elements of the system and the material aspects of the life world. With this recognition, it would be easier to see and theorize the kinds of resistance that occur within these spheres as well as that which occurs between them in response to colonization. Fourth, these modifications would clarify that the colonization thesis represents only a partial theory of social activism; it is one very important catalyst but cannot carry the burden of explaining the full range of social movement activism in advanced capitalism. Fifth, this theory must leave open the question of whether new social movements have or will acquire the status of a central conflict that typifies a new social formation, but it is certainly too early to answer this question in the affirmative at this time. Finally, the most important work that needs to be done to extend this framework concerns the conditions under which movements arising in response to colonization dynamics develop in reactionary or progressive directions. Habermas suggests that even initially defensive responses can become progressive if there is a meaningful role for communicative rationality and collective learning during the mobilization process. These processes require both further theorization and empirical research. These suggestions are meant to build on and advance Habermas's central conception of advanced capitalism as a society of conflicting rationalities in which the tension between instrumental rationality as a form of domination and communicative rationality as a type of sociality provides a vital spark to social movement activism.

A reformulated Habermasian approach to social movements based on these principles would have an applicability even beyond the movements that Habermas has specifically discussed. Two examples may be mentioned here as illustrative of the potential of a revised Habermasian framework for theorizing the impact of national structures on social movement dynamics. The first concerns the urban social movements extensively analyzed by Castells (1983), who argues that these movements typically develop around three overlapping themes. First, such movements raise demands for collective consumption that can be provided only by the state, in contrast to the privatized consumption patterns of a capitalist economy. Couched more broadly, this demand represents a struggle over the definition of the city as a site of exchange value according to the capitalist logic of commodification and accumulation versus a site of use value in which development, consumption, and services are organized according to a logic of people's needs and desires without reference to profitability. Second, Castells argues that such movements are also concerned with the defense of a collective identity linked to a given territory. This often involves creating or maintaining autonomous local cultures in direct contrast to the homogenization of culture symbolized by the mass media. Finally, these movements typically seek an expanded role and enhanced power for local government that is closer to citizen control than regional, state, or national administrative structures. For Castells, this requires decentralization that dovetails with a drive for self-management and autonomy, thereby constituting a citizen movement. Although Castells's theory was developed as a cross-cultural theory of urban social movements, Stoecker (1994) demonstrated the utility of this framework in a study of resistance to urban redevelopment in a Minneapolis neighborhood. Theorized as a struggle over social reproduction rather than production, Stoecker finds strong evidence of all three of Castells's themes in the local mobilization to challenge probusiness forms of urban development.

Although neither of these studies of urban social movements makes significant reference to Habermas, their logic fits a revised Habermasian framework quite closely. The movement goal of collective consumption presupposes a type of state intervention that Habermas has explicitly theorized in his analysis of crisis tendencies. Such movements are responding in part to displaced economic crises that assume the form of state-centered rationality crises, and they are likely to exacerbate such rationality crises and contribute to legitimation crises if and when the state proves unwilling or unable to respond meaningfully to movement goals. Although Castells frames this conflict as one between commodified exchange value and social use value, this resonates closely with Habermas's notion of competing logics and rationalities in advanced capitalism, with exchange value standing in for the generalized media of money and power and use value representing the alternative process of democratic and discursive will formation. Castells's second movement theme of defending collective identity fits Habermas's analysis of systemic imperatives threatening to intrude on the construction and maintenance of identity. Although Castells focuses on progressive movements, it is likely (as Habermas suggests) that defensive responses to colonization can take a reactionary as well as a progressive form depending on the scope of collective learning processes in such mobilizations. The third goal of urban movements toward decentralization reflects an even more fundamental striving toward autonomy and self-management on the part of these movements. These ends have a distinctly Habermasian flavor in that they are rooted in the postconventional morality that Habermas sees as central in modern socialization patterns, and they can be fully achieved only through a process of discursive will formation and participatory democracy of the sort Habermas associates with communicative rationality. Thus, despite their different foci and concepts, there is a striking symmetry in the manner in which both Castells and Habermas theorize modern social movements as emerging out of an irreconcilable friction between the instrumental rationality of systemic imperatives and the social or communicative rationality of democratic self-determination.

A second example of the broader applicability of a revised Habermasian approach may be found in the many parallels between this theory and that of the Italian new social movement theorist Alberto Melucci (1996a, 1989). These parallels are perhaps all the more striking because Melucci's writings convey a mistrust of the sort of grand theorizing that is standard fare for Habermas. Nevertheless, Melucci shares some key Habermasian notions concerning the structures against which new social movements mobilize. Melucci (1980) concurs with Habermas that in advanced capitalism, the production system reaches into the realm of consumption, services, social relations, and personal identity. Advanced capitalist societies have thereby created a new field for social movements by intertwining economic and material activity with cultural processes such as the formation of identities and the processing of information (Melucci, 1984). Given these structural developments, Melucci suggests that new social movements may be conceptualized as contemporary forms of resistance to the growing intervention of the system into the world of social relationships, symbols, identities, and needs—i.e., the world that Habermas has conceptualized as a life world under siege by systemic imperatives. On the one hand, this means that social activism has shifted "inward" to what Melucci explicitly identifies as Habermas's "internal nature": a symbolic world of socialization and identity that opposes and resists its reduction to mere inputs and outputs of the system. On the other hand, this means that resistance also shifts "outward" because new social movement activity may be interpreted as an implicit repudiation of the instrumental rationality of the system. Indeed, as Melucci eloquently argues, a major role of the new social movements is to render power visible by openly challenging the authority and domination that otherwise are obscured by the impersonal rationality of administrative procedures. Finally, in advocating the expansion of free spaces and democratic structures that will allow for the consolidation of collective identity, Melucci parallels Habermas's call for an expanded role for communicative rationality in keeping with the goal of collective self-determination. One of the important differences between these theorists concerns their specific accounts of how movements mobilize in response to these systemic pressures. Where Habermas has implicitly relied on notions of strain and anomie (Ray, 1993), Melucci has been insistent and insightful about the socially constructed nature of collective action and collective identity. But on the question of how to characterize the social structures that provoke and shape contemporary forms of resistance, the many parallels between Melucci and Habermas suggest the utility of a revised Habermasian approach for understanding contemporary social activism.

Social Movements in a Post-Fordist World

Although Habermas's approach can be revised internally in this fashion, it can also be complemented externally by the insights of post-Fordist theorists. As we saw earlier, these theorists have mapped a major shift within advanced capitalism from Fordist to post-Fordist modes of accumulation, and this shift has had important consequences for social activism. Perhaps the most important consequence concerns the partial eclipse of working-class activism and the rise of movements rooted in racial and gender identities. These consequences will receive extended treatment in Chapter 5 on regional structures of power. But there are other effects of the transition to post-Fordism that have shaped the climate for all social movements and have promoted new issues for social activism. There is considerable overlap between the movements Habermas describes as responses to colonization dynamics and the movements post-Fordist theorists see in response to the contradictions and demise of Fordism. But the latter theorists provide a somewhat different account of the roots of these movements that is not dependent on the grand theorizing typical of Habermas's approach.

For post-Fordist theorists, several aspects of the Fordist mode of accumulation were crucial in laying the foundation for specific types of social activism. For one, Fordism generated a degree of material affluence for broad sectors of the population that was historically unprecedented. The productive and distributive mechanisms of Fordism underwrote the development of a broad middle class typified by careerist work patterns, extensive home ownership, and access to higher education. Although these patterns of distribution remained highly unequal across lines of class, race, and ethnicity, it was precisely the more privileged sectors that became the basis for much of the social activism associated with the transition from Fordism to post-Fordism. Another important aspect of Fordism was the rise of an interventionist state. Externally, the interventionist state coincided with a period of hegemonic victory and maturity that saw the militarization of state and society. Internally, the interventionist state extended bureaucratization, regulation, and surveillance into new arenas of social life. A third aspect of Fordism involved the rise of a culture industry that fostered homogeneity and conformity promulgated through mass media that increasingly penetrated into the daily lives and routines of large sectors of the population. The combination of material affluence, an interventionist state, and cultural homogenization proved a potent mix that sparked historically specific forms of social activism during the period of high Fordism and the transition to the present post-Fordist mode of accumulation.

A prime example of a movement response to these dimensions of Fordism is the environmental movement, and particularly those strands of ecological activism grounded in an ideology of "limits to growth." These appeals rest on postmaterialist values that question the economic goals of unlimited accumulation by citing the devastating ecological effects of unregulated economic activity. These appeals also challenge the distributive mechanisms of Fordist economics for their promotion of consumerism and the ecologically wasteful and damaging consequences of demand factors on global resources (Aronowitz, 1992). The example of the antigrowth sector of the environmental movement links Habermas's approach and post-Fordism: both theories offer complementary explanations of the roots of this movement. But this is also a case in which post-Fordism offers a subtler analysis because of the greater historical specificity of this approach. For example, post-Fordist theorists have stressed how social movements that have responded to Fordism have also embodied its contradictions, and as a result they have sometimes facilitated the transition to post-Fordism as an unintended consequence of their opposition to Fordism. In the case of environmentalism, the movement call for more decentralized, localized, and limited forms of production and consumption resonates with (thoroughly capitalist) post-Fordist production strategies emphasizing product differentiation, smaller scale production, localized distribution, and market niches. Theorists of post-Fordism thereby provide a more specific benchmark for evaluating the oppositional potential of social movements by detailing how opposition to one form of capitalist production may unwittingly promote new forms of capitalist production rather than meaningful alternatives (Hirsch, 1988).

Environmentalism is by no means the only social movement that comes into clearer focus with an understanding of the crisis of Fordism and the transition to post-Fordism. Countercultural movements from the beats of the 1950s to the present day may be seen as critical responses to the conformity pressures and cultural homogenization associated with high Fordism's mass culture industry and bureaucratized life world in the post-World War II period. The early student movement against university bureaucracy and hierarchy was led by relatively privileged young people with postmaterialist values who challenged the rigidity, regulation, and alienation associated with the university as "knowledge factory." As the militarism of the Fordist state became more evident with the escalation of the Vietnam War, the student movement identified connections between universities and the military–industrial complex and redirected its energy into a challenge to the war. As Fordism's modes of regulation and control penetrated further into everyday life, it sparked numerous neopopulist local and neighborhood movements that challenged such regulation and control of communities. And as a final example, feminist movements and gay and lesbian movements have arisen to challenge prevailing forms of gender and family life that reflect the cultural homogenization of Fordism. Although there are multiple causes and explanations of all these movements, the value of post-Fordist theory is that it brings a degree of historical specificity to our explanations that is often lacking in more general analyses of the roots of social activism.

Although no single theoretical approach can encompass all of the ways in which the national political economy structures contemporary social activism, I hope to have demonstrated that a modified and refined Habermasian framework complemented by theories of post-Fordism can provide a very productive starting point for such analysis. Combining the concepts of crisis theory, colonization dynamics, and post-Fordist capitalism yields a rich characterization of the historically specific nature of advanced capitalist society and its role in generating social activism. As an advanced capitalist society, these national structures in the U.S. political economy are embedded in the larger global structures of the world-capitalist system analyzed earlier. And these structures contain still other regional and local structures with their own consequences for the shape of social activism.

5

Regional Structures and Social Movements

Class, Race, and Gender

Global and national structures intertwine to create the distinctive social and historical contexts in which collective action occurs. For some movements, it is these structures that are most critical in shaping the particular opportunities and constraints that govern movement emergence, mobilization, and success. For many other movements, it is a third level of structure conditioning relations across lines of class, race, and gender that is most salient in producing collective action. This is obvious in working-class mobilization, movements for racial justice, and feminist movements. But these structures are omnipresent in the background of all forms of collective action. Two examples must suffice to suggest a more general point. On the individual level, the class, race, and gender characteristics of individuals are always reflected in patterns of differential recruitment and mobilization; there are no movements whose membership is not shaped by these realities. On the organizational level, movements that challenge some forms of inequality inevitably sustain and recreate other forms of inequality within their ranks, including class, race, or gender relations. The centrality of these dynamics to collective action requires analysis of a third level of sociohistorical structure that is intertwined with global and national structures.

THE REGIONAL LEVEL OF SOCIOHISTORICAL STRUCTURE

The term "regional" is not a spatial reference but rather an analytical one; it is a term of convenience for a level of analysis between global and national structures on the one hand and the local structures of everyday life on the other hand. This level of sociohistorical structure is comprised of various structures of power that involve relations of exploitation, oppression, or domination among specific collectivities of people. Structures of power consist of a dominant group, a subordinate group, and the ongoing, institutionalized relationships between them. To varying degrees, members of dominant groups are the beneficiaries of these relationships in that they receive material or psychic rewards and privileges as a direct result of their membership in a dominant group. Members of subordinate groups, on the other hand, are the victims of these relationships in that they suffer material or psychic penalties and deprivations that derive from their membership in a subordinate group. Conceptualized in this way, structures of power imply that dominant and subordinate groups have conflicting long-term interests concerning the maintenance or the dissolution of these structures that yield privileges or deprivations, respectively. They also imply that in the long run, members of these groups will arrive at a form of social consciousness that recognizes these interests and their implications for action in the world (for a classic statement of this view, see Dahrendorf, 1959).

These points about interests and consciousness are no more than tendential hypotheses, however, because of the myriad factors that may preclude actors in the world from either perceiving or acting on their interests in these ways. The conceptual model of structures of power should not blind us to a world in which some members of dominant groups relinquish their privileges, or some members of subordinate groups accommodate to existing powers, or members of both groups feel a solidarity based on other lines of affiliation. Indeed, the most complex aspect of these structures of power involves their interrelations with one another and the simultaneity of all these group affiliations and sources of identity (Collins, 1990). Although it is possible to isolate each structure for the purposes of analytical discussion, real social actors inhabit multiple, overlapping locations in these structures that make any simplistic predictions from structure to action impossible. Hence, the concept of structures of power has a certain analytical, comparative, and explanatory potential that is nonetheless limited by the complex and variegated nature of the social relations associated with such power dynamics. If the concept is used as a flexible but fallible guide to a complex world, it can take us where we want to go without blinding us to the complexities along the way.

The number of relevant structures of power in any given society or historical moment is an empirical question. Over time, structures may either arise or decline in any one society, and looking across societies we may find that structures that are prevalent in one society are all but lacking in another. In the context of the contemporary United States, there are at least three structures of power that require analytical elaboration: those rooted in class exploitation, racial oppression, and gender domination. It has become fashionable in some circles to lump these phenomena together through casual references to the "isms" (i.e., "classism," racism, and sexism), but I believe this common practice has two unfortunate consequences. First, it implies that the underlying dynamics of each structure of power are essentially the same and do not need to be distinguished. Second, it implies that these problems are ultimately rooted in attitudinal or ideological factors. My usage of the concept of structures of power is rooted in two contrasting assumptions. First, despite the important similarities between dominant and subordinate groups that warrant using a concept such as structures of power across these different cases, it is equally important to theorize the different, specific, underlying dynamics that distinguish one structure from another. Second, as *structures* of power, the main characteristic of these phenomena is their institutional embeddedness within the social fabric at all levels. This is not to deny the ideological component that often accompanies structures of power, but it is to underscore the material foundation that underlies attitudes and ideologies that we might characterize as "classist," racist, or sexist. With these clarifications and caveats, the concept of structures of power provides a promising guide to the regional level of sociohistorical structure. In each of the subsections to follow, I build on some of the more helpful work in the field to characterize these distinct structures of power as a prelude to analyzing their consequences for social movement activism.

The Class Structure of Power

The social class structure of power concerns the production and distribution of material resources as mediated by labor and capital markets and state intervention. Conceptualized in this way, the class structure of power has a close connection with the dynamics of capitalism, which led traditional Marxist approaches to place these two questions on the same analytical plane. A corollary of this analytical fusion of capitalism and class is the tendency to dismiss any other structure of power as a secondary diversion from the centrality of class and class conflict. If there is a single clear lesson to be drawn from the survival of capitalism long after Marx, however, it is that the connections between capitalism and class are more complex and tenuous than he anticipated. The image of an increasingly polarized class structure generating escalating levels of class conflict between homogeneous bourgeois and proletariat classes made for dramatic social theory but weak prognostication. The first task of a theory of class structure that is sympathetically critical of the Marxist tradition is to reject any necessary linkage between capitalism as a system of economic production and class formation as an inevitable process of polarization, antagonism, and escalating conflict. This creates analytical space for the more important task of tracing how the transition from liberal to advanced capitalism transformed the class structure of power. This task can be approached most productively when we do not assume away the most important questions about capitalism and class, nor automatically privilege any one structure of power over any others.

The advantages of a revised Marxist theory of class are clearest when contrasted with conventional sociological approaches to stratification. The latter typically identify one or more dimensions of inequality that are conceptualized as continuous variables. Through single or combined measures, these variables include amount of income, rank of occupation, or degree of prestige. Such approaches depict stratification as a hierarchical ladder of many rungs with no discrete gaps. Despite this conception, this sociological approach often appropriates the language of class by referring to upper, middle, and lower classes, with many possible permutations on these distinctions. Although this is a fairly common practice, such designations are completely arbitrary because there is no clear conceptual guideline as to why and how such lines should be drawn at one place on the ladder of stratification rather than any other place. Alongside the arbitrariness of such class distinctions is another problem. The sociological approach to stratification focuses exclusively on the distribution of a given resource, with no consideration of how resources are themselves produced in a context of class inequality. Although such a focus may be useful for answering some kinds of questions, the sociological approach to stratification is quite limited in what it can tell us about the overall nature of social inequality (Anderson, 1974; Melucci, 1996a, Chapter 13; Wright, 1989).

The conceptual advantages of a revised Marxist approach to class emerge against the limitations of a sociological approach to stratification. First, by virtue of its focus on the relations of production, this approach is clearer about the boundaries between classes because they are defined by source rather than amount of income. In this more robust scheme of qualitatively distinct classes, capitalists derive income from ownership of private property, workers from the sale of labor power, and small business owners and professional managers from both. Although the model can be simple (Anderson, 1974) or complex (Wright, 1985), the advantage is the clarity with which class lines can be drawn. Second, this approach focuses on the production of societal resources. Hence, the most important feature of the capitalist class is that their ownership of property and control of production processes allow them to make exclusive decisions about how societal resources will be deployed. Based on calculations of profitability, decisions are made about what is to be produced, how much is to be produced, by whom it is to be produced, and where it is to be produced. Workers, by contrast, adapt to, suffer from, or occasionally benefit from such decisions, but they are rarely able to influence such decisions in a fundamental way. Thus, capitalists and workers differ not only quantitatively in terms of income distribution, but also qualitatively in terms of social power. Third, the Marxist emphasis on relations of production underscores the role of exploitation in class relations by analyzing how the wealth of one class is derived from the same processes that produce relative (and absolute) poverty for other classes. Although the labor theory of value has become highly questionable even in Marxist circles (Habermas, 1975) and some intriguing alternatives have been proposed (Wright, 1985), the broader point about theorizing class relations as inherently exploitative retains merit because of its relational focus and its ability to identify why classes reap very different life chances as a result of their positions in the class structure.

Having argued for the theoretical superiority of a revised Marxist theory of class over the sociological theory of stratification, it remains to indicate how and why the class structure of contemporary capitalist societies has become so much more complex than Marx anticipated. Although this has happened in diverse ways, the combined result has been to detach the inherent structural features of capitalism as an economic system from any deterministic or necessary developments on the level of class formation. The first factor has been the increasing heterogeneity of the "working class" defined simply on the basis of income derived from labor. To be sure, there are cross-cutting currents here that for a time were captured in the debates over the "embourgeoisiement" of some sectors of the working class (Goldthorpe, 1969) at the same time other occupations were becoming "proletarianized" (Braverman, 1974). But there can be no denying that the internal heterogeneity and differentiation within the broadly defined working class have become so extensive as to preclude any mobilization remotely resembling the Marxist imagery of proletarian revolution. This differentiation has occurred along multiple axes, including skill levels, income levels, unionization, "mental" versus "manual" labor, capital-intensive versus labor-intensive work, goods production versus service production, full-time versus part-time, permanent versus temporary, degree of autonomy in work, prestige levels, and the like. These trends pose the single greatest challenge to a revised Marxist theory of class.

From a slightly different angle, these developments may be posed as the emergence of the middle class(es) in advanced capitalism. Despite my earlier critique of the sociological theory of stratification, it is true that contemporary class structure consists of a significant number of intermediate locations. These complexities have led Marxist scholars such as Erik Olin Wright (1985) to propose a rather awkward and cumbersome model of contemporary class structure as consisting of no less than 12 classes and contradictory class locations. A further way of underscoring this complexity is by contrasting the class structure of power with those rooted in race and gender. Although both racial and gender structures of power have their own versions of internal complexity and intermediate locations, they are easier to see in terms of a fundamentally bipolar opposition between dominant and subordinate groups. In the case of class, most people in the United States do not identify with either pole but rather with some middle position. All these factors help to explain the relatively low degree of class formation and class consciousness evidenced by the contemporary U.S. working class. But it is time to move beyond the problematic of false consciousness and recognize that people's consciousness of the class structure may be a relatively accurate reflection of the complexity, contradictoriness, and ambiguity of the intermediate locations in that structure. In Habermas's (1987) formulation, the new problem is not so much false consciousness as fragmented consciousness. None of this means we have moved to a postcapitalist social formation; it simply means that in advanced capitalism, economic dynamics and class formation have become relatively detached from one another in a way that was not true in liberal capitalism.

Some of the more promising developments for responding to the problem of the middle class(es) underscore the role of cultural capital and the "new class." This general strategy builds on a sociological tradition that extends back to Mannheim's (1936) theory of intellectuals as relatively detached from the class structure and as structurally predisposed to world views that are critical of existing social realities. Aspects of this argument were revived and transformed by Konrad and Szelenyi's (1979) analysis of intellectuals on the road to class power and the role of the intelligentsia in monopoly capitalism and state socialism. The most compelling statement of these ideas remains Gouldner's (1979) analysis of the rise of the new class characterized by specialized knowledge and expert credentials. The new class is quintessentially defined by a culture of critical discourse that is a wellspring of opposition to any structure of authority that cannot legitimate itself in the terms of rational argumentation. In Gouldner's estimation, these characteristics make the new class the most progressive force in history while simultaneously carrying the seeds of new forms of domination based on hierarchies of cultural capital. The political indeterminacy of this class is worth underscoring, for it is precisely these seeds that Habermas (1987, 1984) sees taking root in his analysis of the role of experts colonizing the life world through specialized knowledge as a form of social control.

Although this sociological legacy from Mannheim to Gouldner highlights the specific role of intellectuals, broader analyses of the middle classes in general are needed. Conceptually, such efforts could build on the notion of cultural capital and educational credentials as a major axis of contemporary stratification (Collins, 1979) that sets the new class apart from both poles of the more traditional class system defined by material resources. This approach can be complemented by the notion of a class habitus (Bourdieu, 1984), referring to collective schemata of experience and perception that shape subjective ideas, personality traits, and forms of consciousness in class-distinct ways. These schemata are not so much explicit forms of class consciousness as they are implicit expressions of a collective class unconsciousness that nevertheless reproduces class distinctions. Empirically, such efforts could build on such insightful if impressionistic studies as Ehrenreich's (1989) analysis of the middle class as plagued by a "fear of falling" because of its indeterminate location in the class hierarchy. This fear can create various forms of status anxiety that can motivate participation in social activism across the political spectrum. Although these are helpful starting points, a coherent theory of the middle class(es) is likely to remain elusive because of the complexity, heterogeneity, and variability of the groups we seek to identify with the term middle class. This does not mean that the project is futile, but rather that the product will necessarily have a more tentative and open-ended quality than the old verities about the supposed inevitability of working-class conflict.

Alongside the increased heterogeneity of working- and middle-class locations, another process that has rendered the analysis of class more complex has been the increasingly global context of capitalist production. Although I have located the class structure of power on the "regional" level of sociohistorical structure, this is a somewhat artificial device that uncouples class dynamics within any one nation from the larger international arena. As world-system theory stresses, one link between capitalism and class that is still applicable is that as the process of capitalist accumulation expands across national borders, so do the class relations between the controllers of production processes and those engaged in direct production. The consequences of these developments have been quite different for each of these two major classes, however. Whereas globalization has promoted the formation of an international capitalist class capable of reaching broad agreement on the contours of the global economy (while fiercely competing within those contours), globalization has more often meant division and fragmentation between different national working classes as capital moves restlessly around the globe in search of lower labor costs. This often pressures workers to turn to nationalism as a source of identification that supersedes any meaningful class affiliation. The more basic problem, however, is that the relations between the core and the periphery may make identification as a national working class pitted against other national working classes a rational posture to take. Some political conjunctures will thus make national identity more salient than class, again precluding the process of class formation anticipated by classical Marxist theory.

A final complicating factor is that class relations reflect only one structure of power among others, and other structures are always copresent with this one. Perhaps the most fateful of these has been the racial structure of power. For the entire history of the working class in the United States, the composition of that class has rested as much on racial as class identities. Virtually every reference to the "working class" needs to be recoded as really referring to the "white working class." Race has not simply been a useful device by which capitalists have divided workers against one another (though there has been plenty of that); it has also been a fundamental underpinning of (white) working-class identity. The orthodox Marxist claim that class is more fundamental than other structures of power and their associated identities reflects a metaphysics of class that can no longer be sustained. No structure of power or identity has any priority over any other; they are all simultaneously present and mutually constitutive of one another (Collins, 1990). A similar logic applies to the question of class and gender: just as class positions have always been "raced," so too have they always been "gendered." Once again, the Marxist tradition built its case for the primacy of class by ignoring or naturalizing questions of gender and the division of society into public and private spheres. Once these are seen as social constructions that are inevitably infused with multiple structures of power and identities, it once again become impossible to see class in an isolated and privileged way.

In summary, I have tried to suggest several lines of argument concerning the class structure of power. The roots of class are to be found in the relations of production within capitalism. These relations define classes as qualitatively distinct groups, account for both the production and distribution of societal resources, and locate exploitation at the center of class relations. Beyond these claims, the Marxist analysis of class is tainted with metaphysical, eschatological, and teleological elements that must be rejected. These include assertions about the primacy of class, the directionality of history, and the certainty of change. The processes by which class structures of power generate collective action cannot be read off the structures themselves but rather must be seen as an open-ended set of possibilities within the complex social formation of advanced capitalism. This is particularly true given the heterogeneity of working- and middle-class locations, the globalization of class dynamics, and the intertwining of class with race and gender structures of power. It is to the latter that we now turn.

The Racial Structure of Power

Racial structures of power involve material discrimination and ideological oppression between dominant and subordinate racial groups that are interwoven throughout society's major institutions. It is part of the ideology of racism that racial categories refer to unambiguous, mutually exclusive, biological differences between groups of people, despite the lack of scientific evidence for such claims. This lack of support suggests that racial distinctions are socially defined and socially constructed rather than physiologically grounded (Burkey, 1978). The motive for such a socially constructed system of classifications, in turn, may be traced back to the period of European expansion that began some 500 years ago. As explorers encountered people who were both culturally and physically different from themselves, race became a dominant way of classifying people. But this was never a disinterested process; it was always part of a colonial dynamic of expansion, domination, and control as well as the need to provide justifications of that process by recourse to racist ideologies. Thus, at a certain point in history, race was invented as part of a process of treating groups unequally. The social construction of racial differences was constitutive of a structure of power between dominant and subordinate racial groups.

The fact that racial differences are socially constructed does not mean that they are arbitrary or reducible to some more basic foundation. Once these socially constructed classifications become embedded in societal institutions and cultural codes, they become a fundamental feature of societal organization and relations. But the recognition that race is socially constructed has tempted some analysts into arguing that it can be reduced to something more basic, thereby trivializing the power of such social constructions. There have been at least three reductionist approaches that warrant mention to provide the basis for a richer, nonreductionist theory of the racial structure of power (Omi and Winant, 1986). The first paradigm involves ethnicity-based theories that represent mainstream sociological thinking on the topic of race. In this paradigm, the implicit reference group is white European immigrants and the dominant presumption is that the assimilation of ethnic groups into the dominant society is both desirable and inevitable. Although this model has some applicability to white ethnic groups in the United States, it is foreign to the experience of those who have been socially defined as racially different. By reducing race to ethnicity, this paradigm obscures the differences between these groups and their markedly different treatment at the hands of the dominant society. This paradigm also implies that strategies of hard work and upward mobility that have worked for some whites are also the preferred strategy for racial minorities. Finally, this paradigm equates broad racial categories and specific ethnic categories (as if "blacks" were on the same analytical plane as "Irish"), thereby ignoring ethnic differences within racial categories. For all these reasons, the ethnicity paradigm will not suffice for theorizing racial structures of power.

Although ethnicity-based theory has defined the mainstream of social science thinking on questions of race, there have been two major challenging paradigms whose foci have been class and nation, respectively. Each contributes something to an understanding of the social construction of race, but each remains flawed in its attempt to reduce racial dynamics to some more fundamental set of processes. In the case of class-based theory, race is explained by underlying economic processes that are presumed to be more fundamental. Although there are both Marxist and non-Marxist variations, all these theories view racial dynamics through the lens of class analysis and thereby fail to address racial issues on their own terms. Such approaches can illuminate the manipulation of race through "divide-and-rule" strategies that pit races against each other and blunt class conflict and consciousness. But these approaches also imply that any form of racial identification is a type of "false consciousness" that impedes the appropriate class consciousness postulated by these theories. Despite their utility for understanding some specific circumstances, class conflict theories comprehend race only as it impinges on presumably more fundamental economic dynamics. In contrast to this view, it makes more sense to see race and class as alternative or competing forms of individual and collective identity. Indeed, these are not just competing but interacting modalities of equal significance that mutually shape one another rather than one determining the other.

Nation-based theories are much more attuned to the history of racial groups and the colonial dynamics that have operated from the beginning of such histories. The basic claim of these theories is that colonialism initiated a process of national oppression that has continued into the present in the form of racial oppression. Variations of this approach include Pan-Africanism, cultural nationalism, the "national question" in Marxism, and the theory of internal colonialism. The latter is attentive to the interaction of economic, political, and cultural factors that contribute to racial domination, and to the corresponding interests of different racial groups. But such theories have their own shortcomings. The equation of cultural movements with nationalist aspirations is neither necessary nor automatic. Such approaches often neglect or minimize class differences within racial communities, rivalries among differing minority groups, and the extent of contact and interpenetration between dominant and subordinate groups. In an ironic twist, nation-based theories can be as problematic as ethnicity-based theories by subsuming cultural differences within racial categories for the sake of a broader racial identity. At the extreme, nation-based approaches become essentialist and obscure the social construction of race every bit as much as biological theories. But despite these potential dangers, nation-based theories are not as overtly reductionist as the ethnicity and class paradigms.

Whereas these paradigms represent flawed attempts to understand the racial structure of power, the theory of racial formation (Omi and Winant, 1986) offers a more robust analysis that simultaneously sees racial categories as socially constructed (rather than biological) and as fundamental (rather than epiphenomenal). Racial formation is the "process by which social, economic and political forces determine the content and importance of racial categories, and by which they are in turn shaped by racial meanings" (Omi and Winant, 1986:61). Racialization is the "extension of racial meaning to a previously racially unclassified relationship, social practice, or group. Racialization is an ideological process, an historically specific one" (Omi and Winant, 1986:64). Through racial formation and racialization, race becomes a fundamental organizing principle of social relationships. At the microlevel, this means race permeates the formation of identity; at the macrolevel, this means race is embedded in the formation and perpetuation of social structure. As these processes unfold, they become sedimented in everyday practice and cognitions to provide a kind of common sense amateur biology for dealing with racial matters. Thus, the most impressive accomplishment of the social construction of race is its ability to hide its own sociohistorical origins behind the facade of a seemingly irreducible biological reality. Precisely because race is socially constructed rather than biologically determined, however, it is vital to see it as "an unstable and 'decentered' complex of social meanings constantly being transformed by political struggle" (Omi and Winant, 1986:68).

This struggle over the meaning of race is also embedded in the state. The term "racial state" (Omi and Winant, 1986) suggests that the state does not simply intervene in racial issues, but rather is inherently racial in its constitution. Just as feminists have argued that the social world is "gendered," a parallel argument can be made about how the state is "raced" because racialization permeates all its institutions, policies, conditions, rules, and social relations. The primary challenge to the racial state has come from racially based social movements that have engaged in a kind of interactive dance with the racial state as each side has influenced the other in pursuit of its respective strategies of control and resistance. Such movements have been responsible for the creation and cultivation of collective identity as part of a process of challenging dominant racial structures and ideologies. Thus, once race is seen as socially constructed, it can be theorized not only as a tool of social control within a racially organized structure of power, but also as a basis of resistance as members of a racially defined group contest the meanings of race built into this system. As Omi and Winant (1986) note, to challenge one's own racially defined identity and position is to implicitly challenge the concept of race itself that lies at the heart of these sociohistorical structures of power.

At first glance, the racial structure of power suggests a more bifurcated social relation than the class structure of power. Whereas the latter is characterized by increasingly important intermediate or contradictory locations between obviously dominant and subordinate groups, racial structures of power appear rooted in qualitative distinctions that sharply demarcate dominant from subordinate groups. This bipolar imagery of racial structures of power has considerable validity at the most abstract level of social order, which is indeed divided between those socially designated as "white" and those socially designated as "nonwhite"—a designation that itself reflects power relations by taking whiteness as the standard of racial classification. At this level of abstraction, there are no intermediate or contradictory locations defined in terms of race that are equivalent to the "middle class" in class structures of power (though there often are such groups in other racially heterogeneous societies). The other dramatic feature of racial structures of power is that the dominant group has historically been a numerical majority of the population. Although this is projected to change in the United States in the next century, this historical reality has lent a particularly oppressive cast to racial structures of power in which nonwhite groups have been minority groups in the double sense of both secondary status and demographic realities.

Although these abstract features of racial structures of power are worth noting, they tell us relatively little about the ongoing operation of such structures. In their own way, racial structures of power are every bit as complicated and contradictory as class structures of power, with important consequences for social movement mobilization. Several such complications may be simply noted here. First, within the dominant group of whites defined in racial terms, there are multiple ethnic groups with their own historical and contemporary patterns of inequality. The generic term "white" obscures the very different fortunes of Polish, English, Irish, Italian, Swedish, or Hungarian peoples within the United States. Second, within the subordinate group of "nonwhites" defined in racial terms, there are in fact multiple racial groups that are typically designated as African-American, Latino/a-American, Native American, and Asian-American. The existence of multiple, racially defined subordinate groups creates the potential for extremely complex combinations of structural organization and subjective identity. Third, within each of these racially defined subordinate groups, there are also multiple ethnic groups. In many circumstances, a group's ethnic origins and identity as Puerto Rican, Jamaican, Vietnamese, or Lakota are much more central to social structure and social identity than the broader racial categories within which these ethnicities are located. Finally, each of these groups has its own distinctive history of interethnic and interracial relations with other subordinate groups as well as various dominant groups. These complexities underscore the importance of seeing race as a socially constructed process of racialization and racial formation that is fluid and dynamic in organizing social relations among these groups of people.

Although each structure of power has its own internal complexities, there are additional relational complexities between structures of power. One example is the combined class/race location of middle-class whites. In purely class terms, this may be a contradictory class location because of the conflicting interests built into the class structure for these individuals. This is also a contradictory class/race location in keeping with the following logic. Racial structures of power create deeply embedded interests tied to locations in these structures. Privileged whites in positions of power and authority benefit from the operation of racial structures of power because, among many other things, historical patterns of economic discrimination against racial minorities have provided a large pool of cheap labor. As a result, we can postulate a strong group interest among elite whites in perpetuating racial structures of power. Members of racial minorities suffer from these practices, and we can postulate an equally strong group interest in the transformation and elimination of racial structures of power on their part. The group for whom it is most difficult to postulate a strong set of interests either way consists of "ordinary whites" located between these two poles. In many immediate situations of group conflict and interaction, their racial privileges may create short-term interests in maintaining the racial structure of power because of the benefits that accrue to ordinary whites when members of racial minorities are subject to discrimination, segregation, or exclusion in the distribution of social resources. In the longer term, however, it may well be that ordinary whites lose more than they gain by the persistence of racial structures of power that lend themselves so readily to the tactics of divide-and-conquer on the part of dominant racial/class groups (Reich, 1981). Thus, short-term gains can lead to long-term losses if the former effectively preclude coalitions, alliances, or unions among subordinate groups that might prevent the latter. At the least, these possibilities serve as a reminder that race is a fluid, socially constructed process for the dominant group as well, whose members may have class-specific interests in the racialization or deracialization of social processes.

Racial structures of power thereby share some broad similarities with other structures of power while also possessing their own distinctive characteristics. In historical terms, such structures have existed longer than contemporary class structures given their origins in the period of European global expansion. Throughout this history, racial structures of power have been established and maintained through mechanisms that have been intertwined with economically driven processes of accumulation, commodification, and exploitation as well as politically driven processes of state-making, legitimation, and bureaucratization. Like class structures of power, racial structures have an increasingly global character to them. Hence, my designation of them as regional structures of power is no more than a convenient means of calling attention to racial structures (and corresponding social movements) within a single national context. Unlike class structures of power and more like gender structures of power, racial structures appear to involve ascribed, biological traits of people that sustain everyday belief systems about race, but these appearances do not stand up to scientific scrutiny. Thus, my conceptualization of racial structures of power has relied on Omi and Winant's (1986) theory of racial formation because it simultaneously recognizes the socially constructed nature of racial structures of power while also avoiding the reductionism of race to some other presumably more fundamental social category. As I argued earlier in the case of class structures of power, an understanding of the dynamics of racial structures of power is necessary but not sufficient for understanding the mobilization of racially based movements. It is necessary because such structures comprise the social organization, material interests, and ideological symbols around which racial formation occurs. It is not sufficient because of myriad intervening factors that preclude any simplistic reading of action off of structure.

The Gender Structure of Power

Gender structures of power involve systemic forms of inequality and discrimination between men and women, along with ideological belief systems that seek to justify such differential treatment. As with race, gender is best seen as a socially constructed set of relations, and the concept of a sex/gender system (Rubin, 1975) provides a convenient means of characterizing this social construction. In this conception, the term "sex" refers to biological differences whereas the term "gender" refers to the socially constructed, culturally learned, and normatively reinforced characteristics associated with the scripts of "masculinity" and "femininity." The "sex/gender system" thereby refers to all the societal mechanisms that produce social differences between genders and use those differences as a basis for unequal or discriminatory treatment. On the microlevel, the concept of the sex/gender system is a theory of socialization attentive to the intertwined social construction of both difference and inequality. On the macrolevel, the concept underscores how gender operates as a fundamental principle of societal organization that is so deeply embedded in the daily operation of social institutions that it often goes unnoticed. On this level, gender structures of power involve a society-wide division of labor mapped onto the distinction between public and private spheres. As a result, all social institutions and practices have a gendered character, i.e., gender is omnipresent as an organizing principle of these institutions and practices. As with race, perhaps the best indicator of the power of these processes of social construction is the extent to which societal members come to see such social organization as natural.

The most salient aspects of gender structures of power have been identified by the second wave of the feminist movement, whose main ideological currents provide several angles of vision for theorizing gender structures of power. As the name implies, liberal feminism drew on the precepts of liberal political philosophy and applied them to the situation of women. Liberal feminism thereby envisioned a gender structure of power in which women were denied access, opportunity, and mobility because of discrimination and differential treatment that created advantages for men and disadvantages for women. Because these forms of discrimination were embedded in many different societal institutions, they had a cumulative and reinforcing character that produced systematic inequalities in the life chances of women and men. Nevertheless, liberal feminism envisioned a structure of power that was amenable to gradual reform through the progressive removal of gender barriers. As these barriers were removed, women would move toward parity with men, culminating in an equal participatory role for women in all social institutions. Although illuminating some aspects of the gender structure of power, liberal feminism was criticized for naturalizing the division of society into public and private spheres and devoting most of its attention to inequality and discrimination in public sphere institutions. By ignoring the private sphere, envisioning paid labor as the path to emancipation, and embracing individualist solutions, liberal feminism implicitly envisioned a gender structure of power more amenable to progressive reform than has proven to be the case (Friedan, 1963; Jaggar, 1983).

If liberal feminism envisioned a gender structure of power open to gradual reform, the opposite may be said for radical feminism, which sought to do for gender what classical Marxism had done for class. That is, radical feminism envisioned all women as constituting a sex class subject to various forms of exploitation, oppression, and domination at the hands of men who constituted the dominant sex class. These relations were embedded in patriarchal forms of social organization that systematically privileged men over women. In this theory, gender was the single, overriding principle of social organization and form of oppression. Radical feminists argued that patriarchy predated other forms of social inequality, provided the model for later forms, and could never be reduced to any other form (Lerner, 1986). For many radical feminists, patriarchy included ideological and psychological oppression that created "false consciousness" that in turn necessitated "consciousness raising" as a necessary component of political struggle against patriarchal domination. Although broadening and deepening the analysis of gender structures of power, radical feminism also had its characteristic weaknesses. Its vision of patriarchal domination was too monolithic and universal to recognize the variable and historically specific aspects of gender structures of power. And its vision of women as a potentially universal and revolutionary class was also too monolithic by failing to recognize diversity and difference among women that prevented any single feminist analysis or strategy from having universal applicability. Despite these limitations, radical feminism advanced the understanding of gender structures of power by analyzing their operation in both the public and the private spheres, by recognizing the systemic nature of gender oppression, and by underscoring the inherently collective nature of both gender oppression and effective responses to it (Echols, 1989; Jaggar, 1983).

Socialist feminism sought a theory that was less individualistic than liberal feminism but less monolithic than radical feminism. It proposed that the position of women in society is the interactive product of two systems of inequality. In "dual system theories" of capitalist patriarchy, class inequalities derived from capitalism were intertwined with gender inequalities derived from patriarchy, and these systems were presumed to reinforce one another. This theory was attentive to gender dynamics in both public and private spheres and to the ways in which capitalists as a class and men as a gender benefited from the operation of capitalist patriarchy. Thus, in the private sphere of family and household, the sexual division of labor and the nuclear family assign women a disproportionate (if not exclusive) responsibility for domestic labor. This directly benefits men, but it also indirectly benefits capitalism because domestic labor is unpaid and thereby constitutes a major subsidy to the profitability of the overall economic system. In the public sphere of economy and society, the sexual division of labor creates sex segregation and discrimination in employment for women. This directly benefits men who face a somewhat less competitive job market as women are excluded through various mechanisms of discrimination. It indirectly benefits capitalist employers who may use such discriminatory mechanisms to play various groups of workers off one another and minimize labor costs. The most pernicious aspect of these dual systems is that the systems reinforce one another, e.g., women's lower earning capacity in the economy dovetails with their greater responsibility for domestic labor, creating a vicious circle that is difficult to escape. This analysis was more systemic and structural than that of liberal feminism, while also being more sensitive to class differences among women. Despite these improvements, however, this theory remained two dimensional at a time when many were beginning to call for a three-dimensional theory attentive to the dynamics of race along with those of class and gender (Sargent, 1981; Jaggar, 1983).

As the second wave of feminism gathered momentum in the 1970s and then faced a reactionary backlash in the 1980s, these ideological strains were complemented by a variety of newer approaches including cultural feminism, lesbian feminism, international feminism, ecofeminism, and feminist spirituality. For the purpose of understanding gender structures of power, however, the most useful additional perspective to emerge has involved the feminism developed by women of color. Just as socialist feminism responded to the monolithic tendency of radical feminism to focus exclusively on gender, the feminism developed by women of color responded to the dualistic tendency of socialist feminism to focus only on sex and class. Women-of-color feminism rejected the debate about the priority of various locations (race versus class versus gender) by insisting that all such locations are intersecting social realities that are experienced simultaneously rather than in some mechanical, additive fashion. Taken as a statement on the gender structure of power, this theoretical perspective underscores the artificiality of designating and analyzing any single structure of power as if it existed or operated in isolation from any other structure of power. This theoretical stance points rather in the direction of a matrix of interlocking forms of domination that contains "few pure victims or oppressors" (Collins, 1990:229) but rather a complex range of intermediate positions combining various degrees of penalty and privilege.

Although such a view is a useful corrective, it does not obviate the need for a theory that identifies the specificity of the gender structure of power. For this purpose, an analytical focus on gender remains helpful. What this focus reveals is that women and men are proportionally distributed into most collectivities defined by race, class, ethnicity, religion, locality, and the like. Put differently, women are dispersed across social groups rather than concentrated together, so that there is little closure (external segmentation and internal integration) for women as a gender group (Kriesi et al., 1995:5). The result is that unlike members of other subordinate groups, women typically live in close proximity and intimate relation with their "oppressors." The typical effect of gender socialization, compulsory heterosexuality, romantic love, maternal mandates, and the nuclear family is to link the fates of individual women with those of individual men rather than with other women. These mechanisms include expectations of harmony and complementarity that can mask the ways in which gender inequality operates. This socially mandated intimacy between men and women means that gender forms of control and domination must be more subtly and finely articulated than in power relations between structurally polarized groups. This is why feminists have paid so much attention to psychological forms of internalized oppression and to solutions that address identity and self-esteem. Although all structures of power include psychological or individual dimensions, they are much more central in the case of gender structures of power because they involve a distinctive combination of interpersonal closeness and domination.

The socially mandated closeness between women and men has important implications for how we might impute interests to these groups. A purely macrostructural theory of gender relations suggests that men as a group have a clear interest in maintaining and expanding their privileges and power over women as a group. However, this structural interest can be cross-cut on the microlevel by situational realities that flow from men's familial roles and interpersonal relationships. Although men as a group may benefit from occupational discrimination against women, they do not benefit if this limits the earning potential of their spouses. Although men as a group may benefit because medical research is male oriented, they do not benefit when this precludes an effective response to their mothers' illnesses. Although men as a group may realize some psychic gratification from cultural images that objectify women, they do not gain if other men act on these images against their daughters. What all these hypothetical examples suggest is a tension within the dominant gender between group interests that benefit men as a group and interpersonal relations that link men to women. There is a female counterpart of this tension as well. In this case, a purely macrostructural theory of gender suggests that women as a group have clear interests in transforming all social institutions and practices that perpetuate their inequality. In the classically radical feminist analysis, this maxim would apply with particular force to the nuclear family as the crucible of patriarchal domination. However, a more situational analysis might find that for many women, that very same family is a major source of identity, social worth, and self-esteem, such that these familial links override any abstract notion of gender inequality or oppression.

In our analysis of class and racial structures of power, it was possible to identify "contradictory" structural locations and corresponding interests because of the internal complexity of these structures of power. In the case of gender structures of power, there are several possibilities for analyzing contradictory locations, but they emerge in a somewhat different way. One example is provided by the situations just discussed, in which members of the same gender have highly variable situational locations and perceived interests based on the nature and extent of their familial, affectional, and sexual ties to a member of the other group. The greater the nature and extent of these ties, the more contradictory one's interests as defined by the cross-cutting forces of gender and kinship. All these examples presume heterosexuality, so another important example of a contradictory location in gender structures of power may be found in the case of gays and lesbians. The contradictoriness of these locations and identities flows from the fact that they are unrecognized in the fundamentally bipolar and heterosexual organization of the gender structure of power. For this reason, it is difficult to map these groups onto this structure in a clear and unambiguous fashion. For instance, although it might be tempting to argue that lesbians are doubly oppressed by virtue of gender and sexual orientation, it is this very combination that can distance and free some lesbians from many forms of patriarchal control that heterosexual women cannot escape as easily. In a similar vein, although there are ways in which gay men remain privileged as men even while they are oppressed as gays, they may also be subject to more ferocious repression because they transgress the sexuality of the dominant group of (heterosexual) men, which is ultimately taken more seriously than the sexuality of the subordinate group of (heterosexual) women.

These brief examples are perhaps sufficient to suggest the ways in which gender structures of power generate contradictory locations and interests as well as bipolar oppositions based on gender. All of the examples discussed in this section are perhaps sufficient to suggest that all three structures of power evidence broadly similar patterns of contradictory locations and interests mapped onto an ideal–typical bipolar opposition between a dominant and a subordinate group. The specific dynamics that generate such locations and interests are different in the case of each structure of power because the specific mechanisms of exploitation, oppression, or inequality are different. But the broader lesson is that these structures of power exhibit a high degree of internal complexity. If this is the lesson to be drawn from analyzing each structure of power in analytical isolation, it takes on even more salience when we recall the fundamental insight of women-of-color feminism that these locations and interests are always copresent, intertwined, simultaneous dimensions of a broader societal matrix of domination. What I have sought to do in this discussion of regional structures of power is to underscore the importance of these structures as the context from which collective action emerges without implying any simplistic, mechanical explanations based on structure alone. Understanding structures of power is vitally necessary, but hardly sufficient, for explaining the mobilization of movements based on class, race, and gender.

These regional structures of power are not only interlaced with one another, they are also embedded in national and global levels of sociohistorical structure. It is capitalism as a global and national socioeconomic system that provides the dynamic element in the ongoing operation of these structures of power. This is not an ontological claim about whether certain kinds of power are more fundamental than others. It is rather a sociohistorical claim that capitalist accumulation has been the driving force in this particular social formation. The transformations that have occurred in these regional structures of power have been due less to internal change mechanisms than to the dynamics of a developing capitalist social formation that has shaped and reshaped the specific forms and functions of regional structures of power based on class, race, and gender (Becker, 1989). Although structures of power have long histories of provoking social movements, a profound understanding of earlier movements requires an historically specific analysis of how these structures were articulated with previous stages of capitalist development. By the same token, a solid grasp of contemporary social activism in these areas requires an equally historically specific appreciation of how these structures of power have evolved and developed in the context of advanced capitalism. It is to a consideration of this activism that we now turn.

REGIONAL STRUCTURES AND SOCIAL MOVEMENTS

Regional structures of power exhibit a fundamental bipolarity between dominant and subordinate groups as well as internal complexity and contradictory locations. Whereas the former implies conflicting long-term interests, the latter suggests that historically specific situational factors always shape the perceptions of social actors and their inclination to act collectively. Two obvious processes that intervene between structures of power and forms of activism are collective identity and group consciousness. Without these, it is unlikely that even severe oppression will activate resistance.

Groups may differ, however, in the degree to which their collective identity is already structurally grounded in societal processes and the extent to which it must be explicitly created in the process of movement mobilization (see Chapter 8). My earlier work on women's movements (Buechler, 1990) compared the degree to which collective identity was structurally grounded across subordinate groups based on race, class, and gender. My argument was that African-Americans (and other racial groups) in the United States have had the most consistent identification as members of a subordinate group based on a long and continuous history of slavery, segregation, discrimination, and racism. By contrast, I suggested that women have had the least consistent collective identification as a subordinate group based on their distribution throughout (virtually) all social groups, their proximity to men, and their structural separation from other women. Workers have occupied a middle ground, with a collective identity stronger than that of women but weaker than that of African-Americans, based on the shifting fortunes of working-class resistance and the heterogeneous composition of the U.S. working class. These differences have important implications for the relative ease with which social activism can be mobilized based on these collective identities. Even so, two caveats are in order. First, the fact that some collective identities may be more deeply rooted in societal structures of power than others does not necessarily mean that mobilization is easier for those groups—indeed it may be harder if the collective identity is suffused with fatalistic notions that preclude politicization of that identity. Second, mobilization is obviously affected by other factors such as resource availability and opportunity structures that can weigh more heavily than collective identity. Nevertheless, the extent to which such identities are inscribed in social structure is likely to influence the texture and the strength of the solidarity that develops in the course of social activism.

Another process mediating structural location and social activism is group consciousness. E. P. Thompson's (1963) classic analysis of the British working class emphasized the cultural dimension of class consciousness as giving meaning to a given class location in relation to other classes. Working-class consciousness developed over time through an ongoing struggle that clarified the interests uniting workers and separating them as a class from others. The working class thereby "made itself" in an active process of developing class consciousness and class formation. This approach can be extended to other groups as well through the concept of a "political consciousness" (Morris, 1992) that does not privilege class or class consciousness but rather considers how various systems of domination generate corresponding forms of oppositional consciousness as subordinate groups "make themselves" into politically conscious forces. Morris argues that race and gender structures are every bit as real and objective as class structures, and that these interlocking systems of domination promote various forms of oppositional political consciousness. Just as structures of domination can reinforce one another, forms of oppositional consciousness can also reinforce one another. This framework thereby accommodates empirical research suggesting that African-Americans display high levels of both class consciousness and race consciousness, and that African-American women "have developed a three-pronged oppositional consciousness to address their reality of simultaneous class, race, and gender oppression" (Morris, 1992:366). Conversely, this framework also helps to understand how one form of hegemonic consciousness—white supremacist race consciousness—has effectively prevented potential alliances between blacks and whites in both the labor movement and the women's movement. Collective identity and political consciousness are thus decisive factors mediating structures of power and collective action. We turn now to more specific examinations of particular structures of power and corresponding forms of social activism.

Class Movements: Au Revoir?

Of the three structures of power, class structures have traditionally received the greatest amount of analytical attention as a basis for social movements. There is now a general perception, however, that class structures of power have lost much of their potential for generating social protest, and that this potential has shifted to other structures of power and to more culturally oriented movements. As noted in Chapter 4, the best of these analyses anchor this shift in historical changes from a Fordist to a post-Fordist accumulation strategy in capitalist society. Fordism was especially likely to promote working-class mobilization because it socially concentrated workers in mass production industries, provided a level of wages that included the discretionary resources needed for effective mobilization, and enlarged the role of the state as a legitimator of working-class organization through unions and as a mediator of the conflicts between capital and labor. Thus, under Fordism, it is not surprising that the social movement sphere was monopolized by the labor movement (Steinmetz, 1994). Indeed, it was the labor movement's success in mobilizing and organizing for a higher standard of living that created one of the pressures toward a post-Fordist accumulation strategy.

With the emergence of this alternative, however, much of the infrastructure of working-class mobilization was undermined, as reflected in rapid deindustrialization, plant relocations, capital flight, service work, and declining unionization. Although these trends created new grievances, they seriously undermined the organizational infrastructure and resource base of working-class political activism. These trends have had a particularly devastating effect on working-class politics in the United States when compared to other advanced capitalist societies that have experienced similar transformations. This is the latest manifestation of the historical reality that the United States has never had the deeply rooted sense of itself as a class society found in most European societies. The American traditions of equality, individualism, mobility, and freedom have always posed a substantial ideological counterweight to the realities of class domination and exploitation. As a result, the subjective identity of class always had a tenuous grip in the context of mass consumption, mass media, mass education, status concerns, and the perception that this is a "classless" or a "middle class" society (Aronowitz, 1992). When the features of Fordism that had previously facilitated working-class mobilization were dismantled, the U.S. working class thus had little to fall back on to sustain its protest potential. Instead of the working class becoming the gravediggers for capitalism, theorists of post-Fordism have become the (reluctant) gravediggers for traditional working-class politics and social activism. In contrast to most European societies, the low salience of old class cleavages in the United States has been seen as creating the political space for other group identities as the bases for protest politics (Kriesi et al., 1995:241).

It is here that the dubious dichotomies of new social movement theory are often invoked to proclaim a shift in social activism from old to new, materialist to postmaterialist, class to caste, political to cultural, interest to identity, and the like. Before considering this argument directly, it is worth noting that although post-Fordism may have undermined the basis of traditional working-class struggles, it has not displaced capitalism as the source of many grievances and the provocation for many movements. Indeed, it is striking how consistently this point is made by diverse theorists and researchers. For example, in a theoretical piece on Antonio Gramsci and new social movements, it is claimed that "despite the emergence of new sites of struggle that cannot be comprehended in terms of class dynamics, capitalism remains the dominant structure in the contemporary world" (Carroll and Ratner, 1994:16–17). In an analysis of regulation theory and post-Marxism, it is argued that "capital accumulation remains the mainspring of advanced societies, even if the sociologically defined working class is declining in size . . . and . . . this process will continue to define the main positions in social conflict" (Steinmetz, 1994:185).

Such claims are not just found in abstract theoretical arguments. Stoecker's (1994) empirical study of community movements also keeps capitalism at the center of the analysis even while acknowledging the shifting base of social protest.

> Increasingly into the late twentieth century, social movements and citizen protests have been neither derived from clear class antagonisms nor directly focused on class issues. . . . The class dynamics of capitalism continue to generate the issues around which citizens mobilize, but the issues are generated

at the output end of capitalism rather than at the input end. Instead of organizing as workers over issues related to the control of production, people are
organizing as citizens and consumers around issues related to their social roles
in reproducing themselves outside work. (Stoecker, 1994:5)

These formulations recall Habermas's notion of new social movements as resisting life world colonization through nonworker roles, but the resistance is
nevertheless against a system whose central dynamic remains the accumulation
of capital. The centrality of capitalism in provoking both old worker mobilizations and many newer social movements provides one important means of narrowing the artificially wide dichotomy between supposedly old and new movements.

Although there may be some theoretical logic to the claim that the working class has been superseded as a site of social activism, it would be a mistake
to dismiss the potential for such mobilization prematurely. Despite the major
changes that have occurred in capitalist production, it remains a profit-driven,
exploitation-based system that continues to provide numerous incentives (if not
always opportunities) for collective protest. Aside from these empirical possibilities, the rejection of the potential for working-class resistance among new
social movement theorists may reflect a theoretical flaw in their reasoning. As
we have seen, Habermasian social theory tends to dichotomize work and interaction, or system and life world, with unfortunate consequences. The earlier Habermas (1969) reduces work to merely instrumental action; as such, the
activity of work and the organization of workers are not seen as having the potential for transcending the domination of instrumental rationality. The later
Habermas (1987, 1984) locates production in the economic subsystem dominated by the generalized media of money, once again precluding the possibility of emancipatory movements arising in this sphere. What these dichotomized
formulations ignore are the interactional foundations of production and the
normative bases of the system. These create the potential not just for resistance
in the sphere of work and production but for a type of resistance that builds
on the learning processes, communicative rationality, and democratization potential that Habermas artificially restricts to the sphere of interaction and the
life world.

These unfortunate dichotomies reverberate in the overdrawn distinction
between old and new social movements and the implication that new movements are exclusively postmaterialist and that old movements were purely materialist. In point of fact, both "old" and "new" movements typically contain
blends of "material" and "cultural" concerns, but these blends may be over-
shadowed by theoretical formulations suggesting the contrary. Recent work on
a variety of social movements in early nineteenth-century Europe suggests that
such movements had many of the features of supposedly new social movements,
implying that they may be generic to the modern social movements of the last
two centuries rather than specific to "new" movements of the late twentieth
century (Calhoun, 1993). Building on this same logic, a recent study of French
syndicalism suggests that this "old" labor movement had many of the features
of "new" social movements, including reliance on a rationalizing tradition of

republican virtue that led the movement to seek a radical extension of democracy in society (Tucker, 1991). If this is the case, contemporary struggles over worker control could also provide a key to democratization if and when they raise fundamental questions of autonomy, identity, and creativity that are central to realizing noninstrumental rationality and nonalienated labor (Tucker, 1991). The sharp distinction between old and new movements and the corresponding dismissal of the potential for working-class protest are both theoretically suspect and empirically dubious.

The ease with which some contemporary theorists dismiss the potential for working-class resistance (and embrace new social movements) is the flip side of a lingering Marxist infatuation with the proletariat as the agent of revolution (and the quest for a new agent). There is no more theoretical reason to dismiss the potential for working-class activism now than there was earlier to privilege this class on the basis of a dubious philosophy of history. What has passed is not so much the potential for effective working class resistance but the viability of a unidimensional concept of an industrial proletariat as a universal class and revolutionary subject of history. This passing has made it easier to grasp the complexity of class relations and their interpenetration with other group relations that are intertwined with the dynamics of class. Thus, there is an increasing recognition that class acquires its subjective weight as a meaningful identity from cultural elements, and those cultural elements are often provided by ethnic, racial, gender, and other identities. Hence, class never appears in a pure form but is rather alloyed with other identities, discourses, and movements (Aronowitz, 1992). This recognition would certainly please those feminists who have been arguing for some time that social actors are constituted by multiple, overlapping, simultaneous identities that shape one another through mutual determination (Collins, 1990).

This recognition makes it easier, in turn, to begin to see the concerns of "old" and "new" social movements as additive or complementary rather than contradictory and mutually exclusive. Rather than seeing a conflict between old worker movements and new social movements, it is possible to see the latter as simply expressing other needs of workers above and beyond their role as laborers (Carroll and Ratner, 1994). Although worker-based activism may have declined in recent years in response to the same post-Fordist transformations that have devastated many communities, there have been many neopopulist, Alinsky-style community organizations and movements that have emerged in the United States in the last decade. With the decline of worker mobilization, these community movements based on race, gender, community, or citizen identities have become the main arenas for insurgency and the defense of social life. However, rather than dichotomizing material and cultural concerns, these contemporary community movements represent the addition of cultural and identity issues to ongoing equity and distributive issues traditionally associated with working-class politics (Fisher and Kling, 1991). Other studies of community organizing also reveal not so much an opposition between class and community identities but rather a seamless blending of both into an oppositional movement that addresses a broad range of movement issues

(Stoecker, 1994). We need theoretical starting points that neither privilege nor dismiss a given form of activism if we are to understand what may be truly new in these movement dynamics.

One example of what may be truly new about contemporary movement activism derives from the shifting demographic realities of the working class. As a theoretical concept, the "working class" has always been implicitly white and male, but this concept is increasingly out of touch with the heterogeneous composition of the contemporary work force. Yet another interpretation of the "death of working-class protest" theme is that it presumes an increasingly out-moded and homogeneous base for protest that is being displaced by a much more diverse group of workers. Although this poses all the familiar difficulties of organizing across various potential divides, it also suggests new possibilities for mobilization. Surveying the current labor organizing scene, Peter Rachleff (1994) strikes a rare note of optimism that we are witnessing not the revival of traditional labor movements but rather a new form of labor movement al-together—one that resembles social movements more than conventional trade unionism. Activist campaigns among immigrant workers, minority groups, and women workers implicitly challenge the dichotomous distinctions between (white male) class movements and (noneconomic) identity movements by be-ing both. These innovative forms of organization prefigure new union struc-tures that link workplaces and communities, build on rank-and-file participa-tion, utilize new technologies and forms of communication, seek alliances with other movements, and acquire an international dimension (Rachleff, 1994). Al-though it remains to be seen whether this new labor organizing will realize all these potentials, it is vital that social movement theorists refocus their theo-retical lenses so as to bring these possibilities into view.

To this point, the discussion of class structures of power has focused on the potentials and pitfalls of working-class protest. I have suggested three main lines of argument. First, although empirically sound, many arguments about the demise of working-class protest in advanced capitalism draw on faulty the-oretical premises about both the past and present nature of the working class. Second, the more untenable arguments about the eclipse of working-class protest often rest on a problematic dichotomy between old and new social movements that is both theoretically and empirically questionable. Third, there is ongoing potential for working-class protest in advanced capitalist societies, though it will emerge from a more heterogeneous working class, and only when fractions of that class can overcome the considerable mobilization obstacles of a post-Fordist environment.

The working class does not exhaust the range of potential class-based so-cial movements. Indeed, one of the central claims of new social movement the-ory is that these movements are much more likely to reflect middle-class aspi-rations than working-class interests. There is, however, considerable debate and confusion over the referent of the term "middle-class" and its implications for understanding social activism. The standard argument about the "new class" as a basis for social protest is that it consists of a growing set of knowledge workers in advanced capitalism who have begun to challenge an older class of entrepreneurs and managers for control and direction of both private and public bureaucracies. The logic is that this class enjoys a degree of self-direction and relative autonomy in its professional work role that is the basis for oppositional political attitudes and action. Although there is some empirical support for these hypothesized links between class position and political activism (Wallace and Jenkins, 1995), the precise class interests that motivate these actors to engage in such activism remain hazy. The fact that there may be a disproportionate share of new class members in progressive social movements does not warrant the conclusion that this reflects (new) class interests. It may simply be that the growth of the new class has increased the number of intellectuals available for all types of involvements, including social movements that are reactionary as well as progressive (Bagguley, 1992). The larger conceptual problem is that it is often difficult to disentangle class effects from other variables (education, occupation, status, generation, etc.) that may have greater explanatory power (Pakulski, 1995; Rootes, 1995).

A major problem thus involves how to specify the interests that motivate members of the middle class, or the new middle class in particular, to participate in social activism. The difficulty arises from the ambiguous and contradictory nature of the middle class(es) as an intermediate location between more well-defined poles of capital and labor. As a result of this location, the new middle class may be characterized as class aware but not class conscious (Giddens, 1975). On the one hand, class location does influence who is likely to participate in certain kinds of movements, leading new middle-class members to be disproportionately represented in new social movements of various types. On the other hand, the goals of these movements do not typically reflect any specific or definable set of class interests, but are rather class unspecific, or universalistic or highly particularistic. The result is "a politics *of* a class but not *on behalf of* a class" (Offe, 1985:833, italics in original). Put differently, a middle-class location shapes a class culture and consciousness but does not determine any particular political content (Rose, 1997). Hence, there are important connections between the middle class and social activism, but they are not nearly as straightforward as the nexus of structure–interest–action in the case of the traditional working class or capitalist class. In contrast to the working-class problematic of false consciousness, the class unconsciousness of the middle class may not be a temporary condition that will fade as class actors gain greater clarity about their social position, but rather a permanent reflection of the ambiguous and intermediate location of the middle class in advanced capitalism.

Following this logic, it may be precisely the intermediate, nonclass character of the middle class that has the greatest explanatory relevance for their role in social movements. This nonclass character is not just a theoretical problem for social analysts; it is even more fundamentally an identity problem for those located within the middle class. Given this premise, the appearance of new social movements with a middle-class mobilization bias may be understood as an "identitarian" struggle on behalf of an ill-defined group to clarify its boundaries and anchor its class identity through social activism (Eder, 1993:158–184). Thus, the cultural, subjective, postmaterial quality of new social movements reflects both the relative privilege and opportunity structure of middle-class actors as well as their attempt to cultivate a class culture that will provide a coherent sense of identity to this group as a whole. This suggests that we envision the middle classes as potential classes undergoing a process of formation through cultural struggles; put differently, this is a middle-class version of the Marxist formulation of class development from a class-in-itself to a class-for-itself. In this reformulation, then, class is less a structural determinant of collective action and more a dialectical outcome of the mobilization of various groups of social actors. In Eder's (1993:184) words, "the new social movements are certainly not a class movement in the traditional nineteenth century sense. They can, however, be seen as a manifestation of a new type of class relationship within which the 'making of the middle class' in advanced modern societies takes place." In this way, the role of social class is still critical in analyzing social activism, albeit in a way rather different from traditional theories of class protest.

The notion that new social movements may be constitutive of the new class (rather than the other way around) is an important thread linking Eder's theoretical speculations with recent empirical analysis of these questions in the Netherlands (Kriesi, 1989). This analysis begins with a careful specification of fractions of the new middle class that distinguishes social and cultural specialists from administrative, commercial, technical, craft, and protective workers. What separates social and cultural specialists from the other fractions of the new class is their relative lack of organizational resources and their ideological reluctance to subordinate their knowledge to purely instrumental uses. These features of social and cultural specialists are hypothesized to predispose them to participate in new social movements, which become an arena of confrontation between the two camps in the new middle class and thus contribute to the formation of that class as a whole. Empirical findings substantiate this hypothesis and help refine the typical claim about links between the new middle class and new social movements. Such claims are both too narrow and too broad. They are too narrow because new social movements attract support from groups other than this segment of the new middle class; they are too broad because it is not the class as a whole that participates in new social movements but rather a distinctive fraction of that class. This research both confirms and specifies new class theory by identifying social and cultural specialists who utilize new social movements to oppose technocratic controls and limitations on their autonomy. If these forms of activism do have these particular class roots, new social movements cannot be dismissed as temporary responses to historical conjunctures, but must rather be seen as deeply rooted manifestations of the structural contradictions of advanced capitalist societies (Kriesi, 1989).

Although the specificity of middle-class activism remains somewhat vague even in this empirical study, it becomes clearer when middle-class activism is contrasted with working-class protest. What quickly becomes evident is that the class divide between middle-class activists and working-class people is a major gulf between political actors who may share certain goals but who find themselves in separate social worlds. The ironic result is that most progressive, left-oriented movements have come to be dominated by white, middle-class activists while the historical constituency of the left—the working class—remains on the sidelines, as alienated from contemporary political struggles as it has traditionally been alienated from exploitative forms of labor (Croteau, 1995). At least three dimensions of class relations contribute to this gulf. As a structure, class separates professional middle-class members specializing in knowledge from workers specializing in manual labor. As lived experience, class separates professional middle-class members who enjoy significant resources, control, and autonomy from workers who receive qualitatively fewer of all these benefits. As a cultural reality, class provides very different cultural tools to each major social class, with the tools of middle-class culture predisposing its members to active political participation while working-class tools predispose people to political withdrawal (Croteau, 1995). From the perspective of progressive politics, this class divide is doubly unfortunate. On the one hand, it means that cultural differences between classes (and their differences on cultural issues in the political arena) often prevent alliances between groups whose redistributive economic agendas and participatory political goals are often quite similar. On the other hand, it leaves the working class vulnerable to the appeals of right-wing movements that benefit from "false consciousness" and the politics of division at the expense of working-class interests (Croteau, 1995).

When class analysis was used to analyze traditional working-class political activism, it was assumed that the long-term interests of workers could be "read off" of their structural class location, and issues were framed in terms of whether workers would "see" their real interests and acquire the capacity to act on them. Middle-class locations in the class structure do not lend themselves to such an easy reading of middle-class interests, so it is often assumed (or explicitly argued) that middle-class movements are classless, or universal, or based on some other identity. It is time to recognize that a middle-class location shapes people's participation in social movements every bit as much as other class locations do. The consequences of this shaping include not just a class divide that keeps working people out of social movements led by middle-class activists (Croteau, 1995), but class-distinct organizing styles across a range of social movements (Lichterman, 1995) and even efforts by middle-class activists to deny their own class roots through elaborate justifications for the middle-class homogeneity of their movements (Croteau, 1994). There can be little doubt that these dynamics represent the politics *of* a class, even if we cannot always fit them into the model of a politics *for* a class.

In sum, the role of class remains critical in the analysis of social activism, but the ways in which it is critical have changed significantly in the twentieth century. With regard to working-class protest, these changes require a definitive break with all metaphysical notions about a proletariat as a revolutionary agent of social change. However, rejecting the inevitability of working-class protest is not only distinct from, but probably a prerequisite for, exploring the new potentials for working-class resistance that are arising alongside new forms of organizing the workplace. With regard to middle-class protest, we need to explore more deeply the role of such an ambiguous and contradictory class location in social protest, as well as the ways in which such protest is consciously and unconsciously used to clarify and perhaps to entrench such class locations. Finally, productive approaches to the nexus of class and activism must struggle with the fact that class actors are always also "raced" and "gendered" in ways that have yet to be adequately conceptualized. For starters, however, we may turn to the role of racial structures in social activism.

Racial Movements: New Social Movement Prototypes?

As we have seen, it is a commonplace observation among new social movement theorists that traditional class-based movements have been displaced by newer movements based on race and gender. Although I have argued that the demise of class-based movements is more complicated than this formula recognizes, there can be little doubt that beginning in the 1950s and continuing through the 1960s and 1970s, race- and gender-based movements came to occupy center stage in the arena of social movement activism in the United States. And there can also be little doubt that the civil rights movement served as the major prototype for a cycle of protest associated with these decades. This prototypical role took several forms. The civil rights movement served as a direct model for other race- or ethnicity-based social movements on behalf of Latino/as and Native Americans. It served as an indirect model for other identity-based movements on behalf of students, women, and gays and lesbians who self-consciously copied the ideologies, goals, and tactics of the civil rights movement and adapted them to their own situation. And beyond serving as a model for other movements, the civil rights movement provided the catalyst for the entire spectrum of social activism in the 1960s and 1970s by radicalizing a generation of college students in conjunction with the draft and the Vietnam War. The conventional wisdom thus appears broadly correct. Of the two major waves of social activism and protest in the United States in the twentieth century, the protests of the 1930s were rooted in class structures of power and undertaken by workers and unemployed people, whereas the protests of the 1960s emerged from racial structures of power that sparked resistance by African-Americans that in turn became a prototype for social activism across the political spectrum.

On one level, the emergence, persistence, and transformation of the civil rights movement may be understood as a response to a new set of political opportunities that built on preexisting forms of social organization within the black community to expand the rights of African-Americans (McAdam, 1982; Morris, 1984). On another level, the history of this movement may be seen as a major exemplar of the process of racial formation (Omi and Winant, 1986). It is the latter process that is of greatest interest here, because the concept of racial formation illustrates the social construction of collective identity at the heart of social movements. The case of race and racial structures of power is particularly instructive because race is still often considered a biological category or at least an ascribed status. These perceptions obscure the social construction of racial categories and the social contestation over what those racial categories mean. The power of the theory of racial formation (Omi and Winant, 1986) is that it sees race as a basic organizing principle of social relationships and simultaneously as an unstable and decentered complex of social meanings. Such a theory can help us shift gears from a static notion of race as an ascribed status to a processual view of racialization as an historically variable and indeterminate struggle to extend or contest the racial coding of social relationships.

This theory underscores two major contributions of the civil rights movement to understand how racial structures of power operate in the United States. First, although the early movement began in the South as an ethnicity-based movement challenging segregation, it evolved into a movement that redefined the meaning of race in terms of the competing paradigms of class and nation. Second, this movement challenged the social meaning of race by expanding the arena of struggle from the economic and the political levels of social structure to the cultural and social levels of lived experience, thereby providing a model for other new social movements that would also link the personal and the political. This politicization of black identity and collective subjectivity redefined the meaning of racial identity "from an emphasis on individual survival to one of collective action" (Omi and Winant, 1986:95). This process of redefinition culminated with the radicalization of the movement under the rubric of black power, which drew on colonial analogies to understand racial oppression. Despite subsequent political setbacks, a profound and permanent transformation has occurred in the collective subjective identity of African-Americans as a result of this movement. In Morris's terms (1992), a politicized form of oppositional consciousness has become an almost taken-for-granted element of everyday experience in many communities—particularly in the world views of young African-Americans. In the absence of political opportunity, this consciousness may be predominantly expressed in cultural terms of dress, language, music, mannerism, and demeanor. In whatever form, this consciousness and identity represent both a movement accomplishment and a movement resource, for "the persistence of the new racial identities developed during this period stands out as the single truly formidable obstacle to the consolidation of a newly repressive racial order" (Omi and Winant, 1986:91).

Whereas the 1960s saw movement gains, the 1970s and 1980s were a period of reaction in which the beneficiaries of racial structures reasserted their power and responded to the great transformation initiated by the black movement. The revival of right-wing politics in various guises had a persistent racial subtext in which the gains of racial minorities were cast as causing or exacerbating a range of social problems; thus "'racial' issues have become central to the agenda of those forces and projects seeking a rightward realignment in US politics" (Omi and Winant, 1986:113). With the exception of the explicitly racist far right, the dominant strain of reaction claims to favor racial equality and a colorblind society, but these lofty goals are strategically deployed to argue against any progressive policy that takes race into account (e.g., affirmative action) as somehow creating reverse discrimination. Although the resurgence of right-wing politics has often been interpreted as a backlash to the gains of the feminist movement, the leading themes of reactionary politics are as much a response to the gains of the civil rights movement as to those of the feminist movement, and thereby represent an attempt to restore traditional racial as well as gender structures of power. Thus, the antistatism of the right (expressed in its opposition to "big government") may be interpreted as a rejection of the historically new role of the state as sponsor of racially progressive policies won by the civil rights movement. The most sophisticated version of reactionary politics is the neoconservative rejection of the concept of collective equality and group rights in favor of a reassertion of individual equality. In theoretical terms, this represents a return to the ethnicity paradigm and its associated ideologies of individual effort, upward mobility, and integration as the only viable option for racial minorities (Omi and Winant, 1986).

The initial successes of the civil rights movement thereby provoked a sophisticated and multifaceted reaction that has led to a complex standoff in race relations. One useful means of understanding this standoff is to see this outcome as a shift from an era of racial domination to an era of racial hegemony (Winant, 1995). The former refers to the explicit, legally sanctioned forms of discrimination and segregation that were directly and successfully challenged by the civil rights movement. In important ways, this challenge to racial domination was successful because the target of the movement was clear and the constituency of the movement included the entire African-American community, all of whom experienced the direct or indirect effects of traditional discrimination and segregation. When the right combination of organization and opportunity materialized against this backdrop (McAdam, 1982; Morris, 1984), a powerful movement emerged and met with considerable success. In the face of this challenge, the racial state responded with some concessions to civil rights demands within a broader strategy of absorption and insulation. Although not entirely successful, these strategies fed into fragmentation and strategic divisions within the black movement that, in tandem with direct state repression, ensured that the latter phases of the movement were not as successful as the earlier stages. In part, the movement's failure to radically alter the racial structure of power in the United States was due to the fact that each of the major movement strategies (entrism, socialism, nationalism) ultimately reduced race to something else (interest group, class fraction, cultural entity) and suffered from the same faults as the ethnicity, class, and nation paradigms (Omi and Winant, 1986). This failure also reflects the complex, multilayered nature of the racial structure of power. The relative success of the early civil rights movement altered one important layer of this racial structure of power by turning back formal, legally sanctioned forms of discrimination and segregation as well as reducing forms of social and political terror against blacks (Piven and Cloward, 1977). But it revealed other layers of the racial structure of power consisting of informal practices and institutional linkages that continue to create drastically different life chances for African-Americans.

The victories against direct racial domination thereby helped usher in a more subtle set of controls in the form of racial hegemony. In political terms, this is a system of power that incorporates oppositional elements into the prevailing forms of rule and coopts movement goals while transforming their substantive content. The relative success of the movement against racial domination and the emergence of this new form of control have created significant obstacles to ongoing racial mobilization. One obstacle is the new and more complex political system of racial control itself; when compared to the former system of racial domination it is evident that racial movements have lost the clear targets and obvious enemies that animated the previous round of movement mobilization. Another obstacle ironically derives from the success of the earlier movement in creating limited opportunities for some blacks that have led to greater social and class differentiation within the black community. Although all African-Americans are affected by the current racial hegemony, the effects differ more dramatically across various segments of this group than was the case with the prior system of racial domination.

From a slightly different angle, these developments reveal some of the dilemmas of identity politics, which implicitly assume that all members of a given group experience the same forms of oppression and share a common set of overriding interests. Although this insight may be crucial to gaining initial access to the political system, once this is won (i.e., the transition from racial domination to racial hegemony) it becomes evident that some members are better positioned to take advantage of these new opportunities than others. Thus, some middle-class blacks have benefited from the dismantling of racial domination in ways that make assimilation a plausible strategy for people in this particular combination of class and race locations—which only serves to accentuate the new social distance between middle-class blacks and working-class and poor people of color. With these developments, the logic of identity politics with its presumption of similar experiences and interests loses much of its plausibility (Anner, 1996). The transition from a system of racial domination to one of racial hegemony, in conjunction with the accelerated differentiation of African-Americans, has thus led to a decentering of the former civil rights movement in the absence of a coherent conflict. In place of a relatively unified movement, there is now a major split between pragmatic liberals and radical democrats, reflecting myriad differences over goals, strategy, tactics, and the role of identity politics in an era of racial hegemony (Winant, 1995).

This reading of recent racial politics suggests that it is more important than ever to understand the intersection of race and class locations rather than treating them in isolation. Indeed, it is their fateful intersection that is a crucial underpinning of the system of racial hegemony. A prevailing strategy in this system of control is to represent class issues in racial terms. The racial coding of issues such as crime, welfare, and poverty obscures their roots in a class system of material inequality and thereby allows powerholders to engage in the age-old strategy of divide and conquer (Winant 1995). If this is the form of the current system of control, the most effective forms of resistance would be those that combine both class and race consciousness. Although receiving little media attention, there is evidence that precisely such movements are emerging. In his survey of social justice movements in communities of color, John Anner (1996) and his associates document a number of relatively small but successful mobilizations among poor or working-class people of color that range from school reform and immigrant labor issues to police accountability and antitox-ics activism. Such movements have several common threads. First, they are ex-plicitly multiracial or multiethnic in their approach to organizing and mobiliz-ing. Second, they organize around immediate, tangible grievances of economic survival, political self-determination, or environmental threats. Third, they tend to be relatively small and localized campaigns (hence attracting relatively little media attention). Fourth, they tend to be highly self-reflexive and deliberate about framing issues so as to fuse identity politics and class-based organizing to solidify communities that are usually divided by race and culture. And fifth, despite an apparent lack of conventional resources, these movements have met with a remarkable degree of success. The theoretical significance of these mo-bilizations is that they are the logical counterpart to the newly prevailing sys-tem of racial hegemony. Whereas this system implicitly rests on a more class-differentiated form of racial control and the obfuscation of race and class, these movements are rooted in working-class and poor communities of color and they explicitly strategize around how to combine racial identity politics and tra-ditional class concerns.

In adopting the theory of racial formation as a guiding thread in this dis-cussion, I have also adopted a focus on African-Americans as the major exem-plar of a racial structure of power as well as resistance to that structure. But this conceptual approach is couched at a level of abstraction that makes it ap-plicable to other racial structures and movements as well. Thus, in the context of the United States, mobilizations of Latina/o groups and Native Americans may also be understood as processes of racial formation that transform racial identities by challenging racial structures of power that are ultimately guaran-teed by a racial state. The origins, timing, and outcomes of each of these move-ments are historically specific but the process of racial formation is similar in each case as the traditional meanings and purposes of racial categories are chal-lenged and politicized by each of these racially based mobilizations in broadly parallel ways. Hence, movements on behalf of different racial groups in the modern era have all promoted and built on new forms of collective subjectiv-ity that emphasize group identity and cultural pride while also politicizing those new identities.

The recent history of Latina/o activism in the United States illustrates sev-eral of these claims. Latina/o activism surfaced in the 1960s as part of a larger cycle of protest, and it quickly adopted the concept of institutionalized racism as a master frame for identifying grievances and mobilizing supporters (Garcia, 1996:89; Marin, 1991:117–118). At first glance, this mobilization exhibited many of the characteristics often ascribed to new social movements. These in-cluded emphases on cultural as well as political issues, on the social construc-tion of group identity, and on autonomy and self-determination as central move-ment goals (Garcia, 1996; Marin, 1991; Munoz, 1989). In contrast to most characterizations of new social movements, however, this mobilization directly appealed to working-class identities alongside racial/cultural identities, and it explicitly identified material goals and the political and economic control of communities as part of its overall strategy (Munoz, 1989).

For my purposes, the most striking feature of this mobilization is its cor-
respondence with the model of racial formation. In the immediate post-World
War II era, Mexicans in the United States "emphasized the American part of
their Mexican American identity. In their minds, political accommodation and
assimilation were the only path toward equal status in a racist society" (Munoz,
1989:49). In promoting an image of Mexican Americans as a white ethnic
group, this form of consciousness mirrored the ethnicity paradigm (Omi and
Winant, 1986). Given this backdrop, and given the internal diversity of
Latina/os in the United States, it was perhaps inevitable that the cycle of protest
that arose in the 1960s would eventually problematize the issue of identity and
place it at the center of Latina/o mobilization. Collective identity was ongo-
ingly reconstructed in this movement, with an eventual coalescence around Chi-
cana/o identity as a way of reclaiming a pejorative, class-bound label and redefining it as a source of pride and a mobilizing point for an important
component of youth-based activism in the 1960s (Munoz, 1989:79). This was
not just an internal movement struggle. The racial state intervened in these
identity battles by bureaucratically mandating the category of "Hispanic" as a
generic term to identify Spanish-speaking residents in the United States. This
top-down imposition of an artificial identity ignored vast cultural and class differences among Spanish-speaking peoples, and it obscured the movement's own
efforts to cultivate a more authentic, pan-Latina/o collective identity defined
by the movement and its various communities. Perhaps the ultimate commentary on the social construction of race and the process of racial formation is the
ongoing debate among academics, activists, and citizens about whether
Latina/o groups are better characterized as a racial group or an ethnic group.
In all these ways, the recent history of Latina/o activism illustrates the process
and politics of racial formation in the context of social movement activism and
the dialectic between movements and the state.

This entire family of movements illustrates how the identification of racial
movements as new social movements becomes problematic. Racial movements
do provide rich examples of the social construction of collective identity and
the culturalist themes that are central to new social movement theorizing. However, racial movements depart from the prevailing imagery of new social movements in at least two fundamental ways. First, they do not even approximate
the image of a movement espousing postmaterialist values and world views.
Second, they do not typically divorce cultural projects of identity formation
from political goals of challenging structures of power. In contrast to much
new social movement theorizing about postmaterialist, culturally oriented activism, racial movements have typically spoken on behalf of materially deprived
constituencies and pursued a variety of political strategies to win concessions
from the racial state. This is not to say that these movements have necessarily
enjoyed lasting success in achieving these broader goals. Indeed, it may well
have been the difficulty of achieving material goals that contributed to a greater
emphasis on cultural expressions of collective subjectivity and solidarity as an
alternative (and perhaps predecessor) to achieving material gains. The exploration of such possibilities is preempted by formulations that equate racial move-

ments with new social movements and define the latter as postmaterialist and culturally oriented. This conceptualization may obscure as much as it reveals about the dynamics of racial movements.

This brief overview of racial movements suggests the parallels between social theorists seeking to understand racial dynamics and social activists seeking to change them. Social theorists have arrived at a social-constructionist language for capturing the initially arbitrary but subsequently "real" status of racial categories and their meanings. Social activists have engaged in a process of racial formation that has exposed the relative and arbitrary status of the categories and their older meanings by cultivating newer and more politicized meanings for those categories as part of a process of movement mobilization. The parallels go further. Social theorists have often committed the conceptual error of reducing race to a manifestation of ethnicity, class, or nation. Social activists have sometimes committed the strategic error of embracing integration, socialism, or nationalism as exclusive movement goals. The common thread uniting both kinds of errors is the inability or refusal to see race itself as fundamental and not reducible to something else. In the case of racial politics, it is not just activists who may misconstrue their constituency; the forces of reaction and resistance also utilize reductionist categories as strategic ploys to blunt the momentum of racial movements, as exemplified by right-wing attempts to reassert the ethnicity paradigm in recent years. In addition to these movement pitfalls, the overlapping nature of structures of power poses powerful challenges to racial movements. In multiracial societies such as the United States, there is always the potential for racial resistance to be diverted from a vertical challenge to the power structure into a horizontal struggle with other racial minorities over artificially scarce resources. And the simultaneous crisscrossing of other structures of power with that of race creates the potential that collective subjectivities based on class or gender will fragment efforts at building racial unity. Hence, struggles around racial formation become two degrees more complex in societies with multiple racial groups and multiple structures of power. This warrants a closer look at the third major category of movements that challenge these structures of power.

Gender Movements: The Longest War?

This processual view of the social construction of group identity is also appropriate for understanding feminist movements that challenge the gender structure of power. Indeed, the gender structure of power is itself a social construction rooted in a sex/gender system that superimposes gendered characteristics on biological differences. This system operates as an institution for organizing social relations throughout society at the macrolevel, and it operates as a socialization mechanism for producing appropriate masculinities and femininities at the microlevel. Like the ethnicity paradigm in the case of racial structures, the sex/gender system presumes a uniform definition of a subordinate group of people that also downplays the formation of any collective identity that might challenge the dominant group. As I suggested earlier, the emergence of collective identity among women may be particularly difficult for two structural reasons. First, women are distributed throughout other social groups in numbers roughly proportional to men, rather than being socially concentrated as often is the case with racial or class groups. Second, through a variety of mechanisms, the sex/gender system promotes social intimacy between individual men and women while discouraging any politicized form of social cohesion among women. Transcending these obstacles to collective identity is a necessary prerequisite for any successful mobilization of women hoping to challenge the gender structure of power. Although gender structures of power may involve the "longest war," these structural realities help explain why it is often a subterranean and individual war that only intermittently takes the form of collective action.

One puzzle in the study of gender movements thereby involves how women's movements ever manage to mobilize in the face of these obstacles. One important factor appears to be the prior involvement of women in "parent movements" that provide resources and create opportunities for feminist mobilization (Buechler, 1990). A second puzzle is why such movements have historically had such a white, middle-class mobilization bias when they did mobilize. An answer to the second question may be found by considering how simultaneously experienced, overlapping structures of power impinge on women's social networks and group consciousness, and hence their propensity for particular types of activism. That is, women are not just subordinate members in a gender structure of power; they also occupy diverse locations with respect to other axes of social differentiation and structures of power. Even the most simplified model of social order suggests at least four possible locations for women: in dominant class and racial groups, in dominant class and subordinate racial groups, in subordinate class and dominant racial groups, and in subordinate class and racial groups. The sociology of knowledge suggests that each of these varied locations will promote different sets of interests and forms of consciousness that will inevitably impinge on the likelihood of mobilization into women's movements.

Women who are members of relatively privileged race and class groups may well be attracted to feminist mobilization because it addresses their one subordinate status. Alternately, they may feel that their class and race privileges outweigh their gender disadvantages, that feminist activism might undermine their dominant class and race position, or that such activism might jeopardize aspects of their gendered identity that they value. Depending on how these structural realities interact with other factors, middle-class white women are thereby the most likely recruits to both feminist and antifeminist movements. Women who are members of a subordinate social class, or a subordinate racial group, or both, are logical candidates for recruitment to class movements, or racial movements, or both—in addition to being potential candidates for women's movements. It is here that preexisting forms of social organization and collective identity become crucial in tipping the mobilization balance for those women who are subject to multiple forms of subordination. The socially concentrated nature of class and racial groups and the socially dispersed nature of gender groups mean that preexisting social networks are likely to direct multiply-subordinated women into movements organized around class or race rather than gender. By the same token, those women who experience only gender oppression have one logical outlet for social activism: they will participate in gender movements if they participate in any movements at all. Although actual mobilization patterns are influenced by many intervening factors, the logic of this argument suggests that the white, middle-class mobilization bias of women's movements has deep structural roots.

The structural tendency for multiply-subordinated women to initially be attracted to race or class movements before gender movements is reinforced by the feminism historically developed by the white, middle-class women who do predominate in feminist movements. This feminism can be characterized as a "pure" feminism that can be incisive in analyzing gender oppression in isolation but that is often blind to the additional, overlapping inequalities experienced by poor women, or working-class women, or women of color. In class terms, this world view amounts to a type of "class unconsciousness" on the part of middle-class women that contrasts sharply with the class consciousness of both upper-class and working-class women. Middle-class women are less likely to see the social world as organized around class precisely because of their class location, and this "class unconsciousness" is fostered and expressed through ideological beliefs about individualism, opportunity, and mobility that deny the presence of structural barriers to individual effort. In racial terms, this world view is expressed as a parallel form of "race unconsciousness" in which racial privilege makes one's own group the standard and the norm against which others are defined and categorized. As a result, one's own racial advantages are unseen or normalized while the racial disadvantages of others are obscured or denied. Hence, the structural location of white, middle-class women promotes a world view shaped by class and racial "unconsciousness" that denies class and race privileges and results in a pure form of feminism attentive to gender but blind to race and class.

To the extent that structural location shapes cultural world views along these lines, it follows that white, middle-class women are the one group that is structurally predisposed to see the world as primarily organized around gender. This structural predisposition is an additional factor in explaining the oft-noted mobilization bias of feminist movements. Thus, even though gender dominance may affect all women, may be recognized by all women, and may be resisted by all women, it is middle-class white women whose resistance is most likely to take the form of independent and autonomous feminist movements. The resistance of working-class women or women of color, by contrast, will be informed by class or race consciousness as well as gender consciousness. In Nancy Cott's formulation,

> The woman's rights tradition was historically initiated by, and remains prejudiced toward, those who perceive themselves first and foremost as "woman," who can gloss over their class, racial and other status identifications because those are culturally dominant and therefore relatively invisible. (Cott, 1987:9)

This mobilization bias has arguably been the most distinctive feature of women's movements in the United States, although a closer empirical study of these movements reveals a number of variations on this theme from the mid-nineteenth century to the present (Buechler, 1990).

This mobilization bias in women's movements has had a number of consequences and provoked a variety of responses. If it is white, middle-class women who are the most likely recruits to a feminist movement, that helps to explain the initial predominance and continuing centrality of liberal feminist ideology in most waves of feminist activism. Reflecting the interests, perceptions, and consciousness of this constituency, liberal feminism does not fundamentally challenge social structure as much as it seeks greater access to all parts of that structure for individual women. The very themes that comprise what I have called middle class "unconsciousness" are the core ideas of liberal feminist ideology: individual access, upward mobility, and equal opportunity are the hallmarks of this world view. Although these beliefs are central to every major phase of feminist mobilization, most phases eventually spark a broader proliferation of ideological stances that, in the case of the contemporary women's movement in the United States, included radical feminism, socialist feminism, cultural feminism, and "difference" feminism. These ideological variations broadened and deepened the feminist critique of gender arrangements in many ways. They suggest that despite their mobilization bias, feminist movements have attracted followers with a diverse range of experiences and grievances that found expression in this ideological profusion. And yet, most of the ideologies identified above remain variations on the theme of gender as the most fundamental societal divide and collective identity in society (with the exception of socialist feminism's attentiveness to class as well as gender). In this way, the earlier profusion of feminist ideology during the 1970s stopped short of perspectives that problematized race, class, and other identities alongside gender.

Whereas the first phase of ideological profusion continued to take gender as the primary focus, the second phase of ideological profusion from the 1980s to the present has sought to take feminism beyond the standpoint of one class and one race to encompass the multiple and diverse standpoints of women from all points on the sociostructural landscape. This expansion of a feminist perspective has been due, in large part, to the work of feminist women of color who have been particularly well situated to perceive and expose the traditional mobilization bias of white, middle-class feminism, to sort through those aspects of gender structures of power that do and that do not affect all women, and to argue for an expanded feminist vision that is respectful of differences among women while building on gender commonalities across race and class lines (Davis, 1983; Giddings, 1984; hooks, 1984; Moraga and Anzaldua, 1981). These developments have expanded the potential base for feminist mobilization by adding to and transforming the issues and grievances that the movement addresses. They have also promoted new theoretical understandings about the multiple, simultaneous, and intertwined nature of social locations and collective identities, and the fact that all gender identities are always also "raced" and "classed" identities (Collins, 1990). Although this reality may be easier to see in the case of racial and class identities that are not privileged, I have tried to suggest that it was a peculiar type of "raced" and "classed" gender identity that gave rise to the white, middle-class mobilization bias of mainstream feminism in the first place. Thus, the explicit thematization of race and class issues within feminism in the past 15 years not only reveals who has been marginalized, but also illuminates who has been at the center. In this way, understandings prompted by social movement activism are refracted back into sociological theories and explanations of how the social world is both socially organized and experientially lived by its members.

Like racial movements, women's movements are often casually classified as new social movements. To the extent that new social movements advocate postmaterialist values, this characterization is problematic at best. The problems are evident even in the case of liberal feminism's white, middle-class base—seemingly a secure foundation for pursuing postmaterialist goals. To the contrary, one of the most consistent demands of liberal feminism has been for economic security through more equitable access to the occupational sector as well as a reduction in the segregation and discrimination that still permeates many career paths and workplaces. In a society in which survival is linked to earning a steady income, this clearly constitutes a materialist demand that has been a consistent element in women's mobilization over the past 30 years. The fact that materialist goals have been central to "middle-class" feminism suggests that even middle-class women cannot take economic security for granted. Indeed, the very term "middle-class women" is problematic because the class structure is generally conceptualized as consisting of familial households of male breadwinners and economically dependent wives. Thus, "middle-class women" often turn out to be women with middle-class husbands who are one relationship away from poverty. In the face of this reality, the demands of "middle-class women" for equal access to the occupational structure are a logical materialist response to their precarious position in the overlapping structures of class and gender. If the feminist demands of middle-class women do not qualify as "postmaterialist," the term is even less appropriate for describing the demands of working-class women or women of color, for whom feminism has always included a quest for greater material security.

The identification of women's movements as new social movements would appear to have more accuracy in the case of a second characteristic of such movements: a concern with subjectivity and a focus on the links between individual and collective identity. In its original version, liberal feminism tended to focus on the public sphere, but the proliferation of other forms of feminism problematized subjectivity by arguing that the personal was political and that seemingly private life-style choices contained their own political dynamic in need of feminist resistance. Certain versions of radical feminism (and subsequently cultural feminism) took this insight the furthest by suggesting that the main forms of patriarchal oppression as well as feminist resistance could be located in the realm of subjectivity (Echols, 1989). The concept of "internalized oppression" nicely captured this viewpoint by suggesting that the most pernicious aspect of patriarchal power was the manner in which it made women complicit in their own subordination through its power to shape female psychology. These theoretical and political insights found a more popular echo in the proliferation of self-help literature whose relentless theme was that women's lack of self-esteem was at the root of all the obstacles confronting women in modern society. In both its ideological and popular version, this focus on subjectivity would thus seem to qualify contemporary feminism as a prototypical new social movement.

Although this argument has more merit than the earlier one equating feminism with postmaterialist values, it is not without its own complications. Without denying the descriptive accuracy of this view of contemporary feminism, there is room to challenge the explanatory claim of the theory in this case. Many versions of new social movement theory argue that the focus on subjectivity in contemporary social movements represents a new tactic in the repertoire of social movements and a new mode of expressing resistance to (post)modern forms of social control. In contrast to these claims, it can be argued that feminism's focus on subjectivity and identity has less to do with new forms of control and resistance than with the fact that these are very old forms of control that are especially well developed in gender structures of power and must be challenged by any feminist movement that hopes to alter relations of power between the sexes. We have already seen how gender structures of power tend to be more finely grained and localized because of the unusually close social relations between dominant and subordinate group members in this case. If these are long-established mechanisms of control and domination, it logically follows that resistance to these mechanisms would occur on the same terrain. Thus, women's resistance to patriarchal power has frequently taken subjective and psychological forms not because this is a new social movement but because this is one of the traditional means through which this power has been exercised and through which it must be challenged. Such activism may look like a new social movement, but the reasons have more to do with the specific forms of gender oppression than with a new repertoire of social movement forms. Although beyond the scope of this work, there is evidence to suggest that earlier waves of feminism also had a vital subjective and psychological dimension to their challenge to gender structures of power, even if it was not expressed in the contemporary vernacular of self-esteem and internalized oppression (Buechler, 1986).

This brief overview of gender movements suggests at least three close connections between gender structures of power and the movements that have challenged them. First, the composition of these movements has historically reflected a white, middle-class mobilization bias that is best explained by specific features of the gender structure of power, including the dispersal of women throughout other social groups and the role of preexisting networks, collective identity, and group consciousness in fostering differential participation among women. Second, the very same dispersal of women creates the potential for the eventual emergence of variegated forms of feminism that reflect the variety of social locations occupied by women—a potential that was realized when women of color, working-class women, lesbian women, and others challenged the traditional mobilization bias of the contemporary women's movement. Third, one of the more striking dimensions of feminist movements is a preoccupation with psychological and interpersonal forms of domination, but this is best seen as a logical response to the specific forms taken by gender structures of power and the distinctively intimate forms of control woven into these structures. Although a fuller explanation of any particular mobilization obviously requires attention to many factors, I have attempted to show that some of the most prominent features of contemporary feminist activism are best understood as logical consequences of the specific qualities of gender structures of power.

At this point, some brief concluding remarks on the relation between regional power structures and social movement activism are in order. My initial premise was that structures of power based on class, race, and gender are deeply rooted, institutional features of advanced capitalism in the United States that organize relations of exploitation, domination, and oppression. The class, race, and gender movements that have arisen to challenge these structures are, in an important sense, derivative from these structures. At the same time, there is nothing automatic about the transition from structures of power to actions that challenge those structures. Two crucial intervening processes involve the formation of collective identity and the development of oppositional consciousness. In different ways, each of the structures of power and its associated movements illustrate the socially constructed nature of these processes. Examining multiple structures and movements alongside one another also reveals their differing historical dynamics and trajectories. Whereas a particular type of (Fordist) class structure gave rise to a particular kind of labor movement as the prevailing form of social movement resistance, the demise of this particular form of class relations has led to a waning of working-class movements and perhaps a shift to certain types of middle-class movements. As class structures have changed and class movements have waned, race and gender structures have become more predominant and race and gender movements have been in historical ascendancy. These movements have been especially important in underscoring the socially constructed nature of all collective identities and the simultaneous intertwining of multiple identities in both structures of power and forms of resistance. One lesson yet to be fully learned is that these insights into the social construction of collective identity and the copresence of multiple identities also apply to class movements—both past and future—and indeed to all forms of collective mobilization. And a final lesson to be learned from this analysis is that typical applications of the concept of new social movements to the demise of class movements and the rise of race and gender movements are deeply flawed, often obscuring more than they reveal about these movements and their resistance to prevailing structures of power.

6

Local Structures and Social Movements

The Politics of Everyday Life

The final level of sociohistorical structure is the "local" level of interpersonal relations and lived experience. In some respects, this level can be most sharply distinguished from the other three. Global, national, and regional structures are elongated through social time and space; they involve centuries of history and thousands of miles. As such, they dwarf individual experience with all the classic characteristics of transcendent, eternal, and omnipotent Durkheimian social facts. Local structures, by contrast, are compressed in social time and space because they involve slices of social reality that are meaningful from the perspective of individual biography. Local structures thereby raise phenomenological and social–psychological issues concerning consciousness, identity, and interaction. Although some sociological traditions have made helpful contributions to understanding this level of social reality, sociological theory has, for the most part, divorced its analyses of macro- and microlevel structures. This has begun to change in the past 20 years, as more and more approaches seeking to integrate or synthesize our understanding of micro- and macrolevels of social reality have appeared. In the following section, I very briefly review some of the more promising approaches for characterizing local levels of microstructure, with a view toward how these are linked both to other structural levels and to prevailing forms of social activism.

THE LOCAL LEVEL OF SOCIOHISTORICAL STRUCTURE

The Social Construction of Reality

One such approach is rooted in social phenomenology as a foundation for understanding the social construction of reality (Berger and Luckmann, 1967). A central puzzle for this approach is how a world that we typically experience as immutable and fundamentally "real" is nevertheless a relative and arbitrary construction. Hence, the starting point of a social–phenomenological approach is an understanding of everyday life as a socially constructed world that rests on a series of taken-for-granted assumptions about subjective, intersubjective, and objective reality that constitute "common sense." These assumptions rest on numerous typifications that social actors use to categorize experiences, situations, and people and to confer meanings on their lived experience. Language is central to this enterprise, as are cultural recipes, social stocks of knowledge, and relevance structures that reflect the intentions of actors and allow them to find meaning and coherence in the social world. The fundamental processes involved in the social construction of reality may be summarized under three broad headings. Through externalization, human intentions and actions give rise to a particular kind of social world, reflecting the idea that society is a human product. Through objectivation, these externalizations take on the quality of an independent, free-standing reality, anchoring the equally basic insight that society is an objective reality. Through internalization, this external, objective world is retrojected into individual consciousness, illustrating a third basic insight that people are a social product. At the broadest level, the social construction of reality refers to the continuous, ongoing, and dialectical interconnections among these three processes (Berger and Luckmann, 1967).

These broad categories allow more detailed analyses of society as an objective and a subjective reality. The creation of society as an objective reality occurs more specifically through the process of institutionalization, as habitual actions and reciprocal typifications acquire "objectivity" over time. This process is reinforced with the passage of generations and the sedimentation of tradition that adds to the objective reality of society. Alongside institutionalization are legitimation processes whereby explanations and justifications of this objective social order are provided through symbolic universes and reinforced through various conceptual machineries of universe maintenance. Although these processes become stretched out over time and space, the objective reality of society and its legitimations nevertheless remain human creations rooted in everyday life activity. The internalization of society as a subjective reality occurs through socialization. Primary socialization involves the development of a self in interaction with significant others and eventually with the "generalized other." Secondary socialization involves the internalization of role-specific knowledge relevant to action in institutional subworlds. As a subjective reality, this internalized world requires its own reality maintenance, which routinely relies on significant others and everyday conversation. Successful socialization is measured by the establishment of symmetry between objective and subjective social reality. This analysis underscores the dialectical nature of the social construction of reality, i.e., the world that some actors are internalizing through socialization is the same world that other actors have created through externalization and objectivation. Berger and Luckmann (1967) thereby provide a useful initial handle on the local level of sociohistorical structure while also theorizing its links to other levels.

Structuration Processes

Although social phenomenology recognizes the reflexive qualities of social actors, the implications of these qualities for both the maintenance and transformation of social structure remain somewhat abstract. Structuration theory illuminates these implications more directly, and thereby provides another attempt to overcome the traditional dualism between the macro- and microlevel (Giddens, 1984). Central to this theory is the duality of structure, meaning that the "structural properties of social systems are both medium and outcome of the practices they recursively organize" (Giddens, 1984:25). This theory challenges sociologists to relinquish the traditional notion of structure as external and constraining for a new notion of structuration in which "structure has no existence independent of the knowledge that agents have about what they do in their day-to-day activity" (Giddens, 1984:26). Put differently, the concept of structuration implies that social reality is best seen not as a static collection of structures but rather an unfolding set of processes in which social actors use aspects of what have traditionally been called "structure" to act on intentions and pursue goals whose unintended result is the reproduction (and sometimes transformation) of those same structural elements. This approach puts major emphasis on the knowledgeability of everyday social actors: "[a]ll competent members of society are vastly skilled in the practical accomplishments of social activities and are expert 'sociologists'. The knowledge they possess is not incidental to the persistent patterning of social life but is integral to it" (Giddens, 1984:26). Such actors routinely use a form of practical consciousness to monitor their own behavior as well as that of others, and they readily incorporate both everyday knowledge as well as social–scientific knowledge into their repertoire for understanding social situations and acting within them. Although structuration theory addresses some of the same issues as social phenomenology, it places much greater emphasis on the extent to which knowledge of these social construction or structuration processes becomes a part of the everyday, practical consciousness of ordinary social actors.

Structuration theory also has important implications for how we understand transformations of self-identity in late modernity (Giddens, 1991). The latter is defined by three fundamental processes. The first is the separation of time and space and the stretching of social relations across global systems. The second concerns disembedding mechanisms that separate interaction from specific locales and influences. The third involves institutional reflexivity whereby regularized knowledge about the circumstances of social life becomes a constitutive element in its perpetuation and change. This heightened reflexivity is not just a feature of institutions; self-identity itself becomes a reflexively organized process as well. Sustaining a self in late modernity thus requires the maintenance of ontological security and the management of existential anxiety through the establishment of trust and the avoidance of shame. On this foundation, the self also involves a trajectory, meaning that the individual consciously formulates a life plan that sustains an autobiographical narrative out of a plurality of options. This project is fraught with uncertainty in late modernity because of the range of risks individuals confront; these may create fateful moments when the maintenance or transformation of self-identity becomes an all-consuming task. It is also shaped by the sequestration of experience whereby modernity has repressed some basic moral and existential questions by institutionally separating "normal life" from forms of madness, sickness, death, and criminality. All these factors create distinctively modern tribulations of the self, including problems of fragmentation, powerlessness, uncertainty, and commodification; each poses a distinctive obstacle to the ongoing construction of self-identity through autobiographical life planning (Giddens, 1991).

The Microphysics of Power

Whereas structuration theory underscores the role of reflexivity, it remains somewhat unclear about the role of power in everyday life. A third perspective that analyzes the microphysics of power (Foucault, 1979) can help to redress this omission. This approach rejects the "repressive hypothesis" about power that presumes that power consists of a massive, centralized force that is used in a merely negative way to control, dominate, and repress undesired forms of human activity. Rejecting the repressive hypothesis also means moving beyond viewing power as the possession of certain individuals (and not others) who use it primarily to prohibit or to punish others. This theory does not deny the existence of this type of power as much as it questions the reduction of power to repression, which is a negative, narrow, and skeletal conception of a much more complex process. Indeed, power would be a fragile thing if its only function were to repress; power is really much stronger than this in ways that the repressive hypothesis fails to recognize (Foucault, 1980).

Analysis of the microphysics of power reveals several distinct features. First, power has a positive, productive role in shaping the social world; it does not repress forces coming from elsewhere as much as it constitutes them in the first place by producing effects in terms of desire and knowledge. Second, power is evident in a multiplicity of specific, local, institutional settings rather than in some unitary, centralized location. Third, and closely related, power should be seen as a network of relations or capillaries in the social body that are interwoven with other kinds of social relations. Fourth, power is not so much a thing or a position as it is the operation of concrete and precise disciplinary technologies that act as a mobile force setting up unequal relations. Fifth, power is omnipresent (if not omnipotent); power is always already there and it enmeshes everyone so that one can never be outside the networks of power relations that constitute the social body. Sixth, power becomes invisible, impersonal, and anonymous as it is inscribed in disciplinary technologies; it becomes a machine that no one owns but anyone can use under the right circumstances. This conception of power may become clearer by tracing its implications for the concept of domination. Because power circulates through a netlike organization and is dispersed and localized, it yields multiform relations of domination rather than a fundamentally binary structure of dominators and dominated. Hence, this view of power cannot really be equated to conventional notions of domination because as a field of relations, power is exercised on the dominant as well as the dominated (Foucault, 1980, 1979; Dreyfus and Rabinow, 1983).

The combined approaches of social phenomenology, structuration theory, and the microphysics of power offer a compelling imagery for analyzing the politics of everyday life. With the partial exception of Foucault, these approaches presume microworlds in which human beings operate as active, reflexively knowledgeable agents whose lines of conduct contribute to the maintenance as well as the transformation of the larger social structures in which these microworlds are embedded. Although Foucault is less comfortable with approaches that appear to privilege agency in this way, his comments on the nature of resistance to the microphysics of power (see below) suggest that he may be of two minds on this matter. In any case, what these approaches provide is a general way to conceptualize the relationship between macro- and microlevels of sociohistorical structure by placing particular emphasis on how structure at all levels constrains and enables social actors in their endeavors to maintain and transform those very same structures. These approaches promise a deeper understanding of the connections between multiple levels of sociohistorical structure and the nature of social movement activism.

LOCAL STRUCTURES AND SOCIAL MOVEMENTS

There are two fundamental ways in which local structures are relevant to an analysis of social movement activism. On the one hand, all social movements require microfoundations that transform individual agents into a collective actor that can engage in social activism. All movements rely on processes of recruitment, mobilization, solidarity, and organization that necessarily operate through the capillaries of local structures. Social movement theory and research has addressed these questions quite successfully over the past two decades. This body of work includes major contributions on the role of recruitment (Fireman and Gamson, 1979), motivation (Hirsch, 1986), micromobilization (McAdam, 1988), consensus and action mobilization (Klandermans, 1988), cognitive liberation (McAdam, 1982), framing activity (Snow and Benford, 1992, 1988), and social psychology (Klandermans, 1997, 1984; Gamson, 1992, 1988). These contributions have richly illustrated how the local level of sociohistorical structure constitutes a necessary microfoundation of all types of social movement activism.

On the other hand, some forms of activism not only require such microfoundations but also thematize local structures themselves as the source of grievances, the site of resistance, or the goal of change. By consciously identifying local structures as the appropriate arena of contention, such movements comprise a distinct subset of the larger family of movements that all rely on microfoundations but do not all thematize local structures in this way. Compared to our knowledge about the microfoundations of movements in general, however, we know much less about the subset of movements that thematize local structures as the major or exclusive focus of their activism. They constitute my primary focus here.

Life Politics and Everyday Resistance

Structuration theory provides a point of entry with its distinction between life politics and emancipatory politics. The latter involves liberating people from adverse constraints on their life chances through the reduction or elimination of exploitation, inequality, and oppression, and through the promotion of justice, equality, and participation. Whereas emancipatory politics involves life chances, life politics involves life-styles: "life politics concerns political issues which flow from processes of self-actualisation in post-traditional contexts" (Giddens, 1991:214). Life politics emerge out of the reflexive project of the self in late modernity, and they are reflected in the slogan that the "personal is political" associated with both the student movement and the women's movement. Life politics reach inward in that they concern the most intimate questions of the self, sexuality, reproduction, and the body; they also reach outward to encompass global questions of ecological survival and nuclear devastation. With this double reach, life politics thereby call for a remoralizing of social life (in contrast to modernity's sequestration of experience discussed earlier) because they turn on fundamentally existential questions about our relation to nature, the dilemmas of reproduction, the search for cooperative forms of social life, and the meaning of personhood. Macrolevel developments and processes of modernity have thus transformed self-identity to such an extent that a new form of politics has been established. Although this form of politics originates on the microlevel of personal identity, its effects are not likely to remain confined to this level.

Whereas structuration theory identifies a new form of life politics, the microphysics of power implies the inevitability of everyday resistance. Although power may be a ubiquitous force that none can escape, it nevertheless generates equally universal forms of resistance and counteroffensives against that power (Foucault, 1980, 1979). Put succinctly, if power is everywhere then so is resistance. This is not just an arcane insight of social theory; it echoes in the practical consciousness of everyday activists in the movement slogan that "everything is political." Like the power it challenges, this resistance has some characteristic features. First, these newer political engagements tend to occur at the level of real, material, everyday struggles against specific opponents. Second, these struggles are directed against power effects as such, rather than some auxiliary grievance. Third, these tend to be immediate, quasi-anarchistic conflicts in which people struggle against their most proximate enemy. Fourth, these struggles challenge the "government of individualization" as people seek both the right to be different as well as to sustain community. Fifth, these struggles oppose effects of power that are linked to the knowledge, competence, and qualification that demarcate "experts" from others. Finally, these struggles essentially revolve around the question of identity and challenge forms of power that apply to immediate, everyday life (Foucault in Dreyfus and Rabinow, 1983:211–212).

The specificity of this power and resistance is suggested by how these struggles do not attack an institution or a group but precisely a form of power that categorizes the individual, attaches to individual identity, and makes individuals subjects. "There are two meanings of the word 'subject:' subject to someone else by control and dependence, and tied to his own identity by a conscience or self-knowledge. Both meanings suggest a form of power which subjugates and makes subject to" (Foucault in Dreyfus and Rabinow, 1983:212). Like Giddens's notion of life politics, this form of resistance is explicitly contrasted to more conventional forms of political struggle that may be found throughout history. Thus, struggles against domination involve ethnic, social, or religious forms of power and resistance, whereas struggles against exploitation seek to reclaim what people have produced after its appropriation by others. But it is struggles against subjection that entail distinctive forms of resistance that challenge the microphysics of power described above. Although struggles against domination and exploitation have not disappeared, struggles against subjection have become a third major form of resistance in the modern world (Foucault in Dreyfus and Rabinow, 1983:212–213).

The Battleground of Identity

Although they represent very distinct theoretical traditions, the analyses of structuration processes and the microphysics of power suggest parallel conclusions about the forms of social activism that respond to local structures. For both traditions, identity is a major battleground because it is an active conduit for the exercise of localized power as well as the expression of individualized resistance in the modern world. Life politics arise at the intersection of political issues and processes of self-actualization; as such, they typify the reflexiveness of the self concerning identity, sexuality, reproduction, and the body. This is another example of how a form of social activism can provide the most vivid and concrete expression of a more general sociological conception. It has become a truism that modernity promotes greater reflexivity on the part of social agents, but this process is perhaps nowhere as fully developed as in life politics where virtually all aspects of everyday life become expressions of one's political values and social commitments. In the case of life politics, the politicized self and the self-actualizing self become one and the same (Giddens, 1991). The microphysics of power also points to identity as the battleground in contemporary forms of resistance. These struggles frequently challenge linkages of knowledge, power, and the authority of experts that culminates in the "government of individualization." In these resistances, the notion of the subject may be challenged because so many forms of identity are suffused with forms of power that use identity to impose a regime of control and surveillance. Although this analysis tends to be somewhat obscure, it nevertheless offers a more critical angle of vision on the notion of life politics. Although life politics involve self-actualization, cultural pressures toward the commodification of identity can reduce self-actualization to consumerist choices among prefabricated life-styles in a marketplace of identity. Giddens's insistence on the reflexivity of social agents can obscure the extent to which people's "choices" may be predetermined by a politics of subjection in which being a subject means being subject to these larger social forces. Foucault's analysis thereby provides a critical lens for seeking the elusive line between genuine forms of resistance and more sophisticated avenues of domination.

Whereas the battleground of identity is located on the local level of sociohistorical structure, the forces challenging identity are rooted in other levels of sociohistorical structure. Habermas's (1987, 1984) notion of the colonization of the life world is again helpful for capturing these dynamics. The colonization thesis envisions system imperatives imposing the generalized media of money and power on a cultural life world of symbolic meanings, cultural traditions, and socialization patterns. The result is that the intrapersonal and interpersonal foundations of identity, consciousness, and social interaction become distorted and detached from their communicative foundations. Preserving and restoring these foundations may well require a concerted effort via social activism—both defensive reactions and resistance movements—to defend the life world and its distinctive socialization and interaction patterns from systemic domination. Although this theory provides an intriguing image of how some local forms of social activism might emerge to defend the life world, it suffers from a problem that plagues most general theories of social movements: the most likely responses to colonization dynamics do not take the form of social activism. Indeed, cultural pessimists would argue that the most typical outcome of these dynamics is the spread of alienated and anomic forms of pseudosocial relations and interaction. In addition, when resistance is forthcoming, it is likely to take the form of individual struggles against "personal" circumstances rather than collective forms of social activism. Thus, although the colonization thesis may help to identify some of the broad, background factors that link local structures and social activism, it is far from specifying the exact dynamics that lead to localized social activism rather than some other response (or nonresponse) to colonization processes.

The skeletal framework of the colonization thesis can be specified by other work on new social movements. In Melucci's somewhat more accessible language, advanced capitalism is a society in which the logic of the productive system has permeated economic consumption, human services, social relations, and personal identity. These dynamics constitute new forms of social monitoring, control, and regulation that create conformity pressures (and forms of deviance) that reach deeply into personal life and interpersonal relations. The role of media, symbols, codes, and signs in extending these forms of control is becoming ever more central in the fabric of everyday life. In addition to these purposive efforts at social control, the sheer pace of change, plurality of memberships, and abundance of messages in modern society combine to weaken and destabilize traditional points of reference and sources of self, creating a homelessness of personal identity. Given the array of systemic forces that reach deeply into personal life, the defense of identity and the continuity and predictability of everyday life become arenas of conflict, as localized forms of social activism struggle to retain control of time, space, and relationships. Melucci's formulation of these arguments thereby places identity—in its personal, social, and collective forms—at the center of modern conflicts. This insight allows him to respond to the Habermasian dilemma of when these social forces will spark collective resistance by suggesting that the propensity of people to become involved in collective action is closely tied to their differential capacity to define and sustain an identity (Melucci, 1989, 1988a, 1981, 1980).

In his most recent work, Melucci (1996a, 1996b) recasts this theme as a collapse of the structural into the individual and a blurring of this classic dualism: "individuals are becoming the social core of what we would have called in more traditional terms 'the social structure'" (Melucci, 1996b:145); "there is, as it were, a transfer of the structure of society to the individual level" (Melucci, 1996b:146). In positive terms, this means that modern, complex systems place an unprecedented level of symbolic resources at the disposal of individuals to pursue projects of individuation, autonomy, self-determination, and identity. In negative terms, these same dynamics open up the potential for new, intimate forms of manipulation and social control as described above. In theoretical terms, these processes mean that to speak of the individual no longer implies an individualistic or a psychological analysis because individuals "stand in" for complex, structural forces—some chosen and some imposed—that constitute them as such. In describing this process, Melucci resorts to Habermas's language about how complex societies are increasingly concerned with the production of inner nature; the "unprecedented expansion of learning, socialization, and communication processes demonstrates the scope of this transformation" (Melucci, 1996a:109). But where Habermas underscores the controlling and colonizing aspects of this relation, Melucci is quicker to argue that "control of 'inner nature' is a scarce resource, and new conflicts arise over its appropriation" (Melucci, 1996a:109). These conflicts are increasingly likely to express themselves in social movements, just as movements are increasingly likely to build on the basis of individual experience.

The assumptions, language, and imagery of these theoretical traditions are remarkably distinct. Giddens's structuration theory privileges agency and reflexivity, downplaying the forces that shape subjects. Foucault's analysis of the microphysics of power emphasizes how this power constitutes subjects in the first place. Habermas's colonization thesis evokes beleaguered subjects defending cultural practices against impersonal systemic forces. Melucci's analysis of new social movements identifies both losses and opportunities in the increasingly fluid nature of identity in modern society. Despite the fundamental differences between these theoretical traditions, there is a remarkable convergence across these theories that power in late modernity has penetrated and saturated the interstices of everyday life in a new and historically specific way. As a result, the terrain of social conflict has also shifted, both provoking and even necessitating localized forms of activism that are often fought on the battleground of identity. These threads knit together the otherwise very different images of the politics of everyday life variously conceptualized as life politics (Giddens), multiple resistances to a microphysics of power (Foucault), defenses against life world colonization (Habermas), or the assertion of new collective identities (Melucci).

Whither Public and Private?

The forms of social activism that challenge these local structures are often described as politicizing the seemingly personal dimensions of social existence in ways that undermine traditional distinctions between public and private and that recast the conduct of personal life and interpersonal relations as profoundly political actions (Melucci, 1996a:102). Although this is broadly correct, there is a sense in which this description may give these movements too much credit. The theoretical traditions just reviewed suggest that it is not movements but the very structures of advanced capitalism and administrative domination that have collapsed the boundaries between public and private or political and personal. If power has taken up residence in the niches of everyday life, movements that seemingly politicize the personal are simply logical responses to shifting forms of control and domination that have already politicized the terrain of supposedly private life. The fact that movements are typically given credit (or assigned blame) for eroding these barriers is itself revealing. It implies that movements generate a practical knowledge of how power operates that is often richer and more robust than other forms of everyday consciousness. It also implies that movements can act as indicators or early warning systems about changes taking place in social structure that everyday consciousness and many academic theories are slower to notice. In both cases, the development of sociological knowledge of social structures and practices would benefit from more systematic attention to the dynamics of social movement activism.

The erosion of the boundary between public and private has allowed a great many social and political causes to find local roots in "personal" life. Of all the contemporary movements that broadly fit this description, it is modern feminism that provides the prototypical case. Because the mechanisms of gender inequality and oppression are so intricately interwoven into the fabric of everyday life, interpersonal relations, and personal identity, it is only logical that feminist resistance would find such a congenial slogan in the notion that the personal is political. All of the leading themes of life politics—identity, sexuality, reproduction, the body—have a particular relevance to understanding feminist resistances to patriarchal control of these domains of life. Hence, there is virtually no arena of contemporary life in which the struggle between gender dominance and resistance may not be found. Although critics (and some sympathizers) of these movements may bemoan the thoroughgoing politicization of everyday life that is signified by localized resistance, these critics may be misguided. If they are genuinely concerned about (over)politicization, they might better look to the parent structures than the derivative movements for the causes of this politicization. This is not to deny that the politicized nature of everyday life (and resistance to it) does not pose obstacles for social activists. If "everything" is "political," then anything can become a movement litmus test that defines allies and enemies. But this danger is part of a long history of sources of schism and factionalism in social movements that predates the contemporary emphasis on the politics of everyday life. As long as critiques of politicization are directed only to contemporary movements such as feminism, they tacitly support structures of power by ignoring how those structures have already politicized everyday life while attacking those who would challenge these forces.

The example of feminist activism also suggests that resistance to local structures of power is not inconsistent with broader challenges to regional, national, or even global levels of structure. This is another indication of the erosion of older boundaries between public and private. Indeed, one of the striking characteristics of movements associated with the politics of everyday life is that they frequently pose issues of both local and planetary significance (Melucci, 1995b). This is evident in various movements that seek to link the conduct of everyday life with the prospects for planetary survival. But it is perhaps most evident in ecological movements and movements against nuclear weapons; in these cases, the planetary also becomes personal because "there is nowhere anyone can go on earth to escape" (Giddens, 1991:223). These connections are conveniently symbolized in another popular movement slogan that urges participants to "think globally, act locally." If the politicization of everyday life originated in social structures and then appeared in movements that challenged those structures, the same might be said for the globalization of everyday life. It is the technological and communicative capacities of modern society that have drastically altered historical patterns of time–space distanciation so that the rhythms and patterns of everyday life become part of the dialectic of the local and the global (Giddens, 1991:21–22). The consequences of this globalization have now attracted the critical attention of movement activists; once again such movements are acting as early warning systems underscoring crisis potentials of globalizing social structures.

The erosion of the traditional distinction between public and private spheres is thus a double-edged process. It is often described in military metaphors as an invasion, penetration, or colonization of the interpersonal sphere by large, impersonal forces. Although such imagery is provocative, it should not obscure the other side of the process. The politicization of everyday life and the collapsing of traditional boundaries can be new avenues of domination, but they also create new opportunities for sociopolitical resistance. As the texture of daily life has been altered by these politicizing forces, so too has the phenomenological understanding of that world on the part of everyday actors. Berger and Luckmann (1967) provide an eloquent theoretical language for capturing the socially constructed nature of the social world and the various devices people employ to sustain a set of beliefs in what is ultimately a relative and arbitrary sense of social reality. However, whereas Berger and Luckmann write as "insiders" with a privileged understanding of these processes, the increasing reflexivity of everyday actors in modernity leads to a convergence of sociological and everyday knowledges such that there are fewer and fewer "outsiders" who lack insight into the socially constructed nature of the world (Giddens, 1984). As this heightened reflexivity develops amid a plethora of competing and conflicting signs, codes, and symbols, there is an unhinging of traditional points of reference and their corresponding rationalizations for social order (Melucci, 1989) and a growing potential for communicative rationality in which norms must find a discursive justification (Habermas, 1987, 1984). The increasing re-flexivity of everyday consciousness means that power is less able to shield itself behind traditional legitimations; the increasing politicization of everyday life means that all social locations become sites for resistance to power. These trends point in the direction of increasing resistance on the local level of sociohistor-ical structure.

The analytical problem is that such resistance often takes forms that con-ventional social movement theory is ill equipped to understand. The politics of everyday life thereby offer a challenge to social movement theory. If the stan-dard for a social movement is that it consists of an organized, enduring asso-ciation of leaders and followers pursuing deliberately chosen strategies and tac-tics in opposition to other groups, a good deal of contemporary resistance in the interstices of everyday life will not even register on the scale being used to measure social activism. The danger is that such traditional benchmarks of so-cial protest will obscure these historically new forms of social activism that are emerging on the local level of sociohistorical structure. These include individ-ualized resistance around the assertion, defense, or deconstruction of a partic-ular identity (J. Gamson, 1995), subcultural worlds whose challenge is as much cultural as it is political (Kriesi et al., 1995), and loosely organized and episodic forms of protest that vacillate between latency and visibility (Melucci, 1989). Melucci's work (1996a, 1989) on new social movements has done as much as anyone to critique an overly restrictive notion of what constitutes a social move-ment and to delineate the contours of alternative movement forms. But in the end, the concept of a "social movement" may not be sufficient for capturing all the various forms of social activism that appear in (post)modern contexts. The study of local levels of sociohistorical structure and the activism they pro-voke will be central in responding to such questions.

The Return of Collective Behavior

One of the ironies of social movement theory is that attempts to theorize the most recent forms of social activism underscore the importance of an older ap-proach to the field that recent social movement theory has largely rejected or ignored. A brief and selective discussion of some recent collective behavior the-ory will serve at least three purposes. First, it suggests some plausible connec-tions between the immediacy of everyday life on the local level and forms of collective behavior that are also more immediate and spontaneous. Second, it speaks to the episodic nature of many people's participation in collective ac-tion. Even when they participate in social movements that persist over time, most participants phase in and out of active involvement in such movements. From the phenomenological perspective of participants, their involvement is often fleeting, temporary, and episodic rather than ongoing and sustained; the assumptions of the collective behavior approach may resonate more closely with this experience than the assumptions of much recent social movement theory. Third, a brief focus on forms of collective behavior provides some more specific and concrete examples that may anchor the rather abstract theoretical reflections that have been the main focus of this chapter.

An important link between the phenomenological structures of everyday life and the emergence of various forms of collective action is to be found in the concept of "disrupting the quotidian" (Snow et al., 1998). The quotidian character of everyday life is rooted in daily practices, taken-for-granted routines, and the natural attitude. One important stimulus for the emergence of collective action occurs when these quotidian patterns and rhythms are disrupted and the practices, routines, and attitudes of everyday life are thereby rendered problematic. A multiplicity of events may provoke such a breakdown in the quotidian patterns of everyday life. These include sudden and disruptive accidents, intrusions or violations into one's social space by threatening forces, changes in taken-for-granted subsistence routines, or dramatic changes in structures of social control (Snow et al., 1998). Like many theories of the emergence of collective action, this one is problematic because disruptions in the quotidian structure of everyday life can provoke a variety of responses other than collective action. When other requisites of collective action are present, however, we can hypothesize that such disruptions in the quotidian routines that constitute the local level of sociohistorical structure will be an important impetus to collective action in some form. Indeed, the preceding discussion on the battleground of identity suggests that disruptions in or challenges to taken-for-granted identities will be especially provocative sources of collective action.

Another promising means of linking local levels of sociohistorical structure with forms of collective action is to be found in dramaturgical theories and accounts of the interactional processes at the root of such collective phenomena. Goffman's dramaturgical approach to social life provides important conceptual tools for a microlevel analysis of the local level of sociohistorical structure through its emphasis on occasions and gatherings, face-to-face interaction, focused and unfocused interaction, and rules of irrelevance and transformation (Brown and Goldin, 1973:148–163). This approach has proven useful in the analysis of victory celebrations as a form of theater involving distinctive interactional patterns between participants and spectators that transform and reappropriate specific social spaces for new purposes (Snow et al., 1981). Although this analysis does not distinguish between oppositional collective action and purely expressive celebration, it offers a means of understanding solidarity-building rituals on the local level that often sustain collective challenges to dominant forms of power. A variation of the dramaturgical approach that links it more closely to social protest concerns the interplay of narrative and identity in the construction of collective action. For example, during the 1960 student sit-ins, activists constructed dramatic narratives of their conduct that emphasized spontaneity, "independence from adult leadership, urgency, local initiative, and action by moral imperative rather than bureaucratic planning" (Polletta, 1998:137). Such dramaturgical narrative accounts, and their repetition in public settings, helped construct the new collective identity of "student activist" and compel participation by others in high-risk activism. Once again, the role of identity and the links between individual and collective identity are a critical dynamic of collective action connecting everyday life and collective action at the local level of sociohistorical structure.

A final linkage between the local level and collective action may be found in the vast literature on crowd behavior that is extensively reviewed and cogently analyzed by McPhail (1991). After identifying the standard problems with traditional analyses of crowds (including presumptions about group psychology, irrationality, and homogeneity), McPhail reconstructs the study of crowd behavior through an array of microlevel concepts that are free of the biases that have traditionally plagued this field. Although this approach encompasses a broader range of crowd phenomena than my focus on oppositional collective action does, it can nonetheless inform the analysis of such action on the local level of sociohistorical structure. When crowd behavior does include an oppositional element and a specific target, it begins to approximate Oberschall's (1993) notion of loosely structured collective conflict. In this formulation,

> loosely structured collective action refers to collective action that is undertaken by a loose coalition of activists, part timers and sympathizers whose boundaries are ill-defined and shifting, who lack common, central leadership, organization and clear-cut procedures for deciding upon a common course of action. (Oberschall, 1993:67)

The emphasis on collective conflict resonates nicely with a focus on oppositional social movements; it is also reminiscent not only of my own concept of social movement communities (Buechler, 1990) but also of Melucci's notion of new social movements as loose coalitions and submerged networks that vacillate between poles of latency and visibility as their activism waxes and wanes (Melucci, 1989). In all of these ways, the collective behavior approach that has traditionally focused on temporary, spontaneous, unstructured, or loosely organized forms of collective action has much to tell us about how the local level of sociohistorical structure provides the immediate impetus and arena for collective action.

This examination of the local level of sociohistorical structure began with the observation that it is most easily distinguished from the other levels of structure. Unlike global, national, or regional structures, individual actors and lived experience loom large on the local level. Although the analytical distinction may be clear, the historical reality is that the local level of sociohistorical structure has become increasingly integrated and synchronized with larger structures as part of the trajectory of modernity. As a result, although there is a distinctive politics associated with the texture of everyday life at the local level, it is a politics that responds not just to the exigencies of everyday life on the local level, but to all the ways in which that local level is increasingly contoured by other levels of structure. The analytical challenge is to see all the distinctive features of the politics of everyday life without also losing sight of the multilevel causes and consequences of those politics.

A STRUCTURAL APPROACH REVISITED

The structural approach to social movements that I have advocated has distinguished among four levels of sociohistorical structure: global, national, "regional," and local. The interests of exposition and analysis have necessitated a separate, sequential presentation of these four levels. Unfortunately, this may obscure the most important feature of sociohistorical structure: each level is dialectically related to and mutually constituted by all of the other levels. The preceding discussion about the connections between the politics of everyday life and global social forces provides one reminder that the multiple levels of social structure described throughout this book are best seen as dialectically related rather than static strata resting on top of one another. Other examples include the national and global dimensions of the regional structures of power that I have analyzed in terms of class, race, and gender. The levels I have distinguished are thus analytical devices for organizing the discussion about the structural roots of social activism; there is nothing privileged about the identification of four levels of structure, and subsequent research and theorizing may suggest that a larger or smaller number of structural levels is more appropriate for social movement theory. What is essential to my argument is that the notion of social structure needs to be restored to a central place in the analysis of social movements.

In doing so, it is equally important that a return to the concept of structure not lead into the same traps as earlier structural approaches. For too long, the concept of structure has been a reified and deterministic straitjacket that privileged structure over agency and the macrolevel over the microlevel in social analysis. There are now more sophisticated ways of conceptualizing social structures and their significance in human action, but social movement theory has been slow to incorporate these insights. As I indicated in introducing this structural approach, the only workable notion of structure is one that might be (awkwardly) labeled a "historical–dialectical–structurational" concept. The historical component is essential for recognizing that all human activities are temporally rooted between pasts and futures such that prior causes and human intentions shape social action in every present moment. The dialectical component is critical in recognizing the interdependency of the multiple levels of structure, each of which is constituted and mediated by every other level of structure. The structurational component is vital to avoid the tendency toward reification and to underscore the ongoing role of reflexive social agents whose conscious actions and unintended consequences continually sustain and transform the patterns we summarize as "structure."

Although the foregoing brief on behalf of the concept of structure is stated in somewhat abstract terms, my operative notion of structure in this analysis has taken a more historically specific form in which the designation of the United States as an advanced capitalist society has been central. On the global level, this has meant that social activism cannot be understood apart from the structural location and historical trajectory of the United States as a core capitalist nation within a world capitalist system. In speaking of national structures, this has meant that a great many social movements can be understood only as responses to the crisis tendencies, colonization dynamics, and post-Fordist transitions that define advanced capitalism in late modernity. At the level of regional structures, this has meant recognizing the multiplicity and relative autonomy of structures of power based on class, race, and gender, and their historically variable opportunities for collective resistance. And in conceptualizing local structures, this has meant understanding how the microphysics of power in the interstices of everyday life provoke distinctly modern forms of social activism in which the defense of identity becomes a decidedly political act. Although these structures by no means offer a full explanation of contemporary social movements, there are no movements that can be understood apart from them.

Part III

The Political and the Cultural in Collective Action

7

The Political

State Politics and Social Politics

A substantial debate about collective action has recently swirled around an elusive distinction between "the political" and "the cultural," and how social movements exemplify these dimensions in their activism. There are at least three levels on which this discussion is occurring. First, at the level of general social theory, the last two decades have seen dramatic shifts away from the political concerns of much social theory toward more cultural issues. This "culturalist turn" in social theory is evidenced by hermeneutics, poststructuralism, semiotics, deconstructionism, and postmodernism. Second, at the level of social movement theory, the last decade has seen a more gradual shift from the political and organizational concerns of resource mobilization theory toward a more cultural emphasis evidenced by social constructionism and many aspects of new social movement theory. Finally, at the level of social movements themselves, there have been various claims about the extent to which more culturally oriented movements have begun to displace more politically oriented movements. At all three levels, the trajectory has thus been from the political to the cultural.

The structural approach advocated here does not provide any immediate answers to these debates concerning the political and cultural dimensions of social activism, but it does provide some implicit guidance. The complex notion of structure (including historical, dialectical, and processual elements) and the multilevel structural model of society developed earlier imply a theoretically open and synthetic approach to the political and cultural elements of social activism. Rather than a dichotomous categorization of movements as either one or the other, this structural approach recognizes the extent to which all social movements contain both political and cultural elements. Thus, all movements (if indeed they are movements to begin with) contain oppositional elements that warrant the label "political," even though their targets may range from specific state agencies to abstract dominant ideologies. Rather than denying the political status of certain movements, it would seem more promising to explore the range of political targets such movements oppose. In a similar fashion, all movements (by virtue of being forms of social action in general) involve symbolic dimensions that are best designated as "cultural," even though the specific cultural aspects of a given movement may be peripheral to its goals or may provide its fundamental *raison d'être*. Rather than denying the cultural dimensions of so-called "political" movements, it would seem more promising to once again examine the range of cultural expressions and to explore the diverse ways that the cultural and the political are intertwined in contemporary social activism (Polletta, 1997).

The claim that all social movements contain significant political and cultural elements may be illustrated in a variety of ways. One of the best examples is provided by studies of traditional working-class movements that are often taken to be quintessential "political" movements. In reality, the most profound studies of such movements have focused precisely on the cultural underpinnings of such supposedly political movements, as exemplified by the work of E. P. Thompson (1963) in Great Britain and Herbert Gutman (1976) in the United States. A second example is provided by studies of leftist movements in the United States that have once again identified a pervasive intermingling of political and cultural elements in such movements reaching back into the nineteenth century (Zaretsky, 1976; Flacks, 1988). A final example may be found in the theoretical and empirical work of Alberto Melucci (1996a, 1989). Although he has been explicitly critical of theories that reduce movements to narrowly political goals and is widely regarded as a theorist of "culturalist" new social movements, Melucci is insistent that even supposedly "cultural" movements contain oppositional elements that challenge power in the social systems in which they operate. What these examples illustrate is that the terms "political" and "cultural" are best invoked not to support false dichotomies but rather to analytically isolate selected aspects of social activism that always rest on a combination of political and cultural elements.

This chapter and Chapter 8 use these terms in precisely this sense. My goal here is to address the political dimensions of social movements by focusing on the different kinds of power that movements challenge. My goal in Chapter 8 is to explore some central cultural processes that undergird social activism. At all times, this distinction will be used as an analytical construction for talking about dimensions of social movements, rather than as a dichotomy or typology that would deny either the political or cultural aspects of all social movements.

SOCIAL MOVEMENTS AND STATE POLITICS

Much confusion about the political dimension of social movements may be traced to inconsistent definitions of the term "political" and the underlying conceptions of power implied by such definitions. As an initial sorting device, we may distinguish between at least two senses of "the political." The term "state politics" will be used to refer to the more conventional type of power struggle in which social activism is directed toward influencing state policy and leaders, including broad revolutionary challenges to the political order. In this conception, power is centralized and hierarchical, although it can be challenged under the right circumstances by sustained opposition. The term "social politics" will be used to refer to a less conventional type of power struggle in which collective action is directed toward altering power relations inscribed in diverse social institutions and cultural practices, including the seemingly "personal" aspects of everyday life. In this conception, power is diffuse and decentralized, and challenges to this form of power take a wider variety of tactical, strategic, and expressive forms. Both types of politics contain a mixture of oppositional and transformative elements that qualify them as "political." Although social politics are more likely to be designated as "cultural" and sometimes opposed to "political," it would be more productive to recognize the cultural dimensions of state politics as well as the political aspects of social politics.

For somewhat different reasons, social movement theory is underdeveloped with reference to both meanings of the political, and this is a logical if unfortunate result of historical trends in social theory. Social movements were not granted political status for decades because collective behavior theory defined them as psychological, noninstitutional, or irrational; each of these formulations obscured the political status of social activism. At the same time, prevalent theories of the state left very little theoretical space for social movements as agents of state politics. Pluralist models envisioned an open polity in which any group with grievances could utilize existing channels to express their preferences and pursue their goals; hence there was no need for social movements. Elite models theorized a closed polity in which a small number of institutionally powerful groups competed for control of the polity and power over a mass society of inert individuals; hence, there was little possibility that social movements would arise. Class models presumed a world in which political questions revolved around the conflict between capital and labor in capitalist society; hence, class-based activism was the only acknowledged form of political contestation.

The combined effect of these theoretical assumptions made it difficult to conceptualize social movements as state-centered political actors. The absence of social movements in prevailing theories of the state dovetailed with the denial of the political nature of collective behavior to keep the state and social movements in conceptually separate universes. This was an ironic outcome given the intertwined histories of states and social movements. In Chapter 1, I noted the family resemblance between sociology and social movements as twin offspring of modernity. The third sibling in this family is the modern nation-state, which played a dual role as both promoter and product of the rise of modernity. Alongside the emergence of a capitalist marketplace, the consolidation of nation-states and an international state system was one of the fundamental processes in the emergence of modern society. As modern states developed, they expanded their power, increased their control, and extended their reach into all levels of society. Given the nation-state's growing intervention in social life, it was only natural that it would become a logical target of social activism and that the repertoire of collective action would increasingly include state-centered strategies and tactics (Tarrow, 1994; Tilly, 1995). By the end of the nineteenth century, the role of the state had become so central that it virtually usurped the meaning of "the political." But throughout much of the twentieth century, analytical work on states and social movements remained divorced.

It was one of the great contributions of resource mobilization theory to reestablish the political nature of social movement activism, but the full implications of this contribution for theories of the state and social movements have yet to be realized (Zald, 1992). Indeed, as recently as 1995, specialists in this area claimed that "surprisingly little attention has been paid to the interaction between social movements and the state" (Jenkins and Klandermans, 1995:3) and that "studies of social movements frequently ignore the state" (Pickvance, 1995:127). The work that has been done occurred in two phases. An earlier wave of work in the resource mobilization tradition in the 1970s and 1980s challenged the conceptual barriers between states and social movements, illustrated the political nature of collective action, and critiqued theories of state power that ignored social movements (McAdam, 1982; Tilly, 1978). A more recent wave of work in the 1990s has solidified these gains by organizing them around the concept of the state as a political opportunity structure. Much of this work has involved identifying different variables or dimensions of political opportunity, often generating typologies of different kinds or levels of states and their relation to collective action (McAdam, 1996; Tarrow, 1996). Other work has taken a more explicitly comparative approach by exploring how different state and opportunity structures are linked to varying social movement processes and outcomes (Kriesi, 1995; Kriesi et al., 1995; Rucht, 1996). Although this work has taken important steps, studies of political opportunity structures remain one-dimensional without a broader examination of the relation between states and social movements.

Among other things, such an analysis requires moving beyond the mesolevel orientation to political opportunity structures evident in most recent work. This, in turn, may require closer attention by U.S. scholars to the various European approaches to social movements. As several European theorists have noted, "In the United States . . . little attention has been paid to the macrodevelopments that are central to the European discussion" (Kriesi et al., 1995:238). Even with the recent rapprochement between U.S. and European work around the concept of political opportunity structures, the mesolevel, U.S. version of the concept has neglected the statist elements to be found in the more macro-oriented analyses of many European theorists (Kriesi et al., 1995: 241). The implication is that we must theorize political opportunity structures as themselves nested within larger sociohistorical structures if we are to make progress on a more systematic theory of the relation between states and social movements. This implication dovetails with the multilevel structural approach advocated in Part II of this book. At the global level, the state is enmeshed in a world capitalist system and an international state system that influence its policies and frequently provide both the grievances and the opportunities that fuel social activism. At the national level, the state is the paramount social institution and the direct target of an increasing proportion of social activism. At the regional level, the state is the ultimate guarantor of structures of power rooted in the dynamics of class, race, and gender, and is thereby a common target of movements opposing these structures. At the local level, the state in advanced capitalism has intervened ever more broadly and deeply in the rhythms of everyday life, once again becoming a target of both defensive and offensive social movements.

Despite the prevalence of the state in social relations at all these levels, social movement theory has yet to move beyond abstract portrayals of the state as a political enemy, a change target, a repressive agent, or an opportunity structure. Thus, one task confronting social movement theory is to develop a more workable conception of the state and the forms of state politics that link collective action to the state. Such work must recognize the historical trajectory of the modern state, build on existing mesolevel work on political opportunity structures, and move toward a more macro-oriented, multilevel structural analysis. Although important groundwork for analyzing state politics has been accumulating over the past two decades, it was precisely in this period that the meaning of the political began to move away from narrow, state-centered conceptions toward more diffuse and decentralized notions. Social movement theory thereby faces a second task that it has barely begun to address: to articulate less reductionistic, non-state-centered notions of the political that theorize different arenas of collective action and explore the theoretical links between social politics and social movement activism.

The challenge of theorizing social politics will be taken up in the second half of this chapter. In the following sections, I address state politics. There are at least three ideas that hold promise for developing a more systematic theory of the state and social movements. These concern the role of the state as an intermediary between advanced capitalism and social movements, the ways in which the state is a profoundly "classed, raced, and gendered institution," and the operation of the state as a series of "reform filters" ensuring that change is rarely implemented against the interests of dominant groups. Each of these ideas may be briefly discussed in turn.

The State as Intermediary

The structural theory outlined in preceding chapters conceptualized modern society as a form of advanced capitalism, giving priority to capital accumulation as the driving force shaping this society as a whole. Given this theoretical commitment, it is only logical to look to neo-Marxist theories of the state as one basis for developing a deeper understanding of the relation between social movements and the state. Neo-Marxist theories of the state concur that it is not a neutral or independent political actor in capitalist societies, but rather is dependent on and constrained by the actions of capitalist classes or the requirements of capitalism as a whole. There are two major variants on this common theme. The instrumentalist version of the theory views the state as a political tool in the hands of the capitalist class and their close allies. This theory emphasizes direct representation and influence by capitalists and their allies in major positions of state power. By virtue of their highly disproportionate representation in such positions, these political actors can directly translate the imperatives of capitalist accumulation into state policy making and governmental action (Miliband, 1969). The implication of this instrumentalist view of the state is that it could conceivably serve the interests of other, noncapitalist groups if they acquire sufficient positions within the state or mount sufficient pressure on those in such positions to redirect decision making and policy formulation.

The structuralist variant of neo-Marxist state theory places less emphasis on direct occupancy of positions of state power and more emphasis on the relation of the state to capitalist society as a whole. In contrast to the instrumentalist view of direct domination of the state by representatives of the capitalist class, the structuralist view argues that the state actually possesses a significant degree of "relative autonomy" from the direct domination of any particular group of capitalists. It is precisely this relative autonomy that allows the state to formulate and defend the long-term interests of the capitalist mode of production as a whole, as opposed to the short-term interests of whatever particular group of capitalists might happen to dominate the state at a given moment. Hence, in paradoxical fashion, the relative autonomy of the state from any one capitalist faction allows it to serve the broader goal of overall capitalist accumulation even more effectively. By virtue of this relative autonomy, the state is able to organize the capitalist class as a whole while simultaneously disorganizing the working class via electoral and representative procedures that imply an atomized and individualized society rather than a class-divided one. The ultimate guarantor of the state's fealty to capitalist interests resides not in the latter's direct control of the state but in the economic leverage that capitalists can exercise over the state. Since the state is dependent on the health of the capitalist economy for its revenue base, the mere threat of a "capital strike" that would undermine state revenue is usually sufficient to keep state policy in line with capitalist interests. The relative autonomy of the state also serves an ideological function, making it appear that the state is not as (directly) controlled by capitalist imperatives as it (indirectly) really is (Poulantzas, 1978). The implication of this structuralist view of the state is that it can really serve only capitalist interests, and that any attempt to reorient state policy in some other direction will simply precipitate a capitalist-induced political crisis that will reorient that policy in line with capitalist interests.

This is not the place to reproduce the somewhat tortuous path of the "Miliband–Poulantzas" debate between instrumentalist and structuralist versions of the neo-Marxist theory of the state. But it is appropriate to recognize the gradual emergence of a third position in response to this debate. The central problem with both the instrumentalist and structuralist theories is that, in their own ways, they deny the possibility of any meaningful agency on the part of state managers. In the instrumentalist view, state managers are largely capitalists anyway, and it is their interests as capitalists that shape their behavior as state managers. In the structuralist view, it does not matter who the state managers are because even though they may be relatively autonomous from direct capitalist domination, the structural relation between capital and the state ensures that they have no meaningful range of choice in their actions anyway. In both views, state managers are puppets of larger economic forces over which they have no meaningful control. Building on this critique, Block (1987) has proposed a revision in neo-Marxist state theory that recognizes the irreducibility of politics to economics and the fact that both classes and economies are themselves constituted by political actors and actions. This view recognizes a meaningful degree of autonomy for state actors that allows them to respond to their own interests and ideologies as state managers (as well as to the clash of other interests and ideologies). Such a view also recognizes the inconsistency and irrationality of capitalist behavior that is obscured in both instrumentalist and structuralist theories that presume an omniscient and omnipotent capitalist power. These modifications in state theory would encourage a more robust vision of politics as involving at least a three-way struggle between capitalists, workers, and state managers in which standoffs between any two groups can enhance the power of the third. At the same time, Block (1987) also recognizes the increasingly important role of nonclass actors rooted in racial, gender, or other sources of identity, interest, and ideology.

Despite these theoretical variations, a similar image of the state's relationship to social movements is implicit in this overall approach. In this image, the state stands as an intermediary between the grievances, ideology, and politics of social movements on the one hand and the imperatives, requisites, and constraints of an advanced capitalist social formation on the other hand. This imagery suggests that "dominant social relationships set the boundaries and determine the possibility and the limits of action in a political system" (Melucci, 1996a:231). These limits constrain the scope of decision making by defining some issues as nonnegotiable because they would challenge dominant social relations. These limits also "reach down" to shape and constrain the internal mechanisms of decision making within the state and the kinds of decisions that are possible within this structure. To capture this dual process, Melucci resorts to a somewhat more limited version of the classical Gramscian conception: "Hegemony . . . denotes the degree of dependence of the system on dominant social relations, and the way in which the dominant interests are expressed in normative decisions through the action of the political forces that represent them" (Melucci, 1996a:233). As an intermediary between dominant groups and social movement challengers, the state thereby poses formidable obstacles to those seeking to alter such relations of dominance.

While underscoring these obstacles, the differing versions of state theory provide a rich set of hypotheses about the relations between social movements and the state. The instrumentalist view implies that one strategy for achieving social movement objectives is the attainment of positions of state power by individuals and groups who share the goals of a movement (or at least will not be actively opposed to them). A secondary strategy would be to play off the conflicting efforts of various groups to attain state power and to seek the realization of some movement objectives in the context of schisms, factions, and divisions between these groups. The structuralist view implies that the only feasible strategy may be to align movement goals with capitalist interests so as to gain a hearing in a state inevitably dominated by the long-term interests of the capitalist mode of production as a whole. A secondary strategy would be to take advantage of moments of crisis and political uncertainty to push movement objectives while realizing that an eventual return to stability is likely to jeopardize any such gains. The state-centered alternative proposed by Block (1987) implies a broader range of strategies that play on the interests of state managers as apart from or as opposed to capitalist interests. A secondary strategy would be to seek coalitions and alliances with the broader range of political actors implicitly acknowledged in this perspective so as to achieve greater political leverage to achieve movement goals. Although these comments are merely illustrative, they suggest the value of a closer examination of the links between movement strategy and differing conceptions of the state as crucial steps in the development of a theory of state politics.

This is a promising beginning step for unpacking the relation between social movements and the state if it can avoid the twin conceptual traps of far too many Marxist theories of the state. First, there has been a tendency to reify the capitalist imperative of accumulation, leading to an unwarranted functionalist and teleological image of social change. Second, there has been a parallel tendency to presume almost unlimited knowledge and power on the part of capitalist actors. Following the critical comments of Block (1987), it is crucial to recognize that in an era of global capitalism and rapid social change, the most effective ways to advance the imperatives of advanced capitalism are not necessarily clear to any particular set of social actors, including capitalists and their immediate allies. In addition to this uncertainty, the complexity of global capitalism makes it likely that fostering accumulation will require contradictory strategies when implemented over time, across economic levels, or among capitalist factions. This implies the need for a more fluid view of political contestation in advanced capitalism that does not deny the institutional power of dominant economic groups but also recognizes the very real limits on their knowledge of and ability to define and act on their interests. Such recognition underscores the potential for social movements to intervene in complex political relations in ways that produce favorable outcomes for them. Conceptualizing the state as an intermediary between social movements and advanced capitalism in this fashion promises to bring the state into social movement theory in a nonreductionist and nondeterminist fashion that acknowledges how state action can both constrain and facilitate the course of social activism.

The State: Classed, Raced, and Gendered

These neo-Marxist theories offer some promising ways to conceptualize state politics, particularly at the global and national levels of social structure. But even the best neo-Marxist theories of the state retain a lingering and unwarranted essentialism that accords a privileged status to working-class activism and a secondary status to other social constituencies. These limitations become evident on the regional level of social structure, where neo-Marxist theories of the state are helpful with regard to (working-)class-based movements but unhelpful for understanding the relation between the state and movements based on race or gender. It is here that theories of racial domination and gender inequality provide a richer account of the posture of the state in relation to race and gender movements. Given the abstract parallels across all three structures of power, it is not surprising that similar ideas have emerged concerning the role of the state. These ideas are most often expressed in the claim that the state in modern society is a "classed, raced, and gendered" institution that structurally embeds the interests of dominant groups into the very functioning of state institutions.

The "classed" nature of the state is captured by the neo-Marxist theories already discussed. The upshot of these theories is that in a capitalist society, the state is structurally predisposed to act in the interests of capitalists as a class, and thereby to act against the interests of any classes (or other constituencies) that challenge those interests. Whereas instrumentalist and structuralist theories describe the general orientation of the state toward capitalist interests, the notion of a "classed" state takes these arguments further by claiming that the very structure and organization of the state reflect the interests of dominant classes and deflect those of subordinate classes. Hence, the "classed" nature of the state may be seen in the relative power and funding of different state agencies, the ways in which representatives respond to the interests of various constituencies, the methods by which political rhetoric promotes capitalist ideology, the role of money in electoral politics, the impact of procapitalist think-tanks in the policy formation process, the political subtext of the federal budget, and the like. In all these ways, the state is structurally predisposed to favor the interests and the ideology of dominant classes over subordinate ones. This view of the state as a "classed" institution does not mean that dominant classes always prevail in state politics, and there have been important historical moments when subordinate classes have made significant inroads into the formulation of state policy—typically as a result of sustained, class-based social activism. But this view of the state as "classed" does mean that it never provides a neutral arena or a level playing field for class conflict. A "classed" state is one in which the long-term interests of the capitalist class are structurally embedded in the state, such that extraordinary circumstances are required for the state to act against the interests of this class.

The state is not only "classed," it is also "raced." This follows from the theory of racial formation that sees race not as a biologically fixed category but rather as a sociohistorical concept whose meaning and importance are socially constructed and reconstructed through the clash of various social, economic, and political forces (Omi and Winant, 1986). Through the process of racialization, racial meanings are superimposed on social relations such that race becomes a basic organizing principle at both the individual level of identity and

the collective level of structure. The primary actors in racial formation are social movements and the state; their drama consists of a dialectical interplay of
conflict and accommodation. The state has always been organized around the
politics of race, and the prevailing racial policy has been one of repression and
exclusion that can be traced back to the Naturalization Law of 1790 (Omi and
Winant, 1986:75). From that time forward, the state has formulated various
laws and policies that categorize groups of people into a hierarchical and racial-
ized social order. These practices have established the state as the main agent
of racialization throughout U.S. history. This process goes deeper than a state
that merely intervenes in racial matters: "in contrast to this, we suggest that
the state is inherently racial. Far from *intervening* in racial conflicts, the state
is itself increasingly the preeminent site of racial conflict" (Omi and Winant,
1986:76, italics in original).

The inherently racial nature of the state is evidenced in all its constituent
elements. At the level of institutions, every state institution is also a "raced"
institution, although different institutions will have differing degrees of involvement in racial politics and they will sometimes work at cross-purposes from
each other. At the level of policies, the state organizes the racial politics of
everyday life through passage, administration, and enforcement of statutes and
laws concerning discrimination, housing, education, families, crime, and the
like. At the level of conditions, the establishment of rules of the game, normal
procedures, and agency mandates are infused with a racial politics rooted in the
diverse interests of competing and conflicting racially defined constituencies.
At the level of social relations, state actions link this institution to myriad other
institutions, agencies, and interest groups as well as broader social relations that
extend throughout the society. At the level of strategies, policies such as absorption (partial acceptance of radical demands in moderate form) and insulation (confining demands to domains not crucial to the prevailing racial order)
are typically used by the racial state to rebuff the challenges of racial movements (Omi and Winant, 1986). And finally, at the level of ideology, the public discourse surrounding issues such as crime, welfare, and immigration is carried on through a racially coded subtext that is central to shaping domestic
policy as a whole.

The state is also "gendered." The sex/gender system is a fundamental social institution for organizing relations between dominant and subordinate genders. As such, it is only logical that these hierarchical power relations also per-
meate the state. Where some see this as evidence of a "patriarchal state" and
privilege male domination as the defining characteristic of the state, it is more
plausible to conceptualize the state as reflecting the interests and pressures of
multiple systems of power (Eisenstein, 1984). The "gendered" state thus shares
a number of characteristics with the "classed" and "raced" state. Every state
institution is also a gendered institution, with some having more direct implications for gender relations than others. Many state policies and statutes reinforce the gender politics of everyday life and the gendered character of social
structure. There are also gendered conditions and rules that shape the daily
practices, normal procedures, and working culture of both state and nonstate

institutions. State actions and inactions thereby bring legal sanction to formally and informally gendered practices across many social institutions. Finally, at the level of strategies and tactics, the state's attempts at absorption or insulation in the case of racial politics have strikingly similar parallels in the case of gender politics. In both, the long history of such strategies is indirect testimony to the equally long history of racial and gender challenges to the raced and gendered state that comprise state politics.

There are thus numerous parallels in how structures of power based on class, race, and gender become inscribed in the structure and operation of the state in advanced capitalism. The specifically gendered nature of the state is most evident in ideologies and practices that implicitly or explicitly deny the reality of the sex/gender system of power. For example, the ideology of the liberal democratic state presents governmental authority as a neutral and disinterested umpire regulating civil society—implicitly denying the institutionalized character of gender-based domination. The same ideology conceptualizes a polity consisting of abstract, independent citizens with formal rights and liberties—implicitly ignoring the socioemotional and gendered subtext of everyday social relations. And most significantly, the ideology of the liberal democratic state reinforces the "ideology of the family and personal life as private locations, thus naturalizing the family as a sphere of social life where power does not normally impinge" (Bush, 1992). When these ideological notions are embedded into laws and policies, the gendered nature of the state becomes readily evident. Thus, the social welfare system has an "unmistakable gender subtext" in its background assumptions that families should consist of a male breadwinner and female homemaker, and that society is divided into two separate and gendered spheres (Fraser, 1989:149). The inscription of gender politics into state policy is evident throughout the life cycle, from state policies and interventions concerning teenage pregnancy and child-bearing to the organization of a social security system that ties retirement benefits to work history and female homemakers to male breadwinners. In these and many other ways, the gendered nature of the state is a telling example of the power and pervasiveness of the sex/gender system across a range of social institutions.

These analyses undermine the ideological notion of the state as a neutral umpire as well as the reductionistic view of the state as the captive of a single group. Between these two extremes is the more persuasive imagery of the state as having only a relative autonomy from multiple structures of power rooted in class exploitation, racial oppression, and gender inequality. To say that the state is "classed, raced, and gendered" means that the state is systematically predisposed to act favorably on the interests of dominant groups and unfavorably on the interests of subordinate groups. These biases are inscribed in formal structures, policies, and laws as well as informal relations, practices, and mentalities. But precisely because the state is complex and multifaceted, there are always opportunities for social movements to exercise some influence over the state through the practice of state politics. As this happens, struggles that once occurred outside the state may move inside the state, particularly if social movements can exercise significant influence over particular state agencies or representatives. In such situations, the question becomes whether movements can fight through a generally inhospitable state structure to realize their objectives.

The State as a Reform Filter

It is here that it becomes helpful to conceptualize the state as a series of "reform filters" that stand between social movements and their goals. This formulation recognizes that movements sometimes do persist over time, exert some influence, and see their objectives reflected in changes in state policy. But this formulation also recognizes that states grant reforms only as a last resort, and even then in as restricted a form as possible (Melucci, 1996a: 265). On such occasions, "a political system filters demands and selects those of them that can be dealt with through the decision-making process" (Melucci, 1996a:235). When movement demands are not deflected altogether, state structures thereby reshape movement goals by filtering out those elements that pose the most fundamental challenges to powerful constituents and by coopting those elements that can be made consistent with prevailing interests [for an early statement of a similar idea, see Blumer (1971); for a contemporary formulation see Melucci (1996a: Chapter 12)].

The "reform filter" does not involve any single agency, decision, or procedure; it is rather a metaphor for a multilevel process unfolding over time in which radical demands enter the decision-making process only to emerge as pale reflections of their original form. Sometimes this occurs for purely functional reasons that require the translation of movement demands into the systemic logic of "problems and solutions." Other times, this occurs for more conflictual reasons when movement demands challenge dominant interests; indeed, "the more direct the impact of a decision on dominant interests, the narrower the range of choices" (Melucci, 1996a:239). In such cases, measures are likely to pass only as pale reflections of initially radical demands that have been altered fundamentally so as to be in alignment with some dominant interest. The filtering effect may occur at many different points in the formulation of state policy. Sometimes it is evident in formulating agendas themselves. Sometimes it is evident in the initial phrasing of legislative initiatives in order to secure enough votes for passage. Sometimes it occurs later in negotiations over stalled legislation. Sometimes laws or policies may be enacted that are quite consistent with movement goals, only to have their impact filtered out due to a lack of funding or enforcement. At all these levels, "codes and laws establish the boundaries beyond which negotiation is no longer possible because the structure of domination would be attacked in its vital bases" (Melucci, 1996a: 247).

The metaphor of the state as a reform filter brings greater specificity to earlier arguments about the relation between social movements and the state. For instance, one way that the state serves as a buffer between advanced capitalism and social movements is to filter out anticapitalist movement initiatives, promote procapitalist alternatives, and transform the former into the latter wherever possible. The role of the state in translating "antigrowth" environmental demands advanced by social movements into new opportunities for commercial ventures by "proenvironment," profit-seeking corporations provides one example of this process. Corporate cooptation of regulatory agencies and progressive legislation is another example. The metaphor of a reform filter is also helpful in illustrating the "classed, raced, and gendered" nature of the state. As a logical consequence of how these structures of power operate, dominant groups have built-in advantages in state arenas by virtue of filtering mechanisms that rebuff fundamental challenges through a variety of methods. Thus, when social movement demands are posed in collective terms, the liberal and individualist discourse of state policy making and legislation often responds by framing these demands as individual rights (which can be posed as contradictory to other rights) or reframing them as "special treatment" (which can then be rejected altogether). The imagery of the state as a reform filter captures the process whereby seemingly "successful" movement initiatives can be turned back against the underlying interests of those very same movements.

One example is domestic violence. The long-standing policy vacuum surrounding domestic violence reflects a gendered subtext about the family, private life, and the inappropriateness of state power in this seemingly private realm. The feminist movement has challenged this subtext with calls for more activist state intervention in this problem. When such demands are not dismissed altogether, the "success" that feminist movements have achieved has been tempered by the absorption and bureaucratization of their goals by a state structure that filters out their underlying feminist aspirations. Because the liberal ideology of the state does not recognize the gendered power relations of the family or the private sphere, feminist demands are typically redefined in terms of criminal justice or mental health. These responses criminalize, individualize, medicalize, or psychologize the problem, but none of these recastings acknowledges the broader sex/gender system that stands behind the problem of battered women. Thus, the complex machinery of the state (including legislatures, courts, law enforcement, corrections, and social service) is predisposed to respond to this problem on the state's terms rather than on the movement's terms; that is, the state acts as a reform filter that translates movement initiatives into absorbable and cooptable reforms. In such cases, narrowly defined movement successes may end up reinforcing broader ideologies that stand behind the initial problem, including another gender subtext of female vulnerability and the need for protectionist policies in a supposedly private sphere that is otherwise off limits to state power (Bush, 1992).

The metaphor of the state as a reform filter underscores the degree of entrenched power that is condensed in the structure of the state. It is important, however, not to reify this power into a deterministic model of an omnipotent state. Against this imagery, the following caveats are in order. First, the state is neither monolithic nor omnipotent, so the notion of a reform filter suggests what the state attempts to do in conflict with other forces rather than what the state can automatically accomplish. Second, there are limits on state power because it is the condensation of potentially conflicting interests between various dominant groups from which it has only a relative autonomy. Third, and closely related, some social movement initiatives may have contradictory effects on the various vested interests represented by state power. Fourth, none of the actors involved in reform struggles is omniscient; every initiative for change and every response involves unintended and unanticipated consequences. And fifth, social movement activists are reflexively aware of the fact that the state operates as a reform filter, and this understanding is typically the baseline assumption for planning movement strategies, including a "Trojan horse" tactic of offering seemingly mild reform that contains the potential for more fundamental change in its course. As powerful as the state may be, all of these counteracting forces may limit its ability to succeed as a reform filter defending dominant interests.

The rudiments of a theory of state politics and social movements may thus be found in these three core ideas. First, the state may be conceptualized as a buffer between the goals of all social movements and the imperatives of advanced capitalism. Second, the state may be analyzed as a "classed, raced, and gendered" institution that has only a relative autonomy from the interests of multiple dominant groups. Third, the state may be seen as a series of reform filters that seek to minimize the impact of any movement initiatives that do get translated into state policy. These interrelated ideas suggest that the state in advanced capitalism is structurally hostile but strategically vulnerable to social movement initiatives; they imply that social movement success is possible, but also that it will involve an uphill battle if movements that engage in state politics are to have any lasting impact on the direction of society. By building on these and related notions, it should be possible to address one of the tasks of social movement theory: to consolidate recent work on these issues in the form of a more systematic theory of the relation between social movements and the state.

SOCIAL POLITICS AND COLLECTIVE ACTION

The second task confronting social movement theory is to explore collective action in less centralized arenas by developing a theory of the relation between social movements and "social politics," i.e., forms of collective action that challenge power relations without an explicit focus on the state. Because social politics have received even less attention, it is a major challenge for social movement theory to develop conceptual tools that are as robust for this realm of collective action as those already being developed for state politics. My goal here is a modest one of suggesting some promising directions for such theoretical development. In doing so, we will revisit some of the issues and theorists that were central to analyzing the local level of sociohistorical structure in Chapter 6. In that chapter, my purpose was to establish the importance of the local level as one among several nested levels of sociohistorical structure that provoke resistance; in this section, my purpose is to clarify the distinctive features of social politics in contrast to state politics and to assess their implications for social movement theory.

Social Politics: Confronting Diffuse and Omnipresent Power

Social politics consist of a wide range of resistances to forms of power that are diverse and polyvalent. Whereas state politics challenges power rooted in centralized political institutions, the power challenged by social politics is diffuse and decentralized. This power saturates the fabric of everyday life, but it has no single, central, massive source or manifestation. Because social movement theory lacks a coherent conception of social politics and the decentralized power it challenges, its ability to analyze movements that resist such power is severely handicapped. As one result, such movements are frequently tagged with a bewildering array of descriptions such as prepolitical, apolitical, metapolitical, or cultural (in contrast to political). The only common denominator across these designations is that they rely on a narrow conception of power that is more suited to state politics, and hence obscure the genuinely political dimension of such movement challenges. An adequate theory of social power would recognize a much broader range of social action as involving a "political" dimension, and it would thereby expand the universe of phenomena that need to be included in a workable theory of social activism.

As we have seen previously, the notion of a microphysics of power (Foucault, 1979) is one provocative if flawed means of conceptualizing the power resisted by social politics. This concept refers to a type of power that flows through the capillaries of the social body and takes up residence in all the interstices of social life. Such a view displaces the image of a massive and centralized power that is a source of repression with a view of power as a decentralized set of relations that produces power effects, including the subjection of individuals. An important consequence of this view of an omnipresent but impersonal and decentralized power is that no action is really "apolitical" (in the broad sense of the term) because social actors are always enmeshed in networks of power that are "already there" and cannot be avoided. In the face of such unavoidable power dynamics, the anxious search for a genuinely "political" response to power that characterizes some proponents of the narrow conception of power and state politics is rendered irrelevant. In a Foucauldian world, every social relation is both a site for the circulation of capillary power and a locus of resistance to that power. Hence, resistance, like power, is omnipresent. Foucault's theory resolves one problem because every social relation is unavoidably political in the broad sense of the term, and hence there are no apolitical, prepolitical, or metapolitical actions.

The flaw in this approach is not in the conception of power but in the conception of resistance, because Foucault's poststructuralist antagonism to humanism almost precludes any notion of agency, i.e., of conscious, rational, subjects acting collectively on their own interests. This is precisely the issue addressed by structuration theory. Just as Foucault has challenged the notion of power as centralized and hierarchical, Giddens (1984) has questioned the concept of structure as external and constraining. His theory of structuration offers an alternative means of capturing a process by which social actors reflexively use elements of "social structure" to pursue their goals while unintentionally reproducing as well as transforming those very same structural elements. In contrast to Foucault, however, Giddens operates with a more conventional theory of the acting subject as a reflexive agent rather than a decentered product of the effects of knowledge and power. His conception thereby opens the door to more traditional social movement variables such as consciousness, ideology, and reflexive awareness that play a role in the emergence of collective action. Such variables have a clear role to play in state politics; at issue is whether Giddens's approach can serve as a bridge between Foucault's concept of a microphysics of power and social politics.

This bridge seems implicit in the concept of life politics, which incorporates political issues deriving from identity, the body, sexuality, and related processes of reflexive self-actualization in late modernity (Giddens, 1991) When described in terms of "self-actualization" or "life-style," it seems at first glance that life politics involves an individualist response to power dynamics in advanced societies. Although this is often the case, processes of self-actualization or identity transformation cannot easily be separated from larger, more collective, and overtly political forms of resistance. Many movements operate at both levels. But even in the case of seemingly individual resistance, the nature of the social power challenged by such resistance renders it both social and political (Taylor and Raeburn, 1995). For instance, when individuals reject socially imposed identities that limit their opportunities by constructing different identities, it is a political act that undermines the privileged status of the imposed identity, establishes the viability of an alternative identity, and challenges the social power behind the imposed identity. Such identity transformation does not occur in a vacuum. There typically is a small group, a subculture, or a network of like individuals who reinforce each other's attempts to transform identities and challenge dominant conceptions. Although such groups may not conform to conventional concepts of social movement organizations, they are nonetheless critical in undergirding what appear on the surface to be individual and isolated acts of resistance to social power. Life politics also transcends the individual level by its recognition of the links between the fate of the individual and the survival of the species. The diffuse and decentralized nature of social power is mirrored at the planetary level where ecological threats to human survival come not from any single, centralized source but from a complex web of interrelationships whose dangers are manifested in diverse ways, times, and places. In all these ways, the seemingly individualist orientation of social politics has deep social roots and extensive social effects.

Social Politics in Social Movements

Concepts such as the microphysics of power and life politics offer intriguing insights into social politics and the political character of action in the social world. But they have yet to find their way into the mainstream of social movement theory. In the latter arena, however, there has been a related debate about the political status of certain types of social activism that invokes a dubious distinction between "political" and "cultural" movements. The distinction carries the unfortunate implication that "cultural" movements lack political effects. My conception of social politics challenges this false dichotomy by broadening the notion of what is political and underscoring the political dimensions of what are often perceived as "merely" cultural movements. Support for this argument may be found in the writings of Alberto Melucci on the nature of collective action. This work has taken a critical stance toward conceptions of social movements that rest on essentialist or teleological elements; Melucci rejects approaches that treat social movements as theoretical givens, unitary objects, metaphysical essences, or historical personages (Melucci, 1988b). The obvious target of these criticisms is the orthodox Marxist imagery of a revolutionary proletariat with an historical destiny to fulfill—as well as any lingering traces of this imagery in more recent formulations of social movements. But this antiessentialist argument is also a recognition of more fluid, situational, or transient forms of social movement resistance and a challenge to the tendency (in European social theory) to equate social movements with a narrow conception of state politics.

These positions have led Melucci's approach to be categorized as "culturalist," with the implication that he eschews any substantive notion of the political. It is far more accurate to see his work as synthesizing the cultural and political, i.e., he has demonstrated the centrality of cultural processes to the conduct of social politics in general and life politics in particular. The political dimensions of his approach are evident in several central assumptions. His working definition of social movements identifies them as purposeful orientations within a field of opportunities and constraints (Melucci, 1989), echoing Giddens' (1984) dual emphasis on reflexive actors who find social structure both enabling and constraining. The core of Melucci's (1989) definition characterizes social movements as involving solidarity, conflict, and actions that break the limits of compatibility of a system. With this working definition, it is difficult to deny the political dimension of social movements in Melucci's work despite his reputation as a "culturalist" in social movement theory. The attributes of solidarity and conflict link his theory directly to conventional notions of political action and struggle between competing groups. The notion that movements challenge the limits of compatibility of a system is more opaque, but would seem to imply that movements pose potentially fundamental threats to the prevailing social order. It is difficult to see how this is not a "political" conception of what a social movement is and what it does in the world.

It could be argued that the subsequent direction of Melucci's research leads away from this political definition of social movements and into a supposedly culturalist realm. But this argument is difficult to sustain for several reasons. First, he frequently describes contemporary social activism as a response to new forms of social control that have emerged in societies increasingly based on symbolic codes and the production of information. Resistance to social control is a political act that challenges prevailing relations of power as well as the groups that establish and benefit from those forms of social control. The fact that such resistance may take a "cultural" form tells us as much about the new forms of social control as it does about the movements resisting them. A second link between the "cultural" and "political" is in descriptions of social activism as symbolic challenges that produce systemic effects by rendering power visible. Without such challenges, power can remain hidden behind the anonymity of administrative logic and procedures. Movements play a political role by unmasking power and revealing the beneficiaries who stand behind the bureaucratic facade of modern authority structures. A related point is that even social activism that takes a primarily expressive form nevertheless poses a challenge to the instrumental rationality of systemic functioning. Such activism reverses dominant codes and definitions of means, ends, roles, values, and identities. In so doing, it invites discussion on ultimate ends that are usually precluded by the one-dimensional focus of instrumental rationality; this is also a fundamentally political act. Finally, Melucci has suggested that collective action is becoming an autonomous subsystem in modern society that is increasingly separate from the conventional political system. He sees new social movements as creating a third space between the state and civil society; it is this intermediate public space that is the province of movements that engage in what I have called social politics. In all these ways, there is a decidedly political cast not just to Melucci's definition of a social movement but also to the central concepts that guide his analysis of social activism in the modern world. Taken as a whole, his work illuminates the political impetus of social movements that engage in social politics, and it thereby challenges untenable dichotomies between the political and the cultural.

Conceptual Resolutions; New Issues

Recent developments in both general social theory and social movement theory jointly suggest the viability of the concept of social politics. First, the notion of a microphysics of power (Foucault, 1979) provides a foundation for a meaningful alternative to centralized and hierarchical notions of power. Second, the concept of life politics (Giddens, 1991) illuminates one way that social actors confront and challenge such decentralized and omnipresent forms of social power. Third, Melucci's approach to social movements provides conceptual bridges for transporting these general theoretical notions into the core of social movement theory. In so doing, Melucci captures the simultaneity and intermingling of "political" and "cultural" elements that characterizes so much contemporary protest. This theory of social politics offers a resolution to debates over what is truly political by providing a robust and inclusive notion of the political that embraces virtually any form of resistance to dominant societal practices as a genuinely "political" response. This solution dispenses with the artificial distinctions between "political" and "cultural" movements and the strained attempts to define some forms of activism as "prepolitical," "apolitical," or "metapolitical." This solution also promises to enrich our understanding of the forms of social activism by contrasting movements engaged in state politics and social politics and by using the contrast to reexamine our conventional wisdom about social movements.

Some well-worn truisms about success, cooptation, institutionalization, and strategy will require rethinking in the context of these contrasts. As difficult as the measurement of success or failure is in the case of traditional social movements, it becomes even more difficult in the case of movements engaged in social politics because there is no centralized, hierarchical form of power to displace or at least influence. It follows that the strategy of cooptation by centralized authorities no longer makes as much sense in the context of social politics. The same might be said for the process of institutionalization that is often regarded as something of a death knell for conventional social movements. When confronting centralized power, institutionalization usually means becoming subordinate to that power. When challenging the microphysics of power associated with social politics, institutionalization implies that forms of resistance and challenge become interwoven with the fabric of this power itself, suggesting a much greater degree of success than is usually associated with the outcome of institutionalization in conventional social movement challenges. A final example is provided by the role of strategy in conventional social movements, which is typically regarded as linking broad goals and specific tactics through a kind of instrumental rationality. Like so many other social movement concepts, this presumes a specific and concrete target of change efforts that is foreign to the logic of social politics. Indeed, at the most fundamental level, social politics would reject the instrumental logic of strategic action as itself part of the problem that such movements seek to transcend more than directly challenge. What these examples suggest is that the theory of social politics renders irrelevant much of the militaristic imagery of conventional social movements and requires a new imagery (and corresponding concepts) to understand this activism. As we begin to develop this imagery, it should become possible to explore an additional range of hypotheses about the circumstances under which movements are likely to adopt state politics or social politics as their modus operandi, how complex movements may include both approaches, and when different approaches have complementary or contradictory effects on a movement's course.

Pursuit of these questions would also encourage a rethinking of the category of social movement itself. Not surprisingly, this is the same issue that emerged from the earlier analysis of social activism on the local level of sociohistorical structure. In the terms of the present chapter, social politics can include action that does not conform to traditional definitions of a social movement. When social politics involves highly individualized life projects or identity claims, these can arguably be called political, but they are not necessarily social movements. A related problem is how to categorize the quiet resistances of everyday life (Flacks, 1988) that are part of social politics but do not in themselves qualify as social movements. As we have seen, Melucci's definition of a social movement (solidarity, conflict, and actions challenging systemic power) encompasses many aspects of social politics, but it also implies that individual resistance without solidarity is not a social movement. The concept of social politics thereby substitutes one conceptual problem (what is a social movement?) for another (what is political?). But there is progress in this substitution. Too much social movement theory has presumed a dichotomy between apolitical individuals and politicized movements. The concept of social politics recognizes an increasingly common middle category of individuals who engage in the quiet resistances of everyday life or the identity projects of life politics without necessarily becoming active in conventional social movements. Recognizing this middle category is crucial if we hope to do justice to the variegated forms of social politics and their complex relationship to social movements in contemporary society.

These abstract reflections find a concrete example in a recent study of the postpartum depression self-help movement that illustrates social politics and how they can stimulate fresh thinking on the nature of social movement activism (Taylor, 1996). The postpartum movement is one of a larger set of self-help movements that are often dismissed as too apolitical and individualistic to merit attention as social movements. Taylor confronts these arguments directly, tracing the historical roots of many self-help groups through the women's health movement and directly to the feminist politics of the 1970s with its emphasis on small groups, consciousness raising, and confronting internalized oppression. The postpartum movement has certainly challenged institutional forces such as the medical establishment and the scientific community that have made it difficult to gain recognition of maternal depression as a legitimate illness. But the movement has been primarily oriented to individual women whose life experiences of pregnancy, childbirth, and childrearing have not conformed to the cultural script of joyous motherhood. As a result of both deviance and resistance, the universality of this script has been challenged, other possibilities have been recognized, and the social power behind conventional notions of femininity and motherhood has been undermined. Although most women who became involved in this issue may not have seen themselves primarily as social movement participants, their experiences and their quest for well-being typify the identity transformations of life politics and the broader notion of social politics. They also provide a powerful illustration of the permeable boundaries between social politics and social movements, and the role of collective identity in transforming the former into the latter. Beyond an examination of a single movement, this study speaks eloquently to the need for a concept of social politics and the value of exploring the connections between social politics and social movements.

This discussion of the political in social movements began with the premise that all movements have political dimensions and that any attempt to distinguish between "political" and "cultural" movements is a conceptual error that invokes a false dichotomy. However, different movements engage in different political struggles, so recognizing the political in all movements also means acknowledging the multiple political forms that movements can assume. Despite the plausibility of the claim that all movements are political, this was not recognized in social movement theory until the resource mobilization approach undermined the collective behavior tradition and its propensity to approach its subject matter as noninstitutional, psychological, or irrational responses to social strains. Whereas resource mobilization theory has been helpful in analyzing group conflict, social movement theory remains ill-equipped to understand two distinct types of politics in which social movements engage. State politics remain undertheorized because until recently, the role of the state has escaped systematic attention in social movement theory. However, the rudiments of a theory of state politics may be found in recent work on the state as a political opportunity structure, as well as a more structural theory of the state that views it as a buffer between advanced capitalism and civil society, as a "classed, raced, and gendered" institution, and as a series of reform filters. Social politics remains undertheorized because we do not have adequate models of diffuse and decentralized forms of power, but the beginnings of a theory of social politics may be found in the work of Foucault on the microphysics of power, the writings of Giddens on life politics, and the theorizing of Melucci on the political underpinnings of seemingly "cultural" forms of social activism. Developments along both these lines promise to consolidate recent work and guide future study toward a fuller understanding of the political dimension of contemporary forms of social activism.

8

The Cultural

Identity, Ideology, and Organization

In turning from the political to the cultural, it bears repeating that this is not a distinction between different types of movements but rather between qualities possessed by all movements. The cultural dimensions of movements engaged in social politics may be more evident because their goals are intertwined with the symbolic practices of everyday life, but this does not mean that they are somehow "more" cultural than movements engaged in state politics. The latter also have important cultural foundations, although they may be obscured by an instrumentalist orientation to social change. Leftist movements in the United States provide particularly rich examples of the relation between the political and the cultural in collective action. Although most such movements have had avowedly political goals and state-centered strategies, their greatest impact and legacy may have been in the cultural arena (Boggs, 1995; Flacks, 1994, 1988). In the same vein, current calls for a revived left place a strong emphasis on the cultural dimensions of moral values and community building (Derber, 1995) alongside conventional political tactics. This recognition of the cultural aspects of what have historically been seen as political struggles is best read not as a criticism of movement tactics but rather as a recognition of the inescapably cultural foundations of all social action, including the social activism in which movements engage. This is why attempts to dichotomize movements as political or cultural obscure more than they reveal about the role of both aspects in all movements. With these provisos in mind, this chapter shifts the focus from the political to the cultural in social activism.

THE ELUSIVE CULTURAL DIMENSION IN SOCIAL MOVEMENT THEORY

Social movement theory has recently become reoriented to the cultural aspects of social movements. The predecessor of this reorientation is Blumer's (1951) symbolic interactionist version of collective behavior theory as developed by Turner and Killian (1987). As I argued in Chapter 2, Smelser's (1962) functionalist version of collective behavior theory was more problematic in its assumptions about social movements than Blumer's symbolic interactionist approach. The subsequent rejection of the collective behavior tradition did not always distinguish between the two strands of the theory, however; there was a tendency to toss out the symbolic interactionist baby along with the functionalist bath water. This meant that some promising symbolic interactionist tools for analyzing cultural aspects of social movements were abandoned—to the detriment of social movement theory. All of these developments were associated with the rise of resource mobilization theory in the 1970s and its swift acceptance as the dominant paradigm for analyzing social movements and collective action. As noted previously, this approach made vitally important contributions by reorienting social movement theory toward an understanding of its subject matter as a rationally motivated, self-interested, formally organized, resource dependent, opportunity driven form of political contestation (McCarthy and Zald, 1977; Tilly, 1978). With this new conception of social movements as strategic actors pursuing instrumental goals, however, a rather sterile and bloodless model of movement organizations and individual participants became ascendant. This was a culturally impoverished image of a social world in which meanings were transparent and action was a mechanistic response to behavioral incentives. For all the analytical leverage that resource mobilization theory provided for understanding political aspects of movements, it was arguably less adequate for understanding cultural aspects of movements than the collective behavior tradition it had displaced.

It is here that the culturalist turn in general social theory finds its echo in the emergence of social constructionism and new social movement approaches in social movement theory. The rise of social constructionism as an independent paradigm for analyzing social movement phenomena may be interpreted as a response to the gaps and weaknesses in resource mobilization approaches. It may also be seen historically as a revival of the symbolic interactionist wing of the older collective behavior tradition. This revival has improved on its predecessor in at least two general ways, however. First, contemporary social constructionism grants social movements an independent conceptual status rather than subsuming them as a minor category within the broader rubric of collective behavior. Second, social constructionism has recognized that movements can be ongoing, patterned, organized, institutionalized, political, and rational phenomena. At the same time, this perspective has cautioned against reifying these features of movements by insisting that they be seen as ongoing, processual, social constructions emerging out of the symbolically mediated activities of individuals engaged in collective action. Many of these insights may also be found in the European tradition of new social movement theory (Melucci, 1996a, 1989). There is thus a strong elective affinity between both social constructionism and new social movement theory on the one hand and the cultural dimensions of social movements on the other hand. These approaches helped move culture to center stage in the study of social movements.

Indeed, by the mid-1990s, devotees of all theoretical perspectives were proclaiming the centrality of culture in collective action; these proclamations produced an explosion of social movement theorizing around the notion of culture (Darnovsky et al., 1995; Johnston and Klandermans, 1995a; Larana et al., 1994). Academically oriented theorists have made numerous efforts to theorize culture and integrate it with existing paradigms. Thus, the leading political process theorist has underscored the inherently cultural aspects of social movements, including cultural facilitation, cultural creation, and cultural consequences (McAdam, 1994). Others have debated the nature of culture itself, distinguishing between systemic and performative views of culture (Johnston and Klandermans, 1995a) and between Weberian and Durkheimian approaches to culture (Swidler, 1995). Still others have called for a more sophisticated, less dichotomized understanding of the interplay between culture and structure, culture and rationality, and culture and politics (Polletta, 1997). Empirically oriented researchers have called for investigations into the varying degrees of culture exhibited by different social movements (Lofland, 1995). Politically oriented theorists have continued a descriptive as well as a normative debate about the role of culture in progressive movements by recognizing the cultural contributions of such movements while urging that traditional political goals not be lost in the valorization of cultural differences or the battles of identity politics (Darnovsky et al., 1995b; Derber, 1995; Flacks, 1995). The return of the cultural in social movement analysis is thus evident everywhere, but it will be most beneficial if it can be integrated with other dimensions rather than producing yet another drastic pendulum swing that will require the rediscovery of "the political" in another 20 years.

Given these developments, the following discussion of the cultural aspects of social activism is highly selective; it will focus on three broad areas. The first concerns the formation and activation of collective identities as a vital part of mobilizing for collective action. Largely ignored by resource mobilization theory, this process has been of interest to social constructionists and has been central to new social movement theory. The second concerns the role of grievances and ideology in social movements. Once again, this topic has been marginalized by resource mobilization theory, but it has been restored to a more central role by new social movement theory's interest in the value base of collective actors and by social constructionism's analysis of framing processes. A third and final area concerns the nature of organization and its meaning for movement participants. Although this has been a major emphasis of resource mobilization theory, the strategic and instrumental focus of the theory has marginalized the cultural dimensions of organization in social movements. Although unavoidably selective, this tripartite focus on identity, ideology, and organization illustrates the range of cultural issues in social movements that have only recently begun to come under systematic scrutiny.

THE CONSTRUCTION OF COLLECTIVE IDENTITY

Modernity and Identity

From a historical perspective, the question of individual and collective identity formation is intertwined with the rise of modernity. As described earlier, the emergence of the modern age promoted a new understanding of the social world as a relative and arbitrary social construction. As the social world came to be seen in this way by increasing numbers of people, their own locations and roles in that world also came to be seen in a more relative and arbitrary fashion. Sociology has recognized this process by distinguishing between traditional societies based on ascribed statuses and modern societies based on achieved statuses. In moving from the former to the latter, a world in which positions (and presumably identities) were fixed, timeless, and unchanging was replaced by a world in which positions and identities are at least partially the outcome of individual volition and accomplishment. In the classical sociological imagery, this was a transition from a world in which identities were granted once and for all to a world in which identities could be gained and lost. Given the sharp contrast between traditional and modern social worlds, it might even be argued that the very concept of identity is an inherently modern one—at least to the extent it connotes a process of self-definition even partially under the control of the individual.

If the rise of modernity relativized identity, late modernity has intensified the process in ways that may undermine the modern notion of identity and the individual subject. Thus, the full historical trajectory is from ascribed and fixed identities in traditional societies to achieved and relative identities in modern societies to fleeting and transient identities in late modernity. Among the many causes of this further relativization of identity is the growing mediatization of contemporary experience whereby multiple signs and symbols with diverse and potentially conflicting meanings continually redefine the phenomenological landscape of contemporary society. These forces produce the plurality and diversity of identifications and memberships typical of many people in late modernity. Alongside these forces, an accelerating pace of social change reinforces the fragility of contemporary identities. Although there is a danger of overstating the extensiveness of these developments and of presuming a uniformity of effects across diverse populations, there can be little doubt that such processes have undermined the more conventional anchors of social life that provided a measure of stability even in modern society. These processes have created a "homelessness of personal identity" that has made the quest for individual identity a central pursuit of modern life (Melucci, 1989: Chapter 5). This formulation recalls Giddens's (1991) understanding of the self in late modernity as involving a reflexive project of social construction. It is against this backdrop of distinctive opportunities and constraints that contemporary social movements seek to construct and transform the collective identities of their participants.

Recent work on collective identity reiterates but also problematizes these claims about broad connections between late modernity and movement mobilization. Although concurring with Melucci that identity construction is a prominent feature of many new social movements, others attribute this to a combination of information overload, confusion over cultural alternatives, and system inadequacies in providing bases for self-identification in a context of material affluence (Johnston et al., 1994). Both formulations thereby postulate causal links between macrostructural features of society and the texture of movement activism. Although provocative, this argument begs an important question. Although it may be true that new social movements revolve around identity questions in some fashion, it is certainly not the case that everyone with identity questions joins a social movement (new or otherwise). Future work needs to address this explanatory gap by specifying why some people find new social movements a congenial locale for meeting identity needs while most turn to any of a wide variety of functional alternatives to meet this same need. Put differently, new social movements compete with a wide variety of other associational activities that could also meet people's identity needs, and we need better understandings of the circumstances under which some people join movements and many people do not. Although such questions are never definitively answered, they help refine the standard argument about identity in social movements by underscoring that this is an identity of a particular type, in which oppositional themes and a politicized orientation are central ingredients.

Dimensions of Identity

Much recent work in this area has addressed differing levels, types, or dimensions of collective identity and their connections to broad structural changes. One such analysis distinguishes between individual, collective, and public identity (Johnston et al., 1994). Individual identities are brought to the movement by each of its participants and then transformed to varying degrees as a result of participation in the movement. Individual identities pose a critical question because participants in new social movements tend to be disproportionately young. Hence, the prominence given to identity in new social movements may reflect the classic Eriksonian identity quests of a young generation rather than the macrostructural features of postindustrial society. Collective identities are fashioned out of ongoing, negotiated processes that can make this phenomenon particularly difficult to analyze in empirical terms. But even if collective identity is empirically elusive, the concept remains crucial because these very processes of collective identity construction are often the major accomplishment of some movements and they are often a necessary prerequisite to the accomplishment of other goals. Finally, the dimension of public identity "captures the influences that the external public have on the way social movement adherents think about themselves" (Johnston et al., 1994:18). Public identity thereby refers to the definition of in-groups and out-groups, the process of boundary maintenance, and the relation of these processes to group solidarity (see also Stoecker, 1995).

Although this typology of individual, collective, and public identities was formulated with reference to new social movement theory as well as "old" collective behavior theory, the perspective of social constructionism has also specified differing types of collective identity involved in collective action. These identities are best seen as ongoing, interactional accomplishments that occur through processes of framing in which interpretive schemata that condense and simplify an external world are constructed and transmitted through social activism (Hunt et al., 1994). Framing processes thus construct "identity fields" that characterize the consciousness and character of three diverse groups in social activism. Protagonist framing establishes distinctions between in-groups and out-groups and a strong we-feeling through boundary maintenance. Protagonist framing is dialectically related to antagonist framing, which specifies the enemies of the movement and may guide strategies for confronting that enemy. Finally, audience framing defines the bystanders in a particular conflict, and it may imply strategies for recruiting or at least neutralizing various audiences to ongoing social conflicts. Taken together, these typologies provide a two-dimensional map of collective identity in social activism. On the vertical dimension, individual, collective, and public identities specify levels of identity across people, groups, and social systems. On the horizontal dimension, protagonist, antagonist, and audience identity fields define combatants and bystanders in a given conflict. Such typologies provide a helpful foundation for ultimately more interesting questions about how different forms of collective identity affect the course of social activism.

The real value of these typological distinctions is in framing our understanding of collective identity as an ongoing process in specific instances of social activism. Lesbian feminist communities provide one particularly rich example of how collective political actors do not exist simply by virtue of structural location, but rather must be created in the course of collective action (Taylor and Whittier, 1992). Identity construction processes are thus central to the translation of structural inequality into subjective discontent. The working definition of collective identity in this analysis includes three elements: a shared salient characteristic, a corresponding form of consciousness, and opposition to some dominant order. Employing this definition to analyze lesbian feminist communities highlights three additional "analytical tools" for understanding the construction of collective identities in social movements. First, the establishment of boundaries (whether social, psychological, or physical) promotes a heightened awareness of group commonalities and structures interaction between in-groups and out-groups; in lesbian feminist communities this typically happens through the creation of alternative institutions and women's culture. Second, the development of consciousness involves interpretive frameworks that emerge out of a group's struggle to realize its common interests; this consciousness contains oppositional elements that are interwoven with the practices of everyday life. Third, the process of negotiation refers to movement efforts to change symbolic meanings in private and public settings so as to advance the movement's cause; negotiation thereby politicizes self and daily life in ways that make identity a fundamental focus of political work. A final contribution of this work is to underscore the inevitably intertwined nature of the cultural and the political. That is, if modern forms of power are diffused throughout everyday life, the very construction of an oppositional collective identity is a political act. Put differently, if hegemony is a valid theory of power, the counter-hegemonic practice of forming oppositional collective identities is a genuine form of resistance.

The Continuum of Collective Identity

Future work on collective identity in social movements will doubtless draw on both general typological distinctions and specific case studies. It will be most productive if it examines the variable dimensions of collective identity and if these variations are examined in explicit comparisons across different movement constituencies. One fruitful means of framing such questions is to conceptualize collective identity as existing on a continuum. At one extreme, some movements build on collective identities that are structurally and historically grounded, i.e., these identities are already a constituent feature of prevailing forms of social organization. At the other extreme, some movements must socially construct collective identities from scratch, i.e., some identities are not salient features of social organization prior to the mobilization of a collective actor in the context of social activism. Locating movements along this continuum and comparing them across this continuum suggest a number of fruitful directions for future research on collective identity in social movements.

Some movements tap collective identities that are structurally and historically grounded in the social organization of society; movements based on race, gender, or class provide obvious examples. There are differing degrees of structural groundedness even across these categories. Thus, blacks have had the most consistent sense of collective identity; women have had the least consistent sense of collective identity; and workers have occupied an intermediate ground between blacks and women (Buechler, 1990:132ff). But the larger point about all of these groups is that even when collective identity is structurally grounded, movement work is still required to cultivate social activism on the basis of this identity. Such work is necessary, if only because the structurally grounded collective identities of subordinate groups are likely to include elements of fatalism or pessimism that deny the efficacy of social activism. In such cases, it might be better to speak of the social "reconstruction" of collective identity as a primary mobilizing task.

Socially reconstructive work in gender movements ranges over four distinct stages of group behavior (Chafe, 1977). In the first stage, women perform similar activities in the social division of labor with no particular sense of doing so because they are women. In the second stage, similarities in women's behavior rest on an implicit understanding of women's place or women's work that mandates such behavior. In the third stage, women consciously articulate and endorse a group identity that becomes the basis for their action. In the fourth and final stage, women act not only consciously and collectively, but also out of a shared sense of grievance about their social position. Cross-referencing these stages with the concept of collective identity suggests that in the first stage gender is part of the social organization of society but is not a basis for collective identity among women. In the second stage, there is only a tacit or nascent sense of collective identity. Genuine group consciousness or collective identity arises only in the third and fourth stages. In the third stage, however, group consciousness of gender identity leads women to accept their socially designated role and act accordingly. It is only in the fourth stage that an oppositional element is added through a feminist challenge to women's position in society. Thus, identities can be structurally grounded (stages one and two) without necessarily giving rise to a conscious awareness of collective identity (stages three and four). Furthermore, collective identity is not necessarily oppositional (stage three versus stage four); these two stages help distinguish between subcultures and movements by making opposition central to the latter (Kriesi et al., 1995). Hence, the task confronting feminist movements is to socially reconstruct the structurally grounded identity of women (stages one and two) so as to make it conscious and explicit (stage three) and oppositional and political (stage four). Whereas the language of stages is problematic because it implies some inevitable and linear progression, these distinctions are helpful conceptual tools for analyzing collective identity in social activism.

A somewhat parallel example of socially reconstructive identity work occurs in racial movements. Race itself is socially constructed; without a process of racialization that extends racial meaning to certain relationships, the biological substratum of physical variations that is construed as "race" would have no meaning. However, the importation of an African labor force for plantation agriculture ensured that the socially constructed category of race would be structurally grounded in the social organization of the United States from the beginning. Because racialization was inherently linked to exploitation, discrimination, and segregation, collective identities based on race developed earlier and more consistently than in perhaps any other group. Such identities nonetheless vacillated between accommodationist stances (stage three) and forms of resistance (stage four). The racial struggles of the last four decades are the latest variation on this theme. The politics of the 1950s and 1960s moved from the ethnicity paradigm with its subtext of gradualist assimilation toward more radical paradigms espousing nationalism, separatism, pluralism, and multiculturalism. The backlash politics of the 1970s and 1980s have sought to restore the ethnicity paradigm for race relations (Omi and Winant, 1986). Thus, like gender movements, racially based movements have also had to engage in the socially reconstructive work of fashioning a politicized collective identity that would sustain social activism. These movements testify to the extent to which even "ascribed" statuses and socially grounded identities do not automatically translate into effective, oppositional, collective identities.

Although some movements face the task of reconstructing structurally grounded identities, movements at the other end of the collective identity continuum face the different challenge of fashioning such identities from scratch.

Many movements are rooted in a set of values or ethical principles that do not correspond to any structurally grounded social status such as gender or race. Animal rights activism, campaigns against drunk driving, antinuclear activism, environmental movements, public interest organizations, and consumer movements provide examples of movements whose real and potential constituencies cannot be read directly off the structural organization of society. Hence, rather than reconstructing structurally rooted identities, these movements must construct their collective identity from the ground up. Such construction involves important strategic choices. One strategy is to build a consensus movement with broad attitudinal support and little organized opposition, but there is reason to think that consensus movements may not be very effective instruments of social change because broad attitudinal support is difficult to translate into committed activism (Schwartz and Paul, 1992). Seen from a slightly different angle, this problem may be conceptualized as a weak sense of collective identity that is likely to pervade movements that have no obvious or organized opposition. Another strategic choice would be to emphasize an opponent (corporations or government bureaucracies) as a means of galvanizing a more passionate sense of collective identity among movement adherents; this strategy involves its own risks of alienating the groups so targeted and risking their sustained opposition.

The collective identity continuum also implies intermediate locations where collective identity is neither as structurally grounded nor as ephemeral as the two extremes. Although it is true that even "structurally grounded" collective identities are social constructions, the case of race defines the extreme in which a social construction has occurred on both macro- and microlevels over centuries so that the construction has become a Durkheimian social fact. Intermediate locations on the continuum involve more temporary, fluid, and situationally constructed identities that undergird intermittent forms of social activism resting on such identities. Such intermediate collective identities may be created when authorities impose policies or laws that categorize people in a certain way and the people so categorized respond based on that identity. They may also involve preexisting but latent identities that become salient in the context of certain policies, conflicts, and interactions that solidify the boundaries of such identities by linking them to privileges and opportunities or to disadvantages and discrimination. For example, gay, lesbian, or bisexual individuals and groups occupy a middle ground on the collective identity continuum, and the same is true of individuals and groups with particular physical handicaps. Both constituencies have engaged in sustained social activism in recent decades, and both have built on an underlying collective identity that is more specific than the pseudoidentities of consensus movements but less structurally grounded than race, class, or gender identities. In addition, both groups have had their own debates between accommodationist stage three identities and oppositional stage four identities. The exact location of any group on the continuum is always debatable, but such debates illuminate how diverse movements construct or reconstruct collective identities. This continuum provides one example of how the concept of collective identity can provide additional analytical leverage if we attend to its variable dimensions across different movements.

The continuum can also frame debates and controversies about collective identity in contemporary social activism. The trajectory of late modernity discussed earlier implies that an increasing percentage of collective action has moved from identities that are structurally grounded to ones that are more flexible and situational. At the extreme, this logic claims that contemporary movements address individuals as individuals rather than as representatives of groups at all (Melucci, 1995b). Although there may be an increasing number of examples in which the individual is the site of political activity (Taylor and Raeburn, 1995), these individuals are still located in interactive networks and collective identities that shape the conflicts in which they engage. Debates over the situational or individualized nature of contemporary protest nonetheless reflect two important insights. The first concerns the multiple, simultaneous collective identities that constitute individuals in late modernity. This multiplicity of identities can lead to a constantly shifting dynamic hierarchy of salient identities in collective action. When movements are ascending, they often have the luxury of creating distinct subgroups or cohorts; when backlash occurs, such fine lines become less relevant compared to a broader frame that unites all activists against their opposition (Whittier, 1995). In a related dynamic, new opportunities or increased scrutiny may lead a formerly unified group to differentiate internally and define new collective identities by excluding some who were formerly included (J. Gamson, 1996). Both of these dynamics also suggest the possibility of "identity deployment" as a conscious movement practice in which different identities are invoked in different movement settings or for different audiences (Bernstein, 1997). The second insight is that because fixed identities are the basis of oppression as well as liberation, the deconstruction of collective identities (or at least their oppressive aspects) may also be a viable movement strategy. For example, queer theory argues that although strong, quasi-essentialist collective identities may be vital in specific struggles, they may be counterproductive to long-term movement success. Alongside constructing or reconstructing identities, there is also a deconstructionist movement strategy that challenges reified categories as a means of liberating the individuals so categorized (J. Gamson, 1995).

A final illustration of the utility of this continuum is the order it can bring to otherwise discrepant or inconsistent findings about collective identity in social movements. For example, there would appear to be a contradiction between recent work suggesting that collective identity is a transient, ever-changing, and fluid element in social protest (Klandermans, 1994) and work demonstrating collective identity to be an ongoing, sustained, and even intergenerational dimension of oppositional subcultures and social activism (Johnston, 1994). The seeming contradiction evaporates when the specific constituencies of this research are examined more closely. Klandermans's conclusions about transient identities were based on a study of the Dutch peace movement that had to fashion its collective identity from scratch on the basis of a broad appeal to values; the movement subsequently saw its identity change with each shift in the proportion of different groups in the movement. Johnston's conclusions about the permanence of collective identity were based on a study of ethnic identities and nationalist movements in politically hostile climates; this structurally grounded identity defines the opposite end of the continuum from the constituency of the Dutch peace movement. What links these movements is that both identities are socially constructed in a broad and generic sense; what distinguishes them is the sociohistorical starting point from which the constructive or reconstructive tasks commenced as well as the solidity of the identities established by these processes.

Another promising direction for future work on collective identity in social movements concerns its relationship to other movement processes. A more profound understanding of collective identity would alter our understanding of virtually every other element of social activism. With regard to resources, basic questions about the resources available to a movement and their probability of delivery will turn on the strength of collective identity within the movement. The same may be said for individual calculations about movement involvement; collective identity is the best antidote to the free-rider dilemma because it precludes an individual calculus of costs and benefits in the first place. With regard to grievances, there is growing evidence that identity construction processes are central in translating structural inequality into subjective discontent (Taylor and Whittier, 1992; Johnston et al., 1994). With regard to strategy, the nature of the collective identity already present in the group will influence strategic choices, and those choices in turn will influence not just movement outcomes but future forms of collective identity in the group. With regard to success, the concept of collective identity suggests that alongside instrumental notions of success such as new advantages or acceptance (Gamson, 1990) there are alternative and more "cultural" ways of measuring success or failure in terms of a group's ability to sustain a collective identity that effectively meets its members' needs. Finally, as we will explore in more detail momentarily, the concept of collective identity is also linked to ideological visions and organizational forms of social activism. These linkages are yet another manifestation of the interconnectedness of "cultural" processes like collective identity and "political" dimensions such as resources, mobilization, strategy, and success.

THE RETURN OF GRIEVANCES AND IDEOLOGY

Alongside collective identity, grievances and ideology also play a vital role in social activism. Once central to social movement theory, grievances and ideology were marginalized by the resource mobilization argument that they are a constant background factor that cannot explain the variable appearance of social movements [see Turner (1981) for an early critique of this marginalization from the collective behavior perspective]. For some 20 years, this paradigm illuminated resources, organization, and opportunity in the emergence of social movements. But the stronger version of the resource mobilization argument that dismissed any meaningful role for grievances and ideology came under increasing challenge, and social movement theory is once again giving serious consideration to grievance formation and ideology articulation in social activism.

This shift in focus is associated with two theoretical contenders to resource mobilization theory. New social movement theory restored attention to grievances and ideology on two levels. On the macrolevel, it called attention to the structural roots of grievances associated with modernity, capitalism, bureaucracy, and the like. And on the microlevel, it analyzed connections between collective identity and the formulation of grievances. An increasing body of theory and research is now available that suggests that the relation between identity and grievances is not linear and sequential but rather reciprocal and dialectical (Buechler, 1990; Taylor and Whittier, 1992; Johnston et al., 1994). If collective identity is as central to social activism as new social movement theory claims, and if collective identity emerges in a dialectical process with grievance articulation, it is appropriate that the role of grievances returns to center stage in the analysis of social movement activism. Although new social movement theory deserves credit for restoring the importance of grievances, it also requires critical scrutiny for the implication that the dialectical relation between collective identity and grievance formation is somehow unique to contemporary movements. The increasingly recognized links between grievances and identity have probably always been a vital part of social movements, but theoretical blinders have rendered these historical links difficult to see (Calhoun, 1993; Johnston et al., 1994). Resource mobilization theory downplayed them altogether, whereas new social movement theory implies that they are important only in contemporary movements. Although there may be something distinctively new about the process of grievance formation in contemporary society (e.g., the role of mass media), this needs to be identified through comparative–historical analysis rather than assumed by theoretical fiat.

The second theoretical contender to resource mobilization theory that has restored the centrality of grievances has been social constructionism. The concept of "framing" has itself framed a wealth of theoretical and empirical contributions to the understanding of grievances in social activism. This approach offers much richer explanations of how grievances motivate activists than were ever available in the resource mobilization imagery of isolated actors engaging in a cost–benefit analysis of the rationality of joining a social movement. The main focus has been on links between movement groups and individual recruits. We consequently know more about how framing processes bridge the meso- and microlevels than we do about how similar processes occur across the macro- and mesolevels. To frame the subsequent discussion, I will thereby use the term "grievances" to refer to the more specific motivating issues that link micro- and mesolevels in social activism, and I will use the term "ideology" to designate broader ideational systems that link meso- and macrolevels. In this terminology, social constructionism has had more to say about grievances than about ideology. One of the challenges to contemporary social movement theory is therefore to use existing work to develop a more robust understanding of ideology in social movements.

The Framing of Grievances

Substantial progress has been made in understanding grievances in social activism. Even before the emergence of social constructionism, some analysts had distanced themselves from resource mobilization theory by calling attention to the centrality of grievances in the emergence of protest. For example, Piven and Cloward's (1977) study of poor people's movements identified three perceptual shifts as necessary preconditions for social activism. First, people must define a situation as unjust, and thus question the legitimacy of social arrangements that create problems for them. Although such a perception may be necessary, it is not sufficient because such an orientation by itself may simply reinforce fatalism and passivity. Hence, a second perception is also vital: people must believe that change is possible and that the world (or some significant part of it) could be organized in a different fashion. The twin perceptions that the world is unjust and that it could be different are necessary but not sufficient to motivate participation in protest. The third required element is a belief in the efficacy of action: people must feel that their own actions will make a difference in changing social arrangements. If people do not believe that their own actions will make a difference, the free-rider problem becomes paramount; if they do not believe that anyone's actions will make a difference, the lack of a sense of agency will preclude social activism even in the face of injustice. These three beliefs thereby constitute subjective prerequisites for successful protest that exist alongside objective factors such as resources and opportunities.

These arguments were developed to help explain the relatively rare appearance of poor people's movements in the United States (Piven and Cloward, 1977). The political process model established these subjective prerequisites as central to a broader range of social movements (McAdam, 1982). This model identifies three sets of causal factors in the mobilization of social movements: external political opportunities, internal indigenous organization, and subjective insurgent consciousness. The latter factor underscores the role of "cognitive liberation" in establishing the efficacy of acting collectively. When these cognitive factors are seen as variable, they return to a central place in the explanation of collective action. Thus, among poor constituencies, a sense of injustice may be fairly common but belief in the possibility of change and the efficacy of action has been anything but common (Piven and Cloward, 1977). Among African-Americans, a sense of injustice has been present for many generations, but it was not until other cognitions about change and action became prevalent that this constituency mobilized into an effective social movement (McAdam, 1982). This work thereby concurred with resource mobilization theory that some groups do have long-standing grievances, but it identified corollary beliefs that are equally necessary for protest but much less common. In so doing, attention was redirected to grievances and related cognitive processes in the generation of social protest.

The emergence of social constructionism as an independent paradigm for analyzing collective action in the 1980s built on these initiatives but took them much further by making grievance articulation a highly variable and causally central factor in the emergence of social movements. This occurred in part by focusing on relatively privileged groups for whom an historically rooted sense of injustice could not be assumed as readily as it could in the case of poor people or racially subordinated groups. But as the perspective developed, it offered an increasingly sophisticated model of the social construction of grievances and motivations that had applicability across a wide spectrum of constituencies. The core notion in this work is the concept of "framing" (Goffman, 1974), which has a particularly rich applicability to grievance construction and articulation in social movements. As detailed in Chapter 2, the core notion of framing has been applied to the social construction of grievances (Snow and Benford, 1988), the types of frame alignment (Snow et al., 1986), and the framing of identities in social movements (Hunt et al., 1994). More specific investigations have examined frame disputes within a movement (Benford, 1993a), vocabularies of motive in movements (Benford, 1993b), dramaturgical elements of social movements (Benford and Hunt, 1992), counterframing and reframing (Benford and Hunt, 1994), and the role of value expectations in mobilization (Klandermans, 1988, 1984).

The analysis of grievances through the social constructionist concept of framing has thus become a cottage industry in the social movement literature. The popularity of this approach has tended to obscure some of its limitations, however. One such limitation is that the focus on framing emphasizes how organizations strategically recruit people rather than how people themselves formulate grievances apart from organizational recruitment efforts (Aguirre, 1994). For my purposes here, a more serious problem is Gamson's (1992) valorization of social psychology as the frontier of social movement theory. There can be little doubt that the social constructionist version of the social psychology of movements is a great improvement over earlier approaches premised on contagion, mass hysteria, irrationality, and social pathology. And it is a major corrective to resource mobilization theory's tendency to ignore grievances, motivation, and recruitment (except via the free-rider problem). The privileging of the social psychology of movements through the framing perspective, however, has directed attention away from questions of ideology at the meso–macrolevel of collective action. There are several related limitations as well. First, this concept has encouraged a reductionist line of research in which individual consciousness becomes the main unit of analysis, sacrificing a genuinely interactionist approach. Second, researchers have invented a plethora of "frames" that are tautologically postulated as causal factors in movement activism without effectively distinguishing between the frames themselves and their alleged effects. Finally, such frames are frequently analyzed in a decontextualized and disembodied manner, so that meaningful links to dominant or alternative cultural themes and imagery are rarely identified. In all these ways, the analysis of framing has been confined to the micro–mesolevel of grievances and had relatively little to say about the meso–macrolevel of ideology and its relationship to the framing of grievances.

Two trends in social constructionist work have the potential to link grievances and ideology. The first is Gamson's work (1995, 1988) on political culture, media discourse, and public opinion. To date, however, this work has focused on how these phenomena heighten the cognitive salience and emotional power of grievances for individuals in social activism. For example, Gamson's research suggests that the most robust movement frames combine media discourse and experiential knowledge; without the latter mass media typically reinforce a sense of powerlessness that denies agency to social actors (Gamson, 1995). When reinforced by personal experience or critical events (Gamson and Modigliani, 1989), however, media discourse can be an important cultural resource in recruitment and mobilization (Gamson, 1995). The second trend concerns the concept of "master frames" (Snow and Benford, 1992) whose generality applies to multiple constituencies, thereby encouraging an analytical shift from individuals to groups. Thus, a master frame emphasizing oppression resonates with many groups, just as the master frame of "threats to survival" links environmental and peace groups. The concept of master frames takes on its richest implications when paired with the idea that social movements often occur in cycles. There is a danger, however, that the concept of master frames will lead to tautological explanations of social movement clustering. The concept might better be defined in terms of "its resonance with the cultural, political or historical milieu in which it emerges rather than its adoption by other social movements" (Swart, 1995:468). This resolution suggests a macrolevel notion of master frame alignment between a movement's activities and its broader symbolic environment that parallels the more conventional notion of frame alignment between movements and individual participants (Swart, 1995).

The most promising direction for framing research would thus involve deploying the notion of master frames in a multilevel analysis that links individuals, groups, and structures in a more historical and contextualized fashion. A good example is provided by a recent study of master framing and cross-movement networking in Canada (Carroll and Ratner, 1996). This work adopts a neo-Gramscian approach in which framing is seen as the cognitive aspect of a counterhegemonic politics that seeks to disorganize consent and organize dissent. In this analysis, the greatest value of a master frame is that it fosters a more comprehensive critique of forms of domination as well as alliances between groups whose specific grievances resonate with the same master frame. The study examines networks across labor, peace, urban/antipoverty, and feminist movements; it also examines how three different frames—political economy, identity politics, and liberalism—facilitate such cross-movement networking. The political economy frame appears to be the most resonant master frame because it defined injustice across many different movements; the activists who espoused this frame were involved in more cross-movement networking than those who invoked other frames. Because it defined power as material and structural, but also as susceptible to transformation, this frame provided a common language for activists to build alliances across specific movements and to articulate a more comprehensive critique of the systemic forms of domination that affected all the movement constituencies in various ways. By contextualizing the notion of framing in an historically specific example of how individuals, groups, and structures interact to produce collective action,

Carroll and Ratner (1996) provide a compelling model of how the framing perspective can overcome its typical limitations.

Ideology: The Orphan of Social Movement Theory?

The concept of master frames extends the social constructionist analysis of framing toward macrolevel social processes. But it does not capture the more elaborate, historically rooted belief systems traditionally denoted by the concept of ideology. "The literature on frames contributes to a better understanding of how actors define their action but it tends to forget the 'ideological' aspect of such a definition. . . . Frames . . .must be located within a theory of ideology" (Melucci, 1996a:348). With its long and tortuous history in the social sciences, ideology has become an orphan in social movement theory. The classical approach to collective behavior treated ideas as irrational generalized beliefs (Smelser, 1962). Resource mobilization theory denied any important role for ideology in order to privilege resources and opportunity. Social constructionism has been attentive to social–psychological framing but has only begun to address the broader connotations of the concept of ideology. New social movement theory is more receptive to analyzing movements on the macrolevel, but it has tended to substitute other analytical concepts for ideology, as suggested by the subtitle of a recent reader on new social movements: "From Ideology to Identity" (Larana et al., 1994). Thus, a major conceptual tool in the social sciences lacks a congenial home in any of the leading theories of social movements. Like other cases of the "end of ideology," this one in social movement theory is premature, and it limits our ability to conceptualize the larger role of ideas in social activism.

There are several reasons to be cautious about the concept of ideology. As a practical matter, there is convincing evidence that most participants in collective action are not motivated by complex and intricate ideologies as much as they are by a relatively simple and straightforward sense of injustice or unfairness (Moore, 1978; Gamson et al., 1982). On an analytical level, the resource mobilization critique is often correct: a sense of injustice and even a more elaborate ideology have historically been easier for aggrieved groups to develop than the resources and opportunities to act effectively on those perceptions. On a philosophical level, the aversion to ideology as a meaningful concept in social movement analysis reflects a healthy suspicion of teleological metanarratives about the direction of history and the destiny of a group in its confrontations with systemic authority. Although these cautions are reasonable, they should not preclude investigations of ideological currents in social movements. This is particularly so when some of the most active movements of the late twentieth century are intensely ideological (Taylor and Whittier, 1992).

The presence and the nature of these intensely ideological social movements suggest the need for a robust concept of ideology that avoids the historically problematic baggage associated with the concept. One promising direction is a concept of ideology that emphasizes its cultural and interpretive functions alongside its instrumental and political ones. Such a concept is implicit in critiques of instrumental rationality offered by thinkers as diverse as Habermas and Foucault. This view underscores ideology as a cultural system of meanings that defines resources and opportunities, fosters political culture, and promotes collective identity and solidarity in social movements (Tucker, 1989). This view conceptualizes ideology as a process of conscious cultural reflection in which movement discourse contributes to a reflexive awareness of the socially constructed nature of both the social movement and the social world. When ideology plays this role in social activism, movements become microcosms of communicative rationality that can challenge the instrumental rationality of systemic power (Habermas, 1987, 1984). In this cultural conception, ideology operates not as a "party line" but rather as an arena for the deliberation of moral and practical questions that movements confront. This approach to ideology is especially well suited for understanding those movements that offer a moral critique of advanced capitalism and the bureaucratic state. At the same time, such "cultural" dimensions of ideology are intertwined with old-fashioned "political" dimensions such as the generation of movement solidarity (Tucker, 1989).

Some contemporary work in cultural studies parallels these ideas by seeing ideology as an aspect of systemic power and implicitly seeing social movements as engaged in the critique of ideology. For instance, Thompson's (1990) study of ideology in modern culture speaks to both political and cultural dimensions while nesting both in the structures of mass communication that characterize the contemporary world. Although not a study of social movements, this analysis is rich in implications for social movement theory. The cultural and political dimensions of ideology are linked in the recognition that ideology is about how meaning establishes and maintains systematically asymmetrical relations of power: ideology is meaning in the service of power. Symbolic forms are not ideological in themselves, but rather become ideological in specific social contexts. Since socially structured contexts always contain asymmetries of power, however, it is very common for symbolic forms to assume ideological overtones in the modern world. This tendency is heightened as mass communication facilitates the one-way transmission of symbolic forms. Audiences are not merely passive, however, since the social world is always already hermeneutically preinterpreted at the level of everyday life. Rejecting a purely passive role for recipients also means rejecting a "social cement" view of ideology as a massive force that simply overwhelms popular consciousness and manipulates individuals at will. To the contrary, the transmission of ideology is frequently contested and intimately linked to the critique of domination. Thompson (1990:68) therefore claims that contestatory symbolic forms should themselves be classified not as ideological but rather as incipient forms of the critique of ideology. My contention is that it is precisely in social movements that such contestatory symbolic forms are most likely to emerge and to direct collective action that challenges dominant ideologies.

It is here that a more specific analysis of the character of dominant ideologies can provide clues to the contestatory challenges that social movements offer to them. There are five distinct modes through which ideology mobilizes meanings in support of domination and asymmetrical relations of power be-tween groups. The first mode is legitimation, whereby ideology portrays rela-tions of domination as legitimate through strategies of rationalization, univer-salization, or narrativization. In different ways, each of these strategies seeks to render domination acceptable. The second mode is dissimulation, in which ide-ology conceals, denies, or obscures relations of domination through strategies of displacement, euphemization, or trope. Each of these strategies seeks to ren-der domination either invisible or positive. The third mode is unification, whereby ideology portrays individuals as part of a false unity through strategies of standardization or symbolization of unity. Once again, the major function of such strategies is to obscure domination. The fourth mode is fragmentation, which divides potential challengers through strategies of differentiation or ex-purgation of the other. Each of these strategies identifies false enemies of a group and thereby redirects their attention away from main axes of domina-tion. The fifth mode is reification, whereby ideology presents a transitory his-torical state as if it were permanent, natural, or timeless through strategies of naturalization, eternalization, nominalization, or passivization. What each of these strategies does is deny the potential alterability of forms of domination (Thompson, 1990:52–67).

If these modalities specify the workings of dominant ideologies, they may be read from the opposite direction to suggest how contestatory symbolic forms can challenge both dominant ideologies and domination itself. Such contestatory forms may be designated as delegitimation, revelation, differen-tiation, solidarity, and relativization. Delegitimation underscores the unac-ceptability of existing social arrangements. Revelation brings power relations to the surface of social consciousness. Differentiation rejects false unities and identifies more fundamental lines of social cleavage. Solidarity creates alliances between groups who share subordinate statuses despite their differences. Rel-ativization underscores the socially constructed nature of existing forms of domination and the possibility of their reconstruction. These counterideo-logical processes suggest the contestatory symbolic forms that constitute the ideational aspects of oppositional social movements; as such, they help to specify how "movements have waged a critical struggle against the represen-tation of the world served up by the dominant models, denying their claim to uniqueness and challenging the symbolic constitution of politics and cul-ture" (Melucci, 1996a:357). Although some of these individual processes re-semble framing activities, the five dimensions taken together suggest a more systemic and holistic endeavor than is usually implied by framing processes. It is this type of conceptual construction that is largely absent from current approaches to social movements that focus on micro–mesolevel framing, and it is this type of cultural construction that can restore a meso–macrolevel analysis of ideological contestation in social movements. My proposal to view movements as engaged in contestatory symbolic forms (delegitimation, rev-elation, differentiation, solidarity, and relativization) exemplifies movement ideology as a cultural process of collective and reflexive self-awareness; it supports a view of social movements as cultural laboratories or learning mechanisms within hierarchically structured social systems.

Two concluding comments on grievances and ideology are in order. The first concerns the interplay between (microlevel) grievances and (macrolevel) ideology. In the preceding discussion of collective identity, I argued that such identities exist on a continuum from structurally grounded to socially constructed. There is a parallel here. Some grievances approximate structural groundedness (the oppression associated with slave labor) whereas others have a higher quotient of social construction (threats to global peace). These variations are likely to overlap with similar variations in the solidity of the collective identity associated with each movement; recall the contrast between the multigenerational ethnic identity analyzed by Johnston (1994) and the transient identities of the peace movement studied by Klandermans (1994). But even in the case of what I have called structurally grounded grievances, they do not lead to collective action without the contestatory symbolic forms we have just analyzed at the level of movement ideology. To make the point somewhat differently, even when the resource mobilization argument is correct (some grievances can be treated as a constant background factor in the life of a collectivity), the counterargument is also correct in that constant grievances do not generate social movements unless they are embedded in a larger dynamic of ideological contestation that involves the dimensions I have labeled delegitimation, revelation, differentiation, solidarity, and relativization.

The second concluding comment concerns the causal and temporal sequencing of grievances and ideology relative to other movement processes. One of the traditional problems with the concept of ideology is that it tends to be used in an overly mechanistic and linear fashion that implies that the formulation of specific grievances and general ideologies is a clear and distinct stage in the emergence of a movement that must precede other stages. A more plausible view of the role of grievances and especially ideology in social movements is a messier one that sees the development of grievances and ideology as a recursive, dialectical, and interactive process in tandem with other processes in social movements. The formation of collective identity is one such process, and as the preceding discussion illustrated, the formulation of such identities is intertwined with the articulation of grievances and ideologies in complex ways. Even more counterintuitive, the formulation of grievances and ideology may actually be as much an outcome of social activism as it is a logically prior step toward that activism. Thus, the counterideological themes that I have identified (delegitimation, revelation, differentiation, solidarity, and relativization) often occur in their most potent form as movement participants or sympathizers witness the response of authorities to initial and tentative rounds of activism. We need theoretical stances that are open to this messier view, as well as empirical efforts to sort out more clearly both the socially constructed nature of grievances and ideology as well as their dialectical relation to other movement processes.

THE SYMBOLISM OF ORGANIZATIONAL FORM

One such movement process is organization. Though conventionally treated as an instrumental "political" aspect of social activism, there is a growing recognition that movement organization is as much a "cultural" as a "political" phenomenon. Conventional discussions of movement organization are often based on a continuum that ranges from centralized, formal, and hierarchical to decentralized, informal, and egalitarian. But there is another source of variation in movement organization that rests on the distinction between the political and cultural aspects of movements. By political aspects, I mean how movements organize themselves to contest for power in conflict with external targets. By cultural aspects, I mean how movements organize themselves to symbolically express their central goals and values and to affirm their collective identities. These two contrasts are at least loosely correlated. Politically oriented movements tend to be more instrumentally and hierarchically organized whereas culturally oriented movements tend to be more expressively and diffusely organized. As I have argued earlier, however, such loose correlations are nothing more than tendencies and we need to remember the exceptions to prevent these categories from becoming mutually exclusive. Thus, even the most politically and instrumentally oriented movement organizations have cultural dimensions, typically evoking themes of loyalty, solidarity, and an *esprit de corps*. Conversely, even the most culturally and expressively oriented movement forms have political dimensions that symbolically challenge the logic of dominant power relations. In addition, the concept of "cultural resources" suggests that culture is not just an internal and expressive phenomenon but can also be seen as a strategic tool kit in the pursuit of movement goals (Williams, 1995). With these provisos in mind, it is the cultural dimensions of movement organization that warrant further attention.

The new left is often taken as a movement that combined a strong political orientation with an explicit emphasis on the cultural aspects of movement organization. In the end, this movement opted for a more expressive form of politics to avoid the specter of oligarchy that was likely to result from pursuing a more instrumentalist course. This does not mean that the movement failed (except by instrumentalist standards); it rather means that the movement succeeded in avoiding a traditional obstacle and exploring an alternative form of organization that created a valuable legacy for subsequent movements (Breines, 1989). The alternative that the new left embraced has come to be known as prefigurative politics, i.e., the movement organized its activities in a manner that prefigured the broader cultural values and social relations that it was seeking in a transformed society. For the new left, this meant a fundamental insistence on participatory democracy, the creation of a range of counterinstitutions in which participatory democracy could be grounded, and the cultivation of a broader community consisting of these counterinstitutions. This instance of prefigurative politics reveals the cultural dimension of movement organization in particularly sharp relief because there was a strong dual commitment to both political and cultural goals, and because the tension between them defined the trajectory of the new left.

Organizational Culture in Women's Movements

The tension between community and organization has been a leading theme in women's movements. In my own research (Buechler, 1990), I found the concept of "movement organization" of limited value and concluded that another concept was necessary to capture the most important organizational forms in the history of women's activism. More specifically, the resource mobilization concept of "social movement organization" (McCarthy and Zald, 1977) had very limited applicability to women's social activism, so I proposed a parallel concept of "social movement community" to capture more typical forms of mobilization in this movement. My initial definition of a social movement community described it as consisting of informal networks of activists with fluid boundaries, flexible leadership structures, and malleable divisions of labor (Buechler, 1990:42). In the first wave of women's activism, such organizational forms were evident at every stage of mobilization. For instance, from the 1840s to 1869 there were no formal movement organizations but there was an informal network of women's rights activists that achieved considerable success in the absence of formal organization. From 1870 to the 1890s, there were formal organizations but they were very ineffective in a period of limited opportunities, and the movement was really sustained by the cultural activities of women's community building more than by formal political organizing. From the 1890s to 1920, the social movement community of women broadened and deepened, becoming a cross-class, multiconstituency alliance resting on a combination of formal organizations, activist networks, and informal groups that won the right to vote. In the second wave of women's activism that began in the 1960s, one major branch of the women's movement (variously described as the younger or more radical branch) was basically defined by its preference for noninstrumental, prefigurative, and community-oriented forms of mobilization. Thus, the history of women's activism is incomprehensible without a category such as social movement community (Buechler, 1990).

My initial use of this concept was meant to expand our conceptual repertoire for analyzing movement forms by recognizing informal, decentralized communities as a viable alternative to formal, centralized organizations. The concept is also relevant to current concerns about the cultural aspects of movement organization. It is relevant because the tendency for women activists to gravitate toward communal forms of organization typically was a conscious and explicit choice to adopt a form of mobilization that was consistent with, and expressive of, the goals and values of their movement. It was not that women settled for what they saw as an inferior mode of organization because they lacked resources or opportunities; it was rather that they consciously sought a form of organization that was consistent with the larger vision of their movement, and they maintained a commitment to those organizational forms even if they decreased the chances of movement success as measured by conventional instrumental criteria. By this evidence, women's movements have always included strong expressions of prefigurative politics. Put differently, movement organization for such constituencies is more a symbolic statement about the values of the group than it is an instrumental tool for winning power. There is a further lesson to be drawn from the history of women's movements. Breines's (1989) focus on one organization in a short historical time frame implied that political/instrumental and cultural/expressive modes of organization involve inevitable tensions and tradeoffs. My focus on multiple organizations over a longer time frame reveals that these tendencies can be mutually complementary for a movement as a whole, if not always for particular organizations. Broadly based movements with multiple constituencies have room for both movement organizations and movement communities, and they often provide a beneficial division of labor within the movement as a whole (Buechler, 1990).

Other work on women's mobilization has spoken even more directly to the role of culture in sustaining social movements. The hiatus between the two waves of women's activism in the United States has traditionally been seen merely as "the doldrums," but the question of how movements survive such doldrums brings the role of culture into sharp relief. The concept of "abeyance structures" refers to processes and forms that allow movements to survive periods of quiescence and to sustain themselves for future rounds of activism when opportunities for mobilization and activism have improved (Taylor, 1989). The women's movement survived the doldrums from 1920 to 1960 by devising abeyance structures that allowed a cadre of activists to survive in organizational niches that sustained protest potentials for later social struggles (Rupp and Taylor, 1987). One specific dimension of movement abeyance structures concerns the role of culture, including the emotions, beliefs, and actions necessary to sustain a base for future mobilization through symbolic and expressive practices (Taylor, 1989). In a more general sense, however, abeyance structures themselves are cultural inventions that help maintain the meaning, motivation, and purpose of women's activism through periods of limited opportunities.

Similar abeyance structures and practices have reemerged in the women's movement in the politically inhospitable climate of the 1980s and 1990s (Taylor and Rupp, 1993; Staggenborg, 1998). In this period, the cultural dimension of social activism and movement organization has become more important than ever, as lesbian feminist communities have made a disproportionate contribution to sustaining feminism in a hostile climate by again maintaining a movement core and allowing activists to sustain oppositional identities. In this context, the emergence of cultural feminism in the 1980s does not represent movement deradicalization (Echols, 1989) as much as movement survival amid social backlash and declining opportunities. In more specific terms, it has been female values, separatist strategy, female bonding, and feminist ritual that have emerged as fundamental cultural processes of movement survival that also have deeply political consequences (Taylor and Rupp, 1993). If the earlier period of doldrums is any guide, movement survival through the current doldrums will vitally shape the next round of feminist activism. In the case of this movement, then, there is cumulative evidence that the cultural dimensions of movement organization have been vital to women's mobilization in major waves of activism and in struggles to survive through less receptive sociopolitical periods.

Organization as a Cultural Resource

Lest this be seen as a peculiarity of women's movements, there is considerable evidence of the centrality of organizational culture in other contemporary movements as well. Examples include activism around nuclear power, peace and justice themes, ecological issues, gay and lesbian concerns, and anti-interventionism. The thread uniting many of these movements is the strategy of direct action. Resting on a shared ideology of feminism, ecology, anarchism, democracy, and spirituality, these movements seek to build community based on egalitarian values while respecting differences within the movement and the larger society (Epstein, 1991). Such movements preserve the legacy of prefigurative politics because their pursuit of utopian goals is recursively built into the movement's daily operation and organizational style. This is evident in affinity groups, decentralized organization, decision making by consensus, respect for differing opinions, and an overall emphasis on the process as well as the outcomes of activism. Such movements do not necessarily seek direct political confrontation as much as they seek to undermine the discursive frameworks that manufacture consent and legitimate authority (Sturgeon, 1995). It is the explicit attention to organization as a semiotic strategy and the attempt to work directly from basic values to daily practice that merits the designation of a "culturalist" orientation; these are movements that actively symbolize who they are and what they want not just as end goals but as daily guides to movement practice. Such movements have a mixed record of instrumental success and predictable tensions between cultural commitments and political aspirations (Epstein, 1991). They nevertheless signify a major trend in contemporary social activism by reframing the Leninist question of organization from a strategic challenge in an instrumental conflict to a symbolic challenge in a cultural struggle.

Lest this be seen as a peculiarity of U.S. movements, it is worth underscoring that significant parallels are evident in new social movements in Italy (Melucci, 1996a:328–331, 1989). Melucci detects a distinctive organizational form in many contemporary movements in which activists eschew traditional, centralized movement organizations because they replicate the instrumental logic of the larger system that these movements seek to challenge. In their place, these movements have constructed loose, temporary, ad hoc, informal networks that link together dispersed and fragmented groups. One remarkable feature of these organizational forms is their intertwining with the rhythms of everyday life, thereby reducing the distance between daily life and movement participation. Another feature of these alternative organizational forms is their self-referentiality. As with the movements discussed above, these organizational forms are deliberate, consciously chosen expressions; to paraphrase McLuhan, the organization is the message in that its form embodies the movement's values and goals in a semiotic statement that can be "read" by proponents, opponents, and bystanders. A final noteworthy feature of these organizational forms is their polarity; they allow movements to alternate between phases of visible public actions and latent cultural experimentation (Mueller, 1994). In all these ways, many new social movements have turned the organizational form of the movement into a cultural statement rather than a political instrument.

Finally, lest this be seen as a peculiarity of contemporary movements, there is some reason to think that cultural self-referentiality and prefigurative politics have been present throughout the history of modern social movements. Like so many of the issues associated with new social movement theory, it is easy to overstate the newness of a phenomenon about which we have much contemporary evidence. Comparative-historical research is the needed corrective for this potential error, and preliminary investigations suggest there are few if any traits that are distinctive to contemporary movements and entirely absent in older movements of the last two centuries (Calhoun, 1993; Tucker, 1991). The more specific question is whether earlier movements brought the same reflexive self-awareness to the question of organizational forms, and whether they were willing to sacrifice strategic success for the sake of preserving movement values and goals (as some contemporary movements seem willing to do). Although not definitive on this question, one recent study of the history of the U.S. labor movement begins to reinterpret organizational questions from a more culturalist orientation (Clemens, 1996). By seeing a movement's organizational form as a kind of frame, it becomes evident that labor's organizational struggles were largely about its relation to the polity and the market and about the collective identities of workers. Experimentation with different organizational models (fraternal, military, union) was not just a political struggle over effectiveness but also a cultural struggle over identity and social relations (Clemens, 1996). Although this study is suggestive, more focused research is required to clarify which (if any) features of movement culture are unique to contemporary movements.

Despite the recent attention paid to organizational culture, it is clear that movements have been more successful at structuring their own activities along participatory lines than at restructuring the larger society along such lines. This outcome has occasionally reinforced a certain inward-looking quality in some of these movements, subjecting them to the criticism that they are no longer really movements at all but rather depoliticized subcultures no longer interested in social transformation. What this criticism ignores is what the concept of abeyance structures (Taylor, 1989) is meant to underscore: that the sheer maintenance of a cultural community of activists who critically reflect on social conditions is both a major accomplishment and the outer limit of what is possible in some sociohistorical circumstances. The implication is that judgments of success and failure cannot be made apart from the opportunities and constraints of historically specific settings. Even so, one benchmark for evaluating the viability of movements across such settings is their promotion of free spaces (Evans and Boyte, 1986) and their capacity to establish and defend such spaces in which critical discourse can flourish. Culturally successful movements cultivate microversions of free spaces within their own movement communities while also retaining sight of the larger goal of renewing the public sphere. Although the latter is inherently more difficult to accomplish, an ongoing commitment to this goal is one important benchmark of a movement seeking broader social transformation.

This analysis of social movement culture has focused on collective identity, grievances and ideology, and organizational forms. Although I have discussed these topics separately, they are more closely connected than this presentation implies. For example, a prefigurative organizational form presumes an explicit ideological statement of a movement's values and a conscious sense of collective identity within the movement. Although movement culture is evident in many other areas, these were chosen to suggest a larger point. Ideology and organization are typically viewed as "political" aspects of social movements and standard components of instrumental action. The same might be said for collective identity in the form of group unity or solidarity. By selecting "political" aspects of movements for closer examination on cultural grounds, I hope to have suggested the duality of the political and cultural in social movements. A final comment on movement culture is in order. The recent rediscovery of the cultural aspects of social activism has been a welcome corrective to overly politicized analyses and a theoretically intoxicating redirection of intellectual energies. The current celebration of the cultural, however, raises the potential danger that social movement theory will continue its wide pendulum swings between artificial polarities. That is why the culturalist corrective was needed in the first place, and that is also why this corrective itself needs to be contextualized vis-à-vis other dimensions of social activism.

THE POLITICAL AND THE CULTURAL

In this and the preceding chapter, I have argued against any approach that dichotomizes movements as either "political" or "cultural," and have argued for the inescapably political and cultural dimensions of all movements. Such a recognition raises new and productive questions about the shifting orientation of movements over time. For instance, there is a strong suggestion in much of the social movement literature that the cultural dimensions of movements become predominant during abeyance periods when opportunities for political change are foreclosed. Whereas this is the specific thesis of Taylor's work (1989) on the women's movement, the pattern may be found in other movements as well. Thus, movement cultures and subcultures are crucial not only in the initial emergence of movements (McAdam, 1994), but also in the survival and reemergence of movements after quieter periods of dormancy. Such dormant periods have traditionally been interpreted as the "death" of a movement by more politically oriented approaches. When a culturalist focus is added, it underscores the role of previously nonvisible networks, oppositional subcultures, or intergenerational relations (Johnston et al., 1994) in ushering movements through periods of latency (Melucci, 1989). When opportunities appear again, it is not that the cultural elements disappear (or that a "cultural" movement suddenly becomes a "political" one). It is rather that the persisting cultural elements become the implicit foundation from which movements once again engage in overt political struggle. A theory that rigidly dichotomizes movements as cultural or political is less likely to recognize these interconnections than one premised on their inseparability.

These interconnections may also be detected in the effects and impacts of movements on the larger society in which they operate. Many movements that have sought explicitly political goals have nevertheless had important cultural consequences that often outweighed their political legacy (McAdam, 1994; Flacks, 1988). These are usually unintended consequences, although in some cases movements undergo a conscious process of goal transformation from more political to more cultural goals. Seen from the opposing side of social control, such cases raise the issue of how authorities invite and welcome a shift in movement goals from more political to more cultural emphases as a means of blunting the movement's impact on prevailing structures of power. Framing and pursuing these research questions requires a fluid understanding of the relation between the political and the cultural in both social movements and social control efforts. In the conceptual language of Chapter 7, this means that most contemporary social movements do not have rigid boundaries between state politics, social politics, and cultural struggles.

In earlier chapters, I argued for a structural theory of social movements that understands movements as responses to multiple levels of sociohistorical structure. Such structures also contain political and cultural elements, and much recent social theory suggests that there has been a fusion of political and cultural elements in social structure. To whatever extent this is the case, the fusion of these elements in contemporary social activism is a logical response to the new forms of social structure such movements challenge. Habermas's (1987, 1984) analysis of modern society identifies the differentiation of an instrumental system and a cultural life world as a major trend of social evolution, but he also suggests that this differentiation has been suspended through the colonization of the life world by the system and by the imposition of instrumental media such as money and power onto cultural questions of meaning and identity. In such a context, social resistance is likely to be articulated in cultural forms, reflecting the immediate terrain of the colonizing effort. But to the extent that such resistance challenges the rationale of the colonization itself, "cultural" struggles have a fundamentally "political" character as well. In a similar vein, Melucci's (1996a, 1989) analysis of new social movements situates them as responses to new forms of social control and conformity pressures that reach down into the interstices of everyday life and operate at the level of symbolic codes and identities. In adopting cultural forms of expression and resistance, contemporary movements respond to these new cultural controls on their own terms. But they also carry the potential for a broader challenge when such resistance becomes an explicit repudiation of the instrumental logic of administrative rationality, when it renders previously hidden power visible, and when it opens up possibilities for socially reconstructing the social order. Such theoretical approaches suggest that the fusion of the political and the cultural in contemporary social activism is not a temporary aberration, but rather a logical response to changes in the dominant social structures of the late modern era.

The broadest argument for the dual nature of social movements as political and cultural phenomena derives from the historical emergence of movements themselves. As I suggested in Chapter 1, social movements are historical products of the age of modernity. They arose as part of a sweeping social, political, and intellectual change that led significant numbers of people to view society as a social construction that was susceptible to social reconstruction through concerted collective effort. Thus, from their inception, social movements have had a dual focus. Reflecting the political, they have always involved some form of challenge to prevailing forms of authority. Reflecting the cultural, they have always operated as symbolic laboratories in which reflexive actors pose questions of meaning, purpose, identity, and change. When social movement theory recognizes this inevitable duality in social movements, it will once again be on a productive path.

Epilogue

Social movements are intentional, collective efforts to transform social order. They are a distinctly modern phenomenon, resting on the sociological insight that society is a social construction that is susceptible to reconstruction through collective action. The unfolding of modernity has enhanced the reflexivity about social order that is the hallmark of both the sociological imagination and social movements.

As the twentieth century draws to a close, there are substantial reasons for pessimism about whether this increased capacity for reflexivity will be used to enhance the quality of life in an equitable manner. And different observers will arrive at very different balance sheets about the cumulatively positive or negative effects of collective action on the shape of the modern world.

There is little doubt that some social movements have and will continue to succumb to revolutionary dogmatism, sectarian infighting, rigid fanaticism, and genocidal hatred. But the sociological imagination requires that our judgments of such movements be tempered with an analysis of the circumstances that provoke such responses, and that we not divorce these movements from their social contexts.

The sociological imagination also requires not just recognition but cultivation of the promise of social movements. Movements can be sites of heightened reflexivity and enhanced capacity to direct the self-production of society. Movements can be opportunities for ordinary people to make their own history. Movements can be carriers of evolutionary alternatives in a rapidly changing world. Movements can be vital learning mechanisms in an era of increasing complexity. Movements can be effective means of resisting instrumental rationality and the commodification of everyday life. Movements can be powerful ways of identifying problems, redistributing resources, broadening participation, and building solidarity. Movements can be havens in a heartless world for developing and nurturing collective identities. Movements can be crucial switching stations in the direction of history. Movements can be vital free spaces that promote democratization and restore a meaningful public sphere. Increasingly, we need movements to be all of these things.

References

Aguirre, Benigno E.
    1994   "Collective Behavior and Social Movement Theory." Pp. 257–272 in *Disasters, Collective Behavior and Social Organization*, edited by Russell R. Dynes and Kathleen J. Tierney. Newark: University of Delaware Press.

Anderson, Charles
    1974   *The Political Economy of Social Class.* Englewood Cliffs, NJ: Prentice-Hall.

Anner, John (ed.)
    1996   *Beyond Identity Politics: Emerging Social Justice Movements in Communities of Color.* Boston: South End Press.

Antonio, Robert J. and Alessandro Bonanno
    1996   "Post-Fordism in the United States: The Poverty of Market-Centered Democracy." *Current Perspectives in Social Theory* 16:3–32.

Aronowitz, Stanley
    1994   "The Situation of the Left in the United States." *Socialist Review* 93(3):5–79.
    1992   *The Politics of Identity.* New York: Routledge.

Bagguley, Paul
    1992   "Social Change, the Middle Class and the Emergence of 'New Social Movements:' A Critical Analysis." *The Sociological Review* 40:26–48.

Becker, Uwe
    1989   "Class Theory: Still the Axis of Critical Social Scientific Analysis?" Pp. 127–153 in *The Debate on Classes*, edited by Erik Olin Wright. London: Verso.

Bell, Daniel
    1960   *The End of Ideology.* Glencoe, IL: Free Press.

Bellah, Robert, Richard Madsen, William Sullivan, Ann Swidler, and Steven M. Tipton
    1985   *Habits of the Heart: Individualism and Commitment in American Life.* Berkeley: University of California Press.

Benford, Robert D.
    1997   "An Insider's Critique of the Social Movement Framing Perspective." *Sociological Inquiry* 67:409–430.
    1993a   "Frame Disputes within the Nuclear Disarmament Movement." *Social Forces* 71:677–701.
    1993b   "'You Could Be The Hundredth Monkey': Collective Action Frames and Vocabularies of Motive within the Nuclear Disarmament Movement." *The Sociological Quarterly* 34:195–216.

Benford, Robert D. and Scott A. Hunt
    1994   "Social Movement Counterframing and Reframing: Repairing and Sustaining Collective Identity Claims." Presented at the Midwest Sociological Society Meeting, St. Louis, March.
    1992   "Dramaturgy and Social Movements: The Social Construction and Communication of Power." *Sociological Inquiry* 62:36–55.

Berger, Peter and Thomas Luckmann
    1967   *The Social Construction of Reality*. Garden City, NY: Anchor.

Bernstein, Mary
    1997   "Celebration and Suppression: The Strategic Uses of Identity by the Lesbian and Gay Movement." *American Journal of Sociology* 103:531–565.

Block, Fred
    1987   *Revising State Theory*. Philadelphia: Temple University Press.

Blumer, Herbert
    1971   "Social Problems as Collective Behavior." *Social Problems* 18:298–306.
    1969   *Symbolic Interaction: Perspective and Method*. Englewood Cliffs, NJ: Prentice-Hall.
    1951   "The Field of Collective Behavior." Pp. 167–222 in *Principles of Sociology*, edited by A. M. Lee. New York: Barnes and Noble.

Boggs, Carl
    1995   "Rethinking the Sixties Legacy: From New Left to New Social Movements." Pp. 331–355 in *Social Movements: Critiques, Concepts, and Case-Studies*, edited by Stanford Lyman. New York: New York University Press.

Bourdieu, Pierre
    1984   *Distinction: A Social Critique of the Judgment of Taste*. Cambridge, MA: Harvard University Press.

Brandt, Karl-Werner
    1990   "Cyclical Aspects of New Social Movements: Waves of Cultural Criticism and Mobilization Cycles of New Middle-Class Radicalism." Pp. 24–42 in *Challenging the Political Order*, edited by Russell J. Dalton and Manfred Kuechler. New York: Oxford University Press.

Braverman, Harry
    1974   *Labor and Monopoly Capital*. New York: Monthly Review Press.

Breines, Wini
    1989   *Community and Organization in the New Left, 1962–1968: The Great Refusal*. New Brunswick, NJ: Rutgers University Press.

Brown, Michael and Amy Goldin
    1973   *Collective Behavior*. Pacific Palisades, CA: Goodyear.

Buechler, Steven M.
1995   "New Social Movement Theories." *The Sociological Quarterly* 36:441–464.
1993   "Beyond Resource Mobilization Theory? Emerging Trends in Social Movement Theory." *The Sociological Quarterly* 34:217–235.
1990   *Women's Movements in the United States: Woman Suffrage, Equal Rights and Beyond.* New Brunswick, NJ: Rutgers University Press.
1986   *The Transformation of the Woman Suffrage Movement: The Case of Illinois, 1850–1920.* New Brunswick, NJ: Rutgers University Press

Burkey, Richard M.
1978   *Ethnic and Racial Groups: The Dynamics of Dominance.* Menlo Park, CA: Cummings.

Bush, Diane Mitsch
1992   "Consequences of Social Movement Mobilization, State Structure, and Ideology: The Case of Women's Movements and Policy Reform." Paper presented at the Culture and Social Movements Workshop sponsored by the CBSM section of the ASA, San Diego, June.

Calhoun, Craig
1993   "'New Social Movements' of the Nineteenth Century." *Social Science History* 17:385–427.

Canel, Eduardo
1992   "New Social Movement Theory and Resource Mobilization: The Need for Integration." Pp. 22–51 in *Organizing Dissent*, edited by William K. Carroll. Toronto: Garamond Press.

Carroll, William K. (ed.)
1992   *Organizing Dissent.* Toronto: Garamond Press.

Carroll, William and R. S. Ratner
1996   "Master Framing and Cross-Movement Networking in Contemporary Social Movements." *The Sociological Quarterly* 37:601–625.
1994   "Between Leninism and Radical Pluralism: Gramscian Reflections on Counter-Hegemony and the New Social Movements." *Critical Sociology* 20:3–26.

Castells, Manuel
1983   *The City and the Grassroots: A Cross-Cultural Theory of Urban Social Movements.* Berkeley: University of California Press.

Chafe, William
1977   *Women and Equality.* New York: Oxford University Press.

Clemens, Elisabeth S.
1996   "Organizational Form as Frame: Collective Identity and Political Strategy in the American Labor Movement, 1880–1920." Pp. 205–226 in *Comparative Perspectives on Social Movements*, edited by Doug McAdam, John D. McCarthy, and Mayer N. Zald. New York: Cambridge University Press.

Cohen, Jean
1985   "Strategy or Identity: New Theoretical Paradigms and Contemporary Social Movements." *Social Research* 52:663–716.
1983   "Rethinking Social Movements." *Berkeley Journal of Sociology* 28:97–113.

Collins, Patricia Hill
    1990   *Black Feminist Thought.* Boston: Unwin and Hyman.

Collins, Randall
    1988   *Theoretical Sociology.* San Diego: Academic Press.
    1979   *The Credential Society.* New York: Academic Press.

Coser, Lewis A.
    1956   *The Functions of Social Conflict.* New York: Free Press.

Cott, Nancy
    1987   *The Grounding of American Feminism.* New Haven, CT: Yale University
            Press.

Cress, Daniel M. and David A. Snow
    1996   "Mobilization at the Margins: Resources, Benefactors and the Viability of
            Homeless Social Movement Organizations." *American Sociological Re-
            view* 61:1089–1109.

Croteau, David
    1995   *Politics and the Class Divide: Working People and the Middle-Class Left.*
            Philadelphia: Temple University Press.
    1994   "Accounting for Class Homogeneity in New Social Movements: The Ne-
            gotiation of Collective Identity." Paper presented at ASA meeting.

Dahrendorf, Ralf
    1959   *Class and Class Conflict in Industrial Society.* Stanford: Stanford Univer-
            sity Press.

Dalton, Russell J. and Manfred Kuechler (eds.)
    1990   *Challenging the Political Order: New Social and Political Movements in
            Western·Democracies.* New York: Oxford University Press.

Dalton, Russell J., Manfred Kuechler, and Wilhelm Burklin
    1990   "The Challenge of the New Movements." Pp. 3–20 in *Challenging the
            Political Order*, edited by Russell J. Dalton and Manfred Kuechler. New
            York: Oxford University Press.

Darnovsky, Marcy, Barbara Epstein, and Richard Flacks (eds.)
    1995a   *Cultural Politics and Social Movements.* Philadelphia: Temple University
            Press.

Darnovsky, Marcy, Barbara Epstein, and Richard Flacks
    1995b   "Introduction." Pp. vii–xxxiii in *Cultural Politics and Social Movements*,
            edited by Marcy Darnovsky, Barbara Epstein, and Richard Flacks. Philadel-
            phia: Temple University Press.

Davies, James
    1962   "Toward a Theory of Revolution." *American Sociological Review* 27:5–19.

Davis, Angela
    1983   *Women, Race and Class.* New York: Vintage.

Derber, Charles (with others)
    1995   *What's Left? Radical Politics in the Postcommunist Era.* Amherst: Univer-
            sity of Massachusetts Press.

Diani, Mario
    1996   "Linking Mobilization Frames and Political Opportunities: Insights from
            Regional Populism in Italy." *American Sociological Review* 61:1053–1069.

Dreyfus, Hubert, L. and Paul Rabinow
1983   *Michel Foucault: Beyond Structuralism and Hermeneutics.* Chicago: University of Chicago Press.

Durkheim, Emile
1897   *Suicide.* New York: Free Press (1951).
1893   *The Division of Labor in Society.* New York: Free Press (1964).

Echols, Alice
1989   *Daring to be Bad: Radical Feminism in America 1967–1975.* Minneapolis: University of Minnesota Press.

Eder, Klaus
1993   *The New Politics of Class.* Newbury Park, CA: Sage.

Ehrenreich, Barbara
1989   *Fear of Falling: The Inner Life of the Middle Class.* New York: Pantheon.

Eisenstein, Zillah
1984   *Feminism and Sexual Equality.* New York: Monthly Review Press.

Epstein, Barbara
1991   *Political Protest and Cultural Revolution: Nonviolent Direct Action in the 1970s and 1980s.* Berkeley: University of California Press.

Evans, Sara M. and Harry C. Boyte
1986   *Free Spaces.* New York: Harper & Row.

Fireman, Bruce and William Gamson
1979   "Utilitarian Logic in the Resource Mobilization Perspective." Pp. 8–44 in *The Dynamics of Social Movements,* edited by Mayer N. Zald and John D. McCarthy. Cambridge, MA: Winthrop.

Fisher, Bob and Joe Kling
1991   "Popular Mobilization in the 1990s: Prospects for the New Social Movements." *New Politics* Winter 1991.

Flacks, Richard
1995   "Think Globally, Act Politically: Some Notes toward New Movement Strategy." Pp. 251–263 in *Cultural Politics and Social Movements,* edited by Marcy Darnovsky, Barbara Epstein, and Richard Flacks. Philadelphia: Temple University Press.
1994   "The Party's Over—So What Is to Be Done?" Pp. 330–351 in *New Social Movements,* edited by Enrique Larana, Hank Johnston, and Joseph R. Gusfield. Philadelphia: Temple University Press.
1988   *Making History: The American Left and the American Mind.* New York: Columbia University Press.

Foucault, Michel
1980   *Power/Knowledge.* New York: Pantheon Books.
1979   *Discipline and Punish: The Birth of the Prison.* New York: Vintage.

Fraser, Nancy
1989   *Unruly Practices.* Minneapolis: University of Minnesota Press.

Friedan, Betty
1963   *The Feminine Mystique.* New York: Dell.

Friedrichs, Robert
1970   *A Sociology of Sociology.* New York: Free Press.

Gamson, Joshua
    1996   "The Excluded Muddle: Internal Disputes in the Making of Collective Identity." Paper presented at the ASA Meeting.
    1995   "Must Identity Movements Self-Destruct: A Queer Dilemma." *Social Problems* 42:390–407.

Gamson, William
    1995   "Constructing Social Protest." Pp. 85–106 in *Social Movements and Culture*, edited by Hank Johnston and Bert Klandermans. Minneapolis: University of Minnesota Press.
    1992   "The Social Psychology of Collective Action." Pp. 53–76 in *Frontiers of Social Movement Theory*, edited by Aldon Morris and Carol Mueller. New Haven, CT: Yale University Press.
    1990   *The Strategy of Social Protest*, 2nd edition. Belmont, CA: Wadsworth.
    1988   "Political Discourse and Collective Action." Pp. 219–244 in *International Social Movement Research*, Volume 1, *From Structure to Action*, edited by Bert Klandermans, Hanspeter Kriesi, and Sidney Tarrow. Greenwich, CT: JAI Press.

Gamson, William, Bruce Fireman, and Steven Rytina
    1982   *Encounters with Unjust Authorities*. Homewood, IL: Dorsey Press.

Gamson, William A. and David S. Meyer
    1996   "Framing Political Opportunity." Pp. 275–290 in *Comparative Perspectives on Social Movements*, edited by Doug McAdam, John D. McCarthy, and Mayer N. Zald. New York: Cambridge University Press.

Gamson, William and Andre Modigliani
    1989   "Media Discourse and Public Opinion on Nuclear Power: A Constructionist Approach." *American Journal of Sociology* 95:1–37.

Garcia, John A.
    1996   "The Chicano Movement: Its Legacy for Politics and Policy." Pp. 83–107 in *Chicanas/Chicanos at the Crossroads*, edited by David R. Maciel and Isidro D. Ortiz. Tucson: University of Arizona Press.

Garner, Roberta
    1997   *Social Movement Theory and Research: An Annotated Bibliographical Guide*. Magill Bibliographies: Salem/Scarecrow Press.

Garner, Roberta Ash and Mayer N. Zald
    1987   "The Political Economy of Social Movement Sectors." Pp. 293–318 in *Social Movements in an Organizational Society*, edited by Mayer N. Zald and John D. McCarthy. New Brunswick, NJ: Transaction.

Geschwender, James
    1968   "Explorations in the Theory of Social Movements and Revolutions." *Social Forces* 47:127–135.

Giddens, Anthony
    1991   *Modernity and Self-Identity*. Stanford: Stanford University Press.
    1984   *The Constitution of Society*. Berkeley: University of California Press.
    1975   *The Class Structure of Advanced Societies*. New York: Harper & Row.

Giddings, Paula
    1984   *When and Where I Enter*. New York: Morrow.

Giugni, Marco
    1998a   "The Other Side of the Coin: Explaining Crossnational Similarities between Social Movements." *Mobilization* 3:89–105.

1998b   "Structure and Culture in Social Movement Theory." *Sociological Forum* 13:365–375.

Goffman, Erving
1974   *Frame Analysis.* New York: Harper Colophon.

Goldthorpe, John
1969   *The Affluent Worker in the Class Structure.* London: Cambridge University Press.

Goode, Erich and Nachman Ben-Yehuda
1994   *Moral Panics: The Social Construction of Deviance.* Oxford: Blackwell.

Gouldner, Alvin
1979   *The Future of Intellectuals and the Rise of the New Class.* New York: Seabury Press.

Gramsci, Antonio
1971   *Selections from the Prison Notebooks.* New York: International Publishers.

Gurr, Ted
1969   *Why Men Rebel.* Princeton: Princeton University Press.

Gusfield, Joseph R.
1994   "The Reflexivity of Social Movements: Collective Behavior and Mass Society Theory Revisited." Pp. 58–78 in *New Social Movements,* edited by Enrique Larana, Hank Johnston, and Joseph R. Gusfield. Philadelphia: Temple University Press.

Gutman, Herbert
1976   *Work, Culture, and Society in Industrializing America.* New York: Knopf.

Habermas, Jurgen
1987   *The Theory of Communicative Action: Lifeworld and System,* Volume 2, translated by Thomas McCarthy. Boston: Beacon Press.
1984   *The Theory of Communicative Action: Reason and the Rationalization of Society,* Volume 1, translated by Thomas McCarthy. Boston: Beacon Press.
1975   *Legitimation Crisis.* Boston: Beacon Press.
1969   *Knowledge and Human Interests.* Boston: Beacon Press.

Halmos, Paul (ed.)
1970   *The Sociology of Sociology.* Keele: University of Keele.

Hirsch, Eric
1986   "The Creation of Political Solidarity in Social Movement Organizations." *The Sociological Quarterly* 27:373–382.

Hirsch, Joachim
1988   "The Crisis of Fordism, Transformations of the 'Keynesian' Security State, and New Social Movements." Pp. 43–55 in *Research in Social Movements, Conflicts and Change,* Volume 10, edited by Louis Kriesberg. Greenwich, CT: JAI Press.

hooks, bell
1984   *Feminist Theory: From Margin to Center.* Boston: South End Press.

Hunt, Scott, Robert D. Benford, and David A. Snow
1994   "Identity Fields: Framing Processes and the Social Construction of Movement Identities." Pp. 185–208 in *New Social Movements,* edited by Enrique Larana, Hank Johnston, and Joseph R. Gusfield. Philadelphia: Temple University Press.

Inglehart, Ronald
   1990   "Values, Ideology, and Cognitive Mobilization in New Social Move-
           ments." Pp. 43–66 in *Challenging the Political Order*, edited by Rus-
           sell J. Dalton and Manfred Kuechler. New York: Oxford University
           Press.

Jaggar, Allison
   1983   *Feminist Politics and Human Nature*. Totowa, NJ: Rowman & Allanheld.

Jenkins, J. Craig and Bert Klandermans (eds.)
   1995   *The Politics of Social Protest*. Minneapolis: University of Minnesota Press.

Johnston, Hank
   1994   "New Social Movements and Old Regional Nationalisms." Pp. 267–286
           in *New Social Movements*, edited by Enrique Larana, Hank Johnston, and
           Joseph R. Gusfield. Philadelphia: Temple University Press.

Johnston, Hank and Bert Klandermans
   1995a   "The Cultural Analysis of Social Movements." Pp. 3–24 in *Social Move-
           ments and Culture*, edited by Hank Johnston and Bert Klandermans. Min-
           neapolis: University of Minnesota Press.

Johnston, Hank and Bert Klandermans (eds.)
   1995b   *Social Movements and Culture*. Minnesota: University of Minnesota Press.

Johnston, Hank, Enrique Larana, and Joseph R. Gusfield
   1994   "Identities, Grievances and New Social Movements." Pp. 3–35 in *New
           Social Movements*, edited by Enrique Larana, Hank Johnston, and Joseph
           R. Gusfield. Philadelphia: Temple University Press.

Killian, Lewis
   1994   "Are Social Movements Irrational or Are They Collective Behavior?" Pp.
           273–280 in *Disasters, Collective Behavior, and Social Organization*, edited
           by Russell R. Dynes and Kathleen T. Tierney. Newark, DE: University of
           Delaware Press.

Kitschelt, Herbert
   1991   "Resource Mobilization Theory: A Critique." Pp. 323–347 in *Research
           on Social Movements: The State of the Art*, edited by Dieter Rucht. Boul-
           der, CO: Westview Press.

Klandermans, Bert
   1997   *The Social Psychology of Protest*. Oxford: Blackwell.
   1994   "Transient Identities? Membership Patterns in the Dutch Peace Move-
           ment." Pp. 168–184 in *New Social Movements*, edited by Enrique Larana,
           Hank Johnston, and Joseph R. Gusfield. Philadelphia: Temple University
           Press.
   1992   "The Social Construction of Protest and Multiorganizational Fields." Pp.
           77–103 in *Frontiers of Social Movement Theory*, edited by Aldon Morris
           and Carol Mueller. New Haven, CT: Yale University Press.
   1991   "New Social Movements and Resource Mobilization: The European and
           American Approaches Revisited." Pp. 17–44 in *Research on Social Move-
           ments: The State of the Art in Western Europe and the USA*, edited by Di-
           eter Rucht. Boulder, CO: Westview Press.
   1988   "The Formation and Mobilization of Consensus." Pp. 173–196 in *In-
           ternational Social Movement Research*, Volume 1, *From Structure to Ac-
           tion*, edited by Bert Klandermans, Hanspeter Kriesi, and Sidney Tarrow.
           Greenwich, CT: JAI Press.

1984   "Mobilization and Participation: Social-Psychological Expansions of Resource Mobilization Theory." *American Sociological Review* 52:519–531.

Klandermans, Bert and Sidney Tarrow
1988   "Mobilization into Social Movements: Synthesizing European and American Approaches." Pp. 1–38 in *International Social Movement Research*, Volume 1, *From Structure to Action*, edited by Bert Klandermans, Hanspeter Kriesi, and Sidney Tarrow. Greenwich, CT: JAI Press.

Konrad, George and Ivan Szelenyi
1979   *The Intellectuals on the Road to Class Power*, translated by Andrew Arato and Richard E. Allen. New York: Harcourt, Brace Jovanovich.

Kornhauser, William
1959   *The Politics of Mass Society*. New York: Free Press.

Kriesberg, Louis
Annual   *Research in Social Movements, Conflicts and Change*. Greenwich, CT: JAI Press.

Kriesi, Hanspeter
1995   "The Political Opportunity Structure of New Social Movements: Its Impact on Their Mobilization." Pp. 167–198 in *The Politics of Social Protest*, edited by J. Craig Jenkins and Bert Klandermans. Minneapolis: University of Minnesota Press.
1989   "New Social Movements and the New Class in the Netherlands." *American Journal of Sociology* 94:1078–1116.
1988   "The Interdependence of Structure and Action: Some Reflections on the State of the Art." Pp. 349–368 in *International Social Movement Research*, Volume 1, *From Structure to Action*, edited by Bert Klandermans, Hanspeter Kriesi, and Sidney Tarrow. Greenwich, CT: JAI Press.

Kriesi, Hanspeter, Ruud Koopmans, Jan Willem Duyvendak, and Marco G. Guigni
1995   *New Social Movements in Western Europe: A Comparative Analysis*. Minneapolis: University of Minnesota Press.

Kuhn, Thomas
1962   *The Structure of Scientific Revolutions*. Chicago: University of Chicago Press.

Larana, Enrique
1994   "Continuity and Unity in New Forms of Collective Action: A Comparative Analysis of Student Movements." Pp. 209–233 in *New Social Movements*, edited by Enrique Larana, Hank Johnston, and Joseph R. Gusfield. Philadelphia: Temple University Press.

Larana, Enrique, Hank Johnston, and Joseph R. Gusfield (eds.)
1994   *New Social Movements: From Ideology to Identity*. Philadelphia: Temple University Press.

Lerner, Gerda
1986   *The Creation of Patriarchy*. New York: Oxford University Press.

Lichterman, Paul
1995   "Piecing Together Multicultural Community: Cultural Differences in Community Building Among Grass-Roots Environmentalists." *Social Problems* 42:513–534.

Linton, Ralph
1936   *The Study of Man*. New York: Appleton-Century-Crofts.

Lofland, John
    1996   *Social Movement Organizations: Guide to Research on Insurgent Realities.* New York: Aldine de Gruyter.
    1995   "Charting Degrees of Movement Culture: Tasks of the Cultural Cartographer." Pp. 188–216 in *Social Movements and Culture*, edited by Hank Johnston and Bert Klandermans. Minneapolis: University of Minnesota Press.
    1993   "Theory-bashing and Answer-improving in the Study of Social Movements." *The American Sociologist* 24:37–58.
    1985   *Protest: Studies of Collective Behavior and Social Movements.* New Brunswick, NJ: Transaction.
    1977   *Doomsday Cult.* New York: Irvington.

Lofland, John, Mary Anna Colwell, and Victoria Johnson
    1989   "Social Movement Strategies as Theories of Social Change." Presented at ASA Meetings.

Mannheim, Karl
    1936   *Ideology and Utopia.* New York: Harcourt, Brace and World.

Marin, Marguerite V.
    1991   *Social Protest in an Urban Barrio. A Study of the Chicano Movement, 1966–1974.* Lanham, MD: University Press of America.

Marx, Gary and Doug McAdam
    1994   *Collective Behavior and Social Movements: Process and Structure.* Englewood Cliffs, NJ: Prentice-Hall.

Mayer, Margit
    1995   "Social Movement Research in the United States: A European Perspective." Pp. 168–195 in *Social Movements: Critiques, Concepts, and Case-Studies*, edited by Stanford Lyman. New York: New York University Press.

McAdam, Doug
    1996   "Conceptual Origins, Current Problems, Future Directions." Pp. 23–40 in *Comparative Perspectives on Social Movements*, edited by Doug McAdam, John D. McCarthy, and Mayer N. Zald. New York: Cambridge University Press.
    1994   "Culture and Social Movements." Pp. 36–57 in *New Social Movements*, edited by Enrique Larana, Hank Johnston, and Joseph R. Gusfield. Philadelphia: Temple University Press.
    1988   "Micro-mobilization Contexts and Recruitment to Activism." Pp. 125–154 in *International Social Movement Research*, Volume 1, edited by Bert Klandermans, Hanspeter Kriesi, and Sidney Tarrow. Greenwich, CT: JAI Press.
    1982   *The Political Process and the Development of Black Insurgency.* Chicago: University of Chicago Press.

McAdam, Doug, John D. McCarthy, and Mayer N. Zald
    1996a   "Introduction: Opportunities, Mobilizing Structures and Framing Processes—Toward a Synthetic, Comparative Perspective on Social Movements." Pp. 1–20 in *Comparative Perspectives on Social Movements*, edited by Doug McAdam, John D. McCarthy, and Mayer N. Zald. New York: Cambridge University Press.

McAdam, Doug, John D. McCarthy, and Mayer N. Zald (eds.)
    1996b   *Comparative Perspectives on Social Movements: Political Opportunities, Mobilizing Structures, and Cultural Framings.* New York: Cambridge University Press.

McAdam, Doug and Dieter Rucht
    1993   "The Cross-National Diffusion of Movement Ideas." *The Annals of the American Academy of Political and Social Science* 528:56–74.

McAdam, Doug, Sidney Tarrow, and Charles Tilly
    1996   "To Map Contentious Politics." *Mobilization* 1:17–34.

McCarthy, John D. and Mark Wolfson
    1996   "Resource Mobilization by Local Social Movement Organizations: Agency, Strategy and Organization in the Movement Against Drunk Driving." *American Sociological Review* 61:1070–1088.

McCarthy, John D. and Mayer N. Zald
    1977   "Resource Mobilization and Social Movements: A Partial Theory." *American Journal of Sociology* 82:1212–1241.
    1973   *The Trend of Social Movements in America: Professionalization and Resource Mobilization.* Morristown, NJ: General Learning Press.

McPhail, Clark
    1991   *The Myth of the Madding Crowd.* New York: Walter de Gruyter.

Melucci, Alberto
    1996a   *Challenging Codes: Collective Action in the Information Age.* Cambridge: Cambridge University Press.
    1996b   *The Playing Self.* Cambridge: Cambridge University Press.
    1995a   "The New Social Movement Revisited: Reflections on a Sociological Misunderstanding." Pp. 107–119 in Lewis Maheu (ed.), *Social Movements and Social Classes.* London: Sage.
    1995b   "The Global Planet and the Internal Planet: New Frontiers for Collective Action and Individual Transformation." Pp. 287–298 in *Cultural Politics and Social Movements,* edited by Marcy Darnovsky, Barbara Epstein, and Richards Flacks. Philadelphia: Temple University Press.
    1989   *Nomads of the Present: Social Movements and Individual Needs in Contemporary Society,* edited by John Keane and Paul Mier. Philadelphia: Temple University Press.
    1988a   "Getting Involved: Identity and Mobilization in Social Movements." Pp. 329–348 in *International Social Movement Research,* Volume 1, *From Structure to Action,* edited by Bert Klandermans, Hanspeter Kriesi, and Sidney Tarrow. Greenwich, CT: JAI Press.
    1988b   "Social Movements and the Democratization of Everyday Life." Pp. 245–260 in *Civil Society and the State,* edited by John Keane. London: Verso.
    1984   "An End to Social Movements?" *Social Science Information* 23:819–835.
    1981   "Ten Hypotheses for the Analysis of New Movements," in *Contemporary Italian Sociology,* edited by Diana Pinto. Cambridge: Cambridge University Press.
    1980   "The New Social Movements: A Theoretical Approach." *Social Science Information* 19(2):199–226.

Merton, Robert
    1968   *Social Theory and Social Structure.* New York: Free Press.

Meyer, David S. and Suzanne Staggenborg
    1996   "Movements, Countermovements, and the Structure of Political Opportunity." *American Journal of Sociology* 101:1628–1660.

Meyer, David S. and Sidney Tarrow (eds.)
    1998   *The Social Movement Society: Contentious Politics for a New Century.* Lanham, MD: Rowman & Littlefield.

Miliband, Ralph
   1969   *The State in Capitalist Society*. London: Weidenfeld & Nicolson.

Mills, C. Wright
   1959   *The Sociological Imagination*. New York: Oxford University Press.
   1956   *The Power Elite*. New York: Oxford University Press.

Moore, Barrington
   1978   *Injustice: The Social Bases of Obedience and Revolt*. White Plains, NY: M.
           E. Sharpe.

Moraga, Cherrie and Gloria Anzaldua (eds.)
   1981   *This Bridge Called My Back: Writings by Radical Women of Color*. Water-
           town, MA: Persephone Press.

Morris, Aldon
   1992   "Political Consciousness and Collective Action." Pp. 351–373 in *Fron-
           tiers of Social Movement Theory*, edited by Carol Mueller and Aldon Mor-
           ris. New Haven, CT: Yale University Press.
   1984   *The Origins of the Civil Rights Movement*. New York: Free Press.

Mueller, Carol
   1994   "Conflict Networks and the Origins of Women's Liberation." Pp.
           234–263 in *New Social Movements*, edited by Enrique Larana, Hank
           Johnston, and Joseph R. Gusfield. Philadelphia: Temple University
           Press.
   1992   "Building Social Movement Theory." Pp. 3–25 in *Frontiers in Social Move-
           ment Theory*, edited by Aldon Morris and Carol Mueller. New Haven, CT:
           Yale University Press.

Munoz, Carlos (Jr.)
   1989   *Youth, Identity and Power: The Chicano Movement*. London: Verso.

Neidhardt, Friedhelm and Dieter Rucht
   1991   "The Analysis of Social Movements: The State of the Art and Some Per-
           spectives for Further Research." Pp. 422–464 in *Research on Social Move-
           ments: The State of the Art in Western Europe and the USA*, edited by Di-
           eter Rucht. Boulder, CO: Westview Press

Oberschall, Anthony
   1993   *Social Movements: Ideologies, Interests and Identities*. New Brunswick:
           Transaction.
   1973   *Social Conflict and Social Movements*. Englewood Cliffs, NJ: Prentice-Hall.

Offe, Claus
   1990   "Reflections on the Institutional Self-transformation of Movement Poli-
           tics: A Tentative Stage Model." Pp. 232–250 in *Challenging the Politi-
           cal Order*, edited by Russell J. Dalton and Manfred Kuechler. New York:
           Oxford University Press.
   1985   "New Social Movements: Challenging the Boundaries of Institutional Pol-
           itics." *Social Research* 52:817–868.

Olson, Mancur
   1965   *The Logic of Collective Action*. Cambridge, MA: Harvard University Press.

Omi, Michael and Howard Winant
   1986   *Racial Formation in the United States from the 1960s to the 1980s*. New
           York: Routledge.

Pakulski, Jan
    1995   "Social Movements and Class: The Decline of the Marxist Paradigm." Pp. 55–86 in *Social Classes and Social Movements*, edited by Louis Maheu. London: Sage.

Parsons, Talcott
    1951   *The Social System*. Glencoe, IL: Free Press.
    1937   *The Structure of Social Action*. New York: McGraw-Hill.

Pichardo, Nelson
    1997   "New Social Movements: A Critical Review." *Annual Review of Sociology* 23:411–430.

Pickvance, Chris
    1995   "Social Movements in the Transition from State Socialism: Convergence or Divergence?" Pp. 123–150 in *Social Classes and Social Movements*, edited by Lewis Maheu. London: Sage.

Piven, Frances Fox and Richard Cloward
    1982   *The New Class War*. New York: Vintage.
    1977   *Poor People's Movements*. New York: Vintage

Plotke, David
    1990   "What's So New About New Social Movements?" *Socialist Review* 20:81–102.

Polletta, Francesca
    1998   "'It Was Like a Fever . . .': Narrative and Identity in Social Protest." *Social Problems* 45:137–159.
    1997   "Culture and Its Discontents: Recent Theorizing on the Cultural Dimensions of Protest." *Sociological Inquiry* 67:431–450.

Poulantzas, Nicos
    1978 *Classes in Contemporary Capitalism*. London: Verso.

Rachleff, Peter
    1994   "Seeds of a Labor Resurgency." *The Nation*, February 21:226–229.

Ray, Larry
    1993   *Rethinking Critical Theory: Emancipation in the Age of Global Social Movements*. London: Sage.

Reich, Michael
    1981   *Racial Inequality: A Political-Economic Analysis*. Princeton, NJ: Princeton University Press.

Reynolds, Larry and Janice Reynolds (eds.)
    1970   *The Sociology of Sociology*. New York: McKay.

Ritzer, George
    1996   *Sociological Theory*, 4th edition. New York: McGraw-Hill.

Robnett, Belinda
    1996   "African-American Women in the Civil Rights Movement, 1954–1965: Gender, Leadership, and Micromobilization." *American Journal of Sociology* 101:1661–1693.

Rootes, Chris
    1995   "A New Class? The Higher Educated and the New Politics." Pp. 220–235 in *Social Classes and Social Movements*, edited by Lewis Maheu. London: Sage.

Rose, Fred
    1997   "Towards a Class-Cultural Theory of Social Movements: Reinterpreting New Social Movements." *Sociological Forum* 12:461–494.

Rosenau, Pauline
    1992   *Post-modernism and the Social Sciences.* Princeton, NJ: Princeton University Press.

Rubin, Gayle
    1975   "The Traffic in Women: Notes on the Political Economy of Sex." Pp. 157–210 in *Toward an Anthropology of Women*, edited by Rayna Reiter. New York: Monthly Review Press.

Rucht, Dieter
    1996   "The Impact of National Contexts on Social Movement Structures: A Cross-Movement and Cross-National Comparison." Pp. 185–204 in *Comparative Perspectives on Social Movements*, edited by Doug McAdam, John D. McCarthy, and Mayer N. Zald. New York: Cambridge University Press.
    1988   "Themes, Logics and Arenas of Social Movements: A Structural Approach." Pp. 305–328 in *International Social Movement Research*, Volume 1, *From Structure to Action*, edited by Bert Klandermans, Hanspeter Kriesi, and Sidney Tarrow. Greenwich, CT: JAI Press.

Rupp, Leila J. and Verta Taylor
    1987   *Survival in the Doldrums.* New York: Oxford University Press.

Sargent, Lydia (ed.)
    1981   *Women and Revolution.* Boston: South End Press.

Schwartz, Michael
    1976   *Radical Protest and Social Structure.* New York: Academic Press.

Schwartz, Michael and Shuva Paul
    1992   "Resource Mobilization versus the Mobilization of People: Why Consensus Movements Cannot Be Instruments of Social Change." Pp. 205–223 in *Frontiers in Social Movement Theory*, edited by Aldon Morris and Carol Mueller. New Haven, CT: Yale University Press.

Seidman, Steven
    1994   *Contested Knowledge: Social Theory in the Postmodern Age.* Oxford: Blackwell.

Shannon, Thomas
    1989   *An Introduction to the World-System Perspective.* Boulder, CO: Westview Press.

Shin, Gi Wook
    1994   "The Historical Making of Collective Action: The Korean Peasant Uprisings of 1946." *American Journal of Sociology* 99:1596–1624.

Smelser, Neil J.
    1962   *Theory of Collective Behavior.* New York: Free Press.

Smith, Jackie
    1997   "Transnational Political Processes and the Human Rights Movement." Pp. 541–563 in *Social Movements*, edited by Steven M. Buechler and F. Kurt Cylke, Jr. Mountain View, CA: Mayfield.
    1994   "The Globalization of Social Movements: The Transnational Social Movement Sector 1983–1993." Paper presented at the ASA meeting.

Smith, Jackie and Ron Pagnucco
1995   "Overcoming Obstacles to Cooperation in Transnational Social Movement Organizations." Unpublished manuscript.

Snow, David A. and Robert Benford
1992   "Master Frames and Cycles of Protest." Pp. 133–155 in *Frontiers of Social Movement Theory*, edited by Carol Mueller and Aldon Morris. New Haven, CT: Yale University Press.
1988   "Ideology, Frame Resonance, and Participant Mobilization." Pp. 197–217 in *International Social Movement Research*, Volume 1, *From Structure to Action*, edited by Bert Klandermans, Hanspeter Kriesi, and Sidney Tarrow. Greenwich, CT: JAI Press.

Snow, David A., Daniel M. Cress, Liam Downey, and Andrew W. Jones
1998   "'Disrupting the Quotidian': Reconceptualizing the Relationship between Breakdown and the Emergence of Collective Action." *Mobilization* 3:1–22.

Snow, David A., E. Burke Rochford, Jr., Steve K. Worden, and Robert D. Benford
1986   "Frame Alignment Processes, Micromobilization and Movement Participation." *American Sociological Review* 51:464–481.

Snow, David A., Louis A. Zurcher, and Robert Peters
1981   "Victory Celebrations as Theater: A Dramaturgical Approach to Crowd Behavior." *Symbolic Interaction* 4:21–42.

Staggenborg, Suzanne
1998   "Social Movement Communities and Cycles of Protest: The Emergence and Maintenance of a Local Women's Movement." *Social Problems* 45:180–204.

Steinmetz, George
1994   "Regulation Theory, Post-Marxism and the New Social Movements." *Comparative Studies in Society and History* 36:176–212.

Stoecker, Randy
1995   "Community, Movement, Organization: The Problem of Identity Convergence in Collective Action." *The Sociological Quarterly* 36:111–130.
1994   *Defending Community: The Struggle for Alternative Redevelopment in Cedar-Riverside*. Philadelphia: Temple University Press.

Sturgeon, Noel
1995   "Theorizing Movements: Direct Action and Direct Theory." Pp. 35–51 in *Cultural Politics and Social Movements*, edited by Marcy Darnovsky, Barbara Epstein, and Richard Flacks. Philadelphia: Temple University Press.

Swart, William
1995   "The League of Nations and the Irish Question: Master Frames, Cycles of Protest and 'Master Frame Alignment'." *The Sociological Quarterly* 36:465–481.

Swidler, Ann
1995   "Cultural Power and Social Movements." Pp. 25–40 in *Social Movements and Culture*, edited by Hank Johnston and Bert Klandermans. Minneapolis: University of Minnesota Press.

Tarrow, Sidney
1996   "States and Opportunities: The Political Structuring of Social Movements." Pp. 41–61 in *Comparative Perspectives on Social Movements*, edited

by Doug McAdam, John D. McCarthy, and Mayer N. Zald. New York: Cambridge University Press.

1994   *Power in Movement: Social Movements, Collective Action and Politics.* London: Cambridge University Press.

1991   *Struggle, Politics and Reform: Collective Action, Social Movements, and Cycles of Protest.* Western Societies Program, Occasional Paper No. 21, Center for International Studies, Cornell University Press.

Taylor, Verta
    1996   *Rock-a-by Baby: Feminism, Self-Help and Postpartum Depression.* New York: Routledge
    1989   "Social Movement Continuity: The Women's Movement in Abeyance." *American Sociological Review* 54:761–775.

Taylor, Verta and Nicole C. Raeburn
    1995   "Identity Politics as High-Risk Activism: Career Consequences for Lesbian, Gay and Bisexual Sociologists." *Social Problems* 42:252–273.

Taylor, Verta and Leila J. Rupp
    1993   "Women's Culture and Lesbian Feminist Activism: A Reconsideration of Cultural Feminism." *Signs* 19:32–61.

Taylor, Verta and Nancy Whittier
    1992   "Collective Identity in Social Movement Communities." Pp. 104–129 in *Frontiers of Social Movement Theory*, edited by Aldon Morris and Carol Mueller. New Haven, CT: Yale University Press.
    1992   "The Women's Movement in the 'Post-Feminist' Age: Rethinking Social Movement Theory from a Feminist Standpoint." Unpublished manuscript.

Therborn, Goran
    1976   *Science, Class, and Society: On the Formation of Sociology and Historical Materialism.* London: New Left Books.

Thompson, E. P.
    1963   *The Making of the English Working Class.* New York: Vintage.

Thompson, John
    1990   *Ideology and Modern Culture.* Stanford: Stanford University Press.

Tilly, Charles
    1995   *Popular Contention in Great Britain, 1758–1834.* Cambridge, MA: Harvard University Press.
    1978   *From Mobilization to Revolution.* Reading, MA: Addison-Wesley.

Touraine, Alain
    1985   "An Introduction to the Study of Social Movements." *Social Research* 52:749–787.
    1981   *The Voice and the Eye: An Analysis of Social Movements.* New York: Cambridge University Press.
    1977   *The Self-Production of Society.* Chicago: University of Chicago Press.

Tucker, Kenneth H.
    1991   "How New Are the New Social Movements?" *Theory, Culture and Society* 8(2):75–98.
    1989   "Ideology and Social Movements: The Contributions of Habermas." *Sociological Inquiry* 59:30–48.

Turner, Ralph
    1996   "The Moral Issue in Collective Behavior and Collective Action." *Mobilization* 1:1–15.

1981   "Collective Behavior and Resource Mobilization as Approaches to Social Movements: Issues and Continuities." *Research in Social Movements, Conflict and Change* 4:1–24.

Turner, Ralph and Lewis Killian
1987   *Collective Behavior*, 3rd edition. Upper Saddle River, NJ: Prentice-Hall.
1972   *Collective Behavior*, 2nd edition. Englewood Cliffs, NJ: Prentice-Hall.
1957   *Collective Behavior*, 1st edition. Englewood Cliffs, NJ: Prentice-Hall.

Wallace, Michael and J. Craig Jenkins
1995   "The New Class, Postindustrialism and Neocorporatism: Three Images of Social Protest in the Western Democracies." Pp. 96–137 in *The Politics of Social Protest*, edited by J. Craig Jenkins and Bert Klandermans. Minneapolis: University of Minnesota Press.

Wallerstein, Immanuel
1990   "Antisystemic Movements: History and Dilemmas." Pp. 13–53 in *Transforming the Revolution*, edited by Samir Amin, Giovanni Arrighi, Andre Gunder Frank, and Immanuel Wallerstein. New York: Monthly Review Press.
1989   *The Modern World-System III: The Second Era of Great Expansion of the Capitalist World-Economy, 1730–1840.* New York: Academic Press.
1980   *The Modern World-System II: Mercantilism and the Consolidation of the European World-Economy, 1600–1750.* New York: Academic Press.
1974   *The Modern World-System: Capitalist Agriculture and the Origins of the European World-Economy in the 16th Century.* New York: Academic Press.

Weber, Max
1947   *The Theory of Social and Economic Organization*, translated by Talcott Parsons. New York: Free Press.

Whittier, Nancy
1995   *Feminist Generations: The Persistence of the Radical Women's Movement.* Philadelphia: Temple University Press.

Williams, Rhys H.
1995   "Constructing the Public Good: Social Movements and Cultural Resources." *Social Problems* 42:124–144

Winant, Howard
1995   "Race Theory, Culture, and Politics in the United States Today." Pp. 174–188 in *Cultural Politics and Social Movements*, edited by Marcy Darnovsky, Barbara Epstein, and Richard Flacks. Philadelphia: Temple University Press.

Wright, Erik Olin
1989   *The Debate on Classes.* London: Verso.
1985   *Classes.* London: Verso.

Zald, Mayer N.
1992   "Looking Backward to Look Forward: Reflections on the Past and Future of the Resource Mobilization Research Paradigm." Pp. 326–348 in *Frontiers in Social Movement Theory*, edited by Aldon Morris and Carol Mueller. New Haven, CT: Yale University Press.

Zald, Mayer N. and Bert Useem
1987   "Movement and Countermovement Interaction: Mobilization, Tactics, and State Involvement." Pp. 247–272 in *Social Movements in an Orga-*

nizational Society, edited by Mayer N. Zald and John D. McCarthy New Brunswick, NJ: Transaction.

Zaretsky, Eli
  1976   *Capitalism, the Family and Personal Life*. New York: Harper & Row.

Zeitlin, Irving
  1987   *Ideology and the Development of Sociological Theory*, 3rd edition. Englewood Cliffs, NJ: Prentice-Hall.

Index